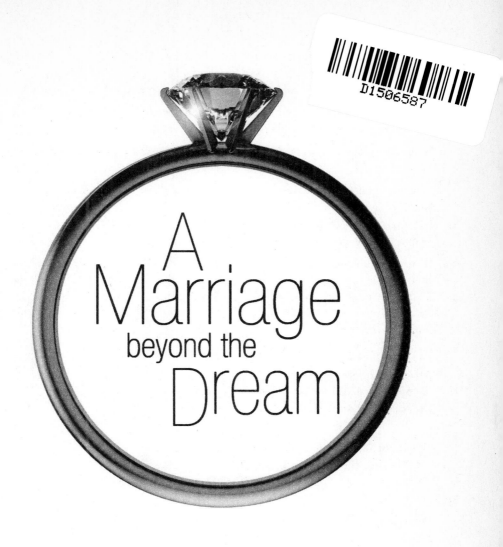

A Marriage
beyond the
Dream

EXPERIENCE MORE THAN YOU COULD
DREAM, HOPE OR IMAGINE...

DRS. THOMAS & MAUREEN ANDERSON

14 13 12 11   10 9 8 7 6 5 4 3 2 1

A Marriage Beyond the Dream:
Experience More than You Could Dream, Hope, or Imagine
ISBN 978-1-60683-345-2

Copyright © 2010 Word for Winners Publishing
3520 E. Brown Road, Mesa, AZ 85213
(480) 964-4GOD

Published by Harrison House, LLC
P.O. Box 35035
Tulsa, Oklahoma 74153
www.harrisonhouse.com

Printed in the United States

Editors: Becky Gilbert and Tammy Zubeck

What Others Are Saying

Drs. Tom and Maureen Anderson have labored to bring rich insight, profound wisdom and practical how to's gleaned from their own lives to help anyone who desires to build a marriage beyond their dream.

Brian Houston
Senior Pastor, Hillsong Church

Tom and Maureen are so well qualified to impart their years of experience to all of us.

Pastor Phil Pringle
Christian City Church, Sydney, Australia

Whether you're married or plan to marry one day, *A Marriage Beyond the Dream* is a true guide for securing "the dream come true" marriage and for making your home heaven on earth.

Jerry Savelle
Jerry Savelle Ministries International

You can be assured that the principles outlined in *A Marriage Beyond the Dream* come from a couple who has based their marriage on the firm foundation of the Word of God.

Reece Bowling
Senior Pastor, Orchard Road Christian Center

This book is rich with life lessons and guidance from Tom and Maureen that will help any marriage improve and move into a deeper, richer and more rewarding relationship.

Dr. Dennis Burke
Dennis Burke Ministries

Drs. Tom and Maureen Anderson in their latest, *A Marriage Beyond the Dream*, have used the power of their pen to get us back in step with the philosophy of God's Word. They move to the heart of the issue when they explain the prescriptions for a great marriage.

Marcus & Joni Lamb
Daystar Television

A Marriage Beyond the Dream will help lay the foundation for strong marriages that go beyond just existing and truly thrive.

John Bevere
Messenger International

TABLE OF CONTENTS

Introduction

1	The Purpose of Genders	11
2	The Motivated Marriage: What Makes You 'Tick'?	31
3	Different Is Good!	45
4	Three Things that Drive a Successful Marriage	63
5	Responsibility Before Authority	75
6	'Where Art Thou,' O Man	97
7	'You Want Me to Do What?'	115
8	If It Takes Two to Tango, Whose Turn Is It to Lead?	135
9	How to Avoid a Train Wreck in Your Marriage	149
10	What to Do When You're 'Just Not Feeling It'	171
11	True Love: The 'Constant' Through Life's Changing Seasons	189
12	Barriers to Intimacy	213
13	Is Your Marriage Overweight?	229
14	When Sex Has Been Abused	239
15	Made for Each Other: Sex and the Covenant of Marriage	255
16	Responsible with Money, Ready for a Bride	271
17	What's Working in You?	285

Dedication

This is dedicated to "the one I love, Maureen."

Dedication and love do not do justice to the fullness in my heart of the depth of love and appreciation I have for the girl I fell in love with when she was 15 and I was 17. She is my inspiration. She's my life. Without her I would not be who I have become, and I will forever be grateful for the investment of love and life she has made in me.

This book reveals the path our lives, love, and marriage has taken. It is a surreal relationship most do not understand and in some cases, believe, but it is available to all who are willing to travel the path and experience *A Marriage Beyond the Dream.*

INTRODUCTION

Marriage was designed by God as a portrait of His love for the world. A marriage relationship should portray the remarkable relationship that exists between Christ and His Bride, the Church. However, in many marriages, it seems that the world is witnessing a skewed image of the love that God has for His people. With the divorce rate in the Church rivaling secular statistics, the true nature of God and His wonderful plan for marriage have been obscured from the eyes of many.

Marriage is much more important than most of us realize. A great marriage can promote success in the workplace, a sense of health and well-being in the home, and the assurance of happy marriages for our children and future generations. A marriage, that portrays "heaven on earth," is a godly witness to our children, families, friends, and the world around us. When others see how much a believing husband and wife love each other, they will draw closer to God, who is the "Master Designer and Architect" of marriage.

Once you understand God's intention and design for marriage, you will see why Satan seeks to destroy individual marriages, as well as the institution of marriage itself. When a Christian divorces, marriage becomes a broken canvas, instead of the beautiful masterpiece that God intended it to be. In *A Marriage Beyond the Dream*, we have endeavored to share the insights that we have gleaned over the years from God's Word, and our own personal experiences. Everyone can benefit from the life-giving truths of God's Word and the insights He has graciously given to us to share with you to help strengthen your marriage relationship.

Today, we are truly "living the dream" in our marriage. However, we did not start out that way. In fact, when we began our lives together, more than forty years ago, we were just in the babyhood stage of learning about marriage. We only knew two things: we loved each other and we desired to build a life together.

Since we both came from broken homes, we decided that we wanted more than what we had, for our own marriage. After we became Christians, our desire to build a happy, successful marriage became even greater. We wanted to bless our children and honor the Lord with our marriage relationship.

Even though our early years of marriage were filled with the same mistakes that most young couples make, we were committed to "on-the-job training" for our marriage! We purposed in our hearts to have a successful, godly marriage, and leave a legacy of honor and blessing for our children and the generations to follow.

Since those early days, we have not only discovered what makes marriages work, but what makes marriages work *well*.

The Lord has equipped us along the way to help others build long lasting, healthy and happy marriages. No matter where you are in your own marriage, God can help you. Whether you simply want to improve a marriage, or rebuild one that has been devastated—there is hope and help in the Lord. It seems that married couples, who are "living the dream," get so much attention in our society today, because they are a minority. However, it is not God's will that these "Heaven-on-earth" marriages, are so few and far between! Marriages thrive as a result of the investment that the husband and wife put into the relationship, as well as the godly patterns that have been established over time. In other words, these marriages did not happen by accident, but on purpose, because the husband and wife esteemed their relationship as valuable and precious.

To be truly successful in marriage and in life, you must value what God values. You must also demonstrate honor for what He honors, not just by your words, but also by your actions. What you value in life will always increase in worth, because of the great respect with which you treat it. If you value something, you will protect it and go to great lengths to ensure its preservation. Consequently, if you value your relationship with your spouse, you will protect and keep it, and it will increase in value over time.

God bless you as you read.

Living the dream for His glory,

Drs. Tom and Maureen

THE PURPOSE
OF GENDERS

Dr. Tom Anderson

God designed the genders and He created us "male and female" (Genesis 1:27; 5:2). Our design is connected to our purpose and value. In other words, when we understand His design for the genders, we will also understand His purpose for the genders. As we gain a new understanding of our purpose, we will learn to value the opposite sex, especially our spouse. "Husbands, likewise, dwell with them with understanding, giving honor to the wife, as to the weaker vessel, and as being heirs together of the grace of life, that your prayers may not be hindered" (1 Peter 3:7 KJV).

One of the most common complaints that I have heard over the years of counseling couples, is "I just don't understand her!" or "I don't get where he's coming from!" We often laugh about our seeming inability to understand the opposite sex. It seems that men especially, just accept and resign themselves to the fact that they will never understand their wives, and they often make jokes about this. Here is one in particular, that comes to mind:

A guy walks along a California beach, where he finds a small bottle. He rubs the bottle and a genie appears before him. The genie says, "You can have anything you'd like; I'll grant you one wish."

The man thinks for a moment and answers, "Well, I've always wanted to see the beaches of Hawaii, but I'm afraid to travel by boat or plane. If you could create a road from here to Hawaii, I could drive over and see the beaches."

The genie responds, "That's a tall order that would require a tremendous amount of power and resources to make happen. Isn't there anything else you'd like?"

After a long moment of silence, the man finally says, "Well, there is one other thing that's really important to me, and that is, I would really like to understand my wife."

The genie replies, "Would you like one lane or two?"

Most would agree and think that this is really funny, but in light of the fact that the Bible commands us, as husbands, to understand our wives, it really isn't. For years, I have heard, read, believed, and even joked about the fact that it is impossible for a man to understand a woman, because men and women are designed so differently. I actually thought that having this understanding was not possible and that it wasn't supposed to be possible. But since the Word of God is my standard for what I believe, live, and teach, I have changed my mind on this matter. It really is possible for a husband to understand his wife, because the Bible says it is! Since God says, "Live with her with understanding," that means we can do it.

'His' and 'Hers' Brains

In recent years, medical science has discovered much concerning the dramatic chemical, hormonal, and even physical differences between "his" and "her" brains. We now understand that these physiological differences impact thoughts, emotions, and virtually every area of human behavior. The bottom line is that men and women are not the same! By God's design, they are uniquely different from one another. In understanding some of the physical and emotional differences between the genders, we will gain a better understanding of the God-given and God-ordained purpose for these differences.

Let's start at the beginning of a person's life. Men and women are created different from the time of conception. In other words, there is no such thing as a "unisex" brain in babies, children, or adults. From the beginning, we were wired male or female with vital differences that are unique to each gender. Some "progressive-minded" individuals accuse traditional society (as if it were a criminal offense) of conditioning boys to be boys, and girls to be girls. These differences between the genders, however, are not "nurtured" as much as they are "natured." Association and environment can play a role in the development of the genders, but the inherent differences are strongly "nature" and "God-ordained." A person is either male or female.

It is possible for a husband to understand his wife because the Bible says it is!

Hormones tend to play the largest role in the development of the male and female brains. At conception, the embryo possesses chromosomes that determine the gender of the child. However, the embryo does not distinguish gender until about six weeks into gestation. Prior to that time, the human brain is a basic female brain, because the egg or ovum in a woman is strictly female-produced—then it is fertilized by the male sperm. If the baby is a male, then the hormone testosterone becomes the messenger to the brain, and the network of connections between the right and left sides of the brain diminishes. On the other hand, if the baby is a female, then more connections grow between the right and left sides of the brain. In laymen's terms, this basically means that mentally, women have greater processing power than men—that's why a man will never win an argument with a woman!

There are also other differences in male and female brains. For instance, the male brain is about ten percent larger than the female brain.

You would think that this would make him smarter, right? Wrong! Women consistently score the same as men in all intelligence testing. Men have 6.5 times more gray matter (thinking matter) in the brain, than women. On the other hand, women have 9.5 times more white matter (processing matter) than men. Women also have multiple connectors between the left (analytical) and right (creative) parts of the brain. One third of the man's brain is sexual-oriented, while the woman's sexual part of the brain is about the size of an almond. Yet one third of the woman's brain is communication-oriented, while his communication part is almond-sized.

As you can clearly see, men and women are different. We should not try to make men more like women, or women more like men, because it doesn't work. Have you ever heard a husband or wife complain about their spouse and say, "I wish she [he] were more like me?" Attempting to "combine" the design of the sexes creates dysfunction and chaos. This is not God's will or design. If husbands and wives honored each other for their differences, instead of criticizing each other, then blessings would begin to flow in their marriages.

> *We shouldn't try to make men more like women or women more like men, because it doesn't work.*

The Best Marriage Advice on the Planet: Find Your Spouse's Need and Meet It!

As we have seen, "different" is God's design for the genders. Since men and women are different, their needs in relationships are also different (remember the disparities in the sexual parts and the communication parts of the brain between the genders?). These "different" needs between the genders must be met in order to develop a successful and thriving relationship. Consequently, this is usually where the problem begins. In general, we don't want to meet each others needs! We simply want to ensure that our own needs are met. However, selfishness will not create a Kingdom marriage, or a marriage that is "Heaven on earth," because a Kingdom marriage is established and brings blessing to both people in the marriage, when each one learns to die to self and give his or her self to the other. The needs of a husband and wife are as different as the "his" and "her" brains that they were created with!

The following is a general list of gender-specific needs—in order of importance—based on various studies. These needs may not match yours perfectly, but you should be able to recognize and identify with many items on the list. This list will help you understand the vast differences between your needs and your spouse's needs.

Male needs:

1. sex
2. ego affirmation
3. physical touch
4. acts of service
5. security
6. unconditional love
7. trust

Female needs:

1. unconditional love and trust
2. communication
3. emotional connection
4. protection
5. security

6. provision

7. affirmation

8. quality time

9. acts of service

10. romance

Some of these needs overlap between the genders, while others are altogether exclusive. In order for love to be true love, both the husband and wife must work to meet the other's needs. For example, men must learn to love unconditionally. They must purpose to be trustworthy. They also must learn to communicate and to be in touch with their emotions, as well as their wife's emotions. Men must be the strength in the relationship and offer companionship, as well as protect, provide for, affirm, serve, and romance their wives.

Women must also love unconditionally, serve and be trustworthy. They must learn to speak sweetly and affirm their husbands. Women must also learn to have and enjoy sex!

However, as I said earlier, meeting one another's needs in marriage has historically posed problems. So many needs have gone unmet due to ignorance, selfishness and indifference. When a husband and wife's needs are met in their marriage, a remarkable transformation takes place in their marriage, as well as in both of them. A happy, fulfilled marriage produces happy, fulfilled lives. So let's pursue understanding each other's differences as "male and female," so we can better understand how to meet each other's needs.

Created in God's Image

Understanding our spouse is the first key to meeting his or her needs; therefore, it is crucial that we understand our differences as male and female.

We have already looked at the difference between the genders from the time of conception. Now let's go back even further to God's creation of the first man and woman on the earth. I believe that everything in God's creation relates to one another, and that there is something we can learn about God by studying or observing His creation. (see Romans 1:20.) Consequently, if we pay attention to the creation of man and woman, we will be able to better understand God, since man is created in His image and likeness (Genesis 1:26-27). In essence, we will also be able to better understand each other, as male and female.

The Bible says that God created both male and female in His own image.

Then God said, "Let Us make man in Our image, according to Our likeness; let them have dominion over the fish of the sea, over the birds of the air, and over the cattle, over all the earth and over every creeping thing that creeps on the earth." So God created man in His own image; in the image of God He created him; male and female He created them."

Genesis 1:26-27

It is important to note that God is a Spirit (John 4:24); therefore, He is neither male nor female, in a human sense. Remember, this passage says that God created both male and female in His image. The Father, Son, and Holy Spirit were all present in the beginning of Creation. We have heard so much teaching about God the Father and Jesus the Son, but we haven't heard as much in-depth teaching about the Holy Spirit, who is often represented as the "feminine" side of God. We know that the Creation relates directly to Jesus, the Word that was "made flesh and dwelt among us." Nothing was created except by the Word of God. (See John 1:1-3,14.)

Now, let's take a look at the Holy Spirit's role in Creation. Genesis 1:2 says, "The earth was without form, and void; and darkness was on the face of the deep...." Then it says, "...And the Spirit of God was hovering over the face of the waters." (NKJV). Notice that even though the Holy Spirit was brooding over the waters, nothing happened until God spoke. "Then God said, 'Let there be light,' and there was light" (Genesis 1:3 NKJV). When God gave the word, the Holy Spirit brought forth that word in power, and gave life and substance to the spoken word. The following pages will reveal how this function of the Holy Spirit relates to the design of the genders, especially the woman.

The 'Wombed Man' — Comparable but Different

Genesis 2:18 says, *"And the Lord God said, 'It is not good that man should be alone; I will make him a helper comparable to him.'"* You can read the recorded account of God's creation of woman in Genesis chapter 2. God put Adam to sleep and took one of his ribs and fashioned a woman— "comparable" but different. She came from man, but she was noticeably different. God had made Adam a helper to carry his seed and to bring forth life. I don't need to give you an anatomy lesson, to simply tell you that a woman was made with reproductive organs distinctly different from a man's. In essence she's a *"wombed man,"* if you will, with the ability to receive seed, and then hold, incubate, nurture and grow that seed, until it is brought forth as a new life. This aspect of woman's design was not an accident; it was a purposeful, deliberate act of the Creator. Remember, in Genesis 1:27, it says, *"...God created man in His own image...male and female...."* At that point, there was just Adam, so when Eve was created (Genesis 2:18-23), God separated the "male" and "female" in Adam, so that there was now—man and woman—two genders, each with a distinct design and purpose.

Weakness or Design?

What is the purpose of a man and a woman, especially as it pertains to marriage? Very simply, men are by design sowers and initiators, while women are by design receivers and responders. Besides the obvious fact that a wife receives "seed" from her husband in pro-creation, in order to bring forth new life, she also receives what he sows into her heart and mind and she "incubates" that until it, too, comes to life. What does she incubate? Words. A woman is especially a good "meditator" of the words and actions of her husband! So if you, as a husband, want to have a good relationship with your wife, you have to sow the right kind of seeds. The right words get the right reaction, and the right seeds get the right harvest.

Every seed that he plants into his wife's life is going to produce after its own kind!

Have you ever noticed that a woman can tell you the same story four times and use different words each time? There's a reason for that. She has meditated on that story over and over again—and when she tells it to you, she's meditating on it again. This irritates a lot of men, but, frankly, men have to hear a story four times before they will remember just part of it! A wife will say something to her husband, and he will think, *Didn't we talk about this yesterday?* But she's simply trying to get something across to him, and her attitude is, if she says it enough, maybe some of it will stick!

Women are by nature great meditators and great communicators. *Meditate* means to imagine, muse, devise, study, mutter, utter, talk, speak, roar, and groan. This word also portrays the idea of a person chewing something—as a cow chews its cud, digesting it until it becomes a part of him. Meditating on the Word of God is something we are all called to do as believers (see Joshua 1:8), but women, by design, are especially good meditators. They are brooders, so to speak, and will brood over words in much the same way a hen will brood over the life that's in the egg, until it is finally brought forth. A woman can give life to everything that is communicated to her—every thought, word, and deed, including body language and tones. She can meditate on it and incubate it until those thoughts, words, or deeds are given life. This is who she is by design, not by weakness. It is her design by God.

Sowing and Reaping in Marriage

One of the most basic things that every husband should know about his wife, is that every seed he plants into her life is going to produce after its own kind. For example, the Bible says, "Husbands, love your wives and do not be harsh with them" (Colossians 3:19). I have searched the Bible and could not find any scriptures that told the wife not to be harsh with her husband. There weren't any, but that doesn't mean that it's okay for a wife to be harsh toward her husband, because it certainly isn't. However, God specifically addresses the husband concerning this. So a husband must sow love, peace, patience, gentleness, and kindness into his wife's life, instead of harshness.

What often happens however, is that a man gets caught up in his work and dealing with frustrations on the job, and then brings that attitude home to his wife. As a result, he sows harshness into her life with his tone of voice and body language, and perhaps even his words. In return, his wife will meditate on that. After all, she's been working hard, too. She's trying to serve her husband, take care of the kids, and perform other tasks in the home. So she begins brooding. He's fussing, and she's fuming. While he's taking his frustrations out on her, she is in deep thought, *I married this guy and gave my life to him. I pledged to honor him, and he's treating me harshly. Okay then, I'll show him harsh!* Consequently, his harvest begins to be multiplied back to him. Some men don't want to hear that, nevertheless it's the truth. Every seed that he plants into his wife's life is going to produce after its own kind! In fact, he will reap a multiplied harvest of everything that he sows into his marriage. This is scriptural and absolutely true.

In light of this truth, how foolish would it be for a husband to sow harshness toward his wife? On the other hand, how wise would it be to sow love, peace, patience, gentleness, and kindness? As a husband, when you truly understand the design and purpose of the genders, and the law of sowing and reaping in marriage, you will wisely and earnestly sow into your wife what God says you should.

In Ephesians 5:21-33, the Lord compares the relationship between a husband and wife to the relationship between Christ and the Church. Christ is the picture of the husband in marriage, and the Church—the Bride of Christ—is the picture of the wife. Just as we, the Bride of Christ, are to receive the Word of God and meditate on it until we bear fruit—or produce life, a woman will meditate on the words her husband speaks and bring life to those words. When we, as believers, receive God's Word into our heart, we become "impregnated" by that Word and life is formed. That Word becomes programmed into our actions and then surfaces in our circumstances. We become recipients of the divine life that is contained in the Word. For instance, when you heard and received the Word concerning salvation, you became "impregnated" with salvation and a new life in Christ was brought forth; you became a child of God. This happened because of the completed picture: God the Father, Jesus the Word, and the Holy Spirit, who is the agent of the godhead that brings forth life.

The Heart of a Woman

Proverbs 4:23 NKJV says, "Keep your heart with all diligence, for out of it spring the issues of life." The heart is a powerful spiritual force in bringing forth new life in the earth. This is especially true concerning women. Women are programmed to meditate on and incubate words until those words bring forth life.

Mary, the mother of Jesus, was a great example of a woman who incubated words. She meditated on and pondered them in her heart.

And they [the shepherds] came with haste and found Mary and Joseph, and the Babe lying in a manger. Now when they had seen Him, they made widely known the saying which was told them concerning this Child. And all those who heard it marveled at those things which were told them by the shepherds. BUT MARY KEPT ALL THESE THINGS AND PON-DERED THEM IN HER HEART.

Luke 2:16-19 NKJV, emphasis mine

In the same chapter, we read again that Mary pondered and held close in her heart the words that were spoken to her. The fact that Mary pondered and meditated on the words that she heard, was important.

His [Jesus'] parents went to Jerusalem every year at the Feast of the Passover. And when He was twelve years old, they went up to Jerusalem according to the custom of the feast. When they had finished the days, as they returned, the Boy Jesus lingered behind in Jerusalem. And Joseph and His mother did not know it; but supposing Him to have been in the company, they went a day's journey, and sought Him among their relatives and acquaintances. So when they did not find Him, they returned to Jerusalem, seeking Him. Now so it was that after three days they found Him in the temple, sitting in the midst of the teachers, both listening to them and asking them questions. And all who heard Him were astonished at His understanding and answers. So when they saw Him, they were amazed; and His mother said to Him, "Son, why have You done this to us? Look, Your father and I have sought You anxiously." And He said to them, "Why did you seek Me? Did you not know that I must be about My Father's business?" But they did not understand the statement which He spoke to them. Then He went down with them and came to Nazareth, and was subject to them, but His mother kept all these things in her heart.

Luke 2:41-51 NKJV

From what we know about Mary from Scripture, it's safe to say that she was a meditator, holding God's words in her heart and pondering them. Mary is typical of most women today. Just as women bring forth natural life, they also bring forth "life" from the words they ponder, whether good or bad. Women are incubators of all things: A good word spoken to a woman's heart will produce a good thing; a bad word spoken will produce a bad thing. Bearing fruit and bringing forth life from God's Word is a picture of the Church. The Body of Christ can learn something from its female members about pondering and bringing forth life from words.

Of course, we know that a woman who has been treated poorly by her husband, must walk in love and forgiveness just as any other believer. In other words, the commandment of God to walk in love is given to the woman, as well as to the man. When God says to meditate on things that are "true, noble, just, pure, lovely, and of good report" (Philippians 4:8), He is talking to both men and women. Women, as well as men, are responsible to take wrong thoughts captive and not dwell on them (2 Corinthians 10:5).

I don't perform marriage counseling for church members anymore, because it robs me of my ability to yield to the Holy Spirit from the pulpit and minister in the area of marriage. For example, I might say something in a church setting, by the unction of the Holy Spirit, that coincides with something someone has said to me in a counseling session. I don't want that person to think I'm talking about him or her publicly, so I've assigned many of those counseling responsibilities to my staff.

Back when I did perform marriage counseling, this was a common scenario. A husband and wife who were separated would come into my office. They had been married for years, but then the wife had given him the boot, so to speak. I addressed the wife first, because in most cases, the husband was clueless. He thought everything was fine until his wife threw him out. He had a wife, kids, job, house, and car, so his attitude was, *We're doing fine. What's the problem?* But he had sown the wrong things into his wife for years. If a man sows bitterness into his wife, it may take ten, fifteen, twenty years, or even more but eventually there will be the birth of a "baby" called "bitterness." This "bitterness" will be a living thing that could very likely destroy their relationship. In other words, once it happens, it is tough to restore what has been lost.

The heart is like a womb, because whatever grows there will produce something. The heart will give life and substance to what has been planted there. It doesn't just give back the seed that was sown; it gives back a multiplied harvest on that seed. This is especially true of women in marriage. Naturally speaking, if you give a woman a seed, she will give you a baby. If you give a woman a house, she will give you a home. If you give a woman a smile, she may give you her heart.

Women were created to multiply fruit and life from seed. They are gifted at turning something small into something large and significant. For instance, Jesus had one conversation with the woman at the well in Samaria (see John 4:4-26), and she turned it into an evangelistic crusade! She multiplied the Word of the Lord that was sown into her life. In the same manner, a husband will always receive a multiplied harvest on the seed he sows into the life of his wife.

The Wonder of Pregnancy and Birth

Just as a woman receives "seed" from the man and conceives a baby, we, as the Bride of Christ, receive the seed of God's Word and hide it in our hearts, where it will grow and produce life. We read, study, meditate on, and talk about the Word until it has "conceived" in our heart and begins to grow. Then we expect a manifestation of what has been conceived, because we have entered into the "rest" of faith, wherein we know that we know that we actually have what we have conceived, although we do not see it yet.

For instance, if you have meditated on God's Word concerning healing and you believe you received your healing while you are still experiencing symptoms, you are "pregnant" with God's Word. You are expecting a "baby"—a manifestation of God's Word in the form of healing. You will begin to make preparations for that "baby" to come forth! In other words, the Word of God, that is hidden and nurtured in a person's heart, creates life, as well as expectancy.

There is an air of excitement that surrounds a person with genuine faith in God's Word. When a woman is pregnant, she usually knows it—and when she knows it no one can talk her out of the fact that she is going to have a baby! She will decorate the nursery and buy diapers, blankets, and other items to prepare for the arrival of her baby. Similarly, when you are in faith about something, you know it. When you are believing God for something, you are expecting it to show up at any time.

Here's another illustration that will help you understand God's design for women. In a physical pregnancy, one of the first things that happens in a woman is that her womb begins to thicken. This is like our heart when we receive the Word of God—it "thickens" so we can hold on to that Word until the answer is brought forth. Consequently, when the enemy comes to steal the Word, that Word is guarded and protected in our hearts.

When God's Word enters your heart, you have to "toughen up." If you want to hold on to what you have received and see it grow and mature in your spirit, you will have to become "thick-skinned." In other words, you can't waver every time a circumstance comes that tells you that God's Word isn't true, or that you are never going to receive what you are believing in your heart. If you ever want to see it, you have to be tough.

Some people don't like hearing that. They will say, "I just can't walk by faith; it's too hard." However, you can be as strong as you need to be. You can be strong in the Lord and in the power of His might (Ephesians 6:10). You need to say, "Yes, I can endure because God says I can. He planted this Word in my heart—and I'm holding on to it! There's going to be a baby soon. Devil, you get out of here! I have received the Word, and you can't have it!"

During pregnancy, after the womb thickens, hormonal changes also begin to take place. In part, these chemical changes are designed to prevent a miscarriage. Similarly, that's what teaching does for the Bride of Christ. "All Scripture is given by inspiration of God, and is profitable for doctrine, for reproof, for correction, for instruction in righteousness" (2 Timothy 3:16 NKJV). If we don't continue in the Word, or if we don't understand how to hold on to and nurture what we have received, we become in danger of losing it. That is where the teaching of the Word comes in, producing the changes necessary in the hearer, so that he does not miscarry and lose what was conceived in his heart.

One way in which people miscarry the Word of God in their heart is through their wrong confession. For example, if they are speaking the Word that is in their heart one day, but the next day they are saying, "Things don't look any different. I'm not sure if this is coming to pass or not," they could miscarry the Word that's in their heart, making it unproductive in their life. Most women who are pregnant will go to great measures to protect the life that's growing within them. They know that if they guard what has been conceived in their womb, in nine months, they will be holding a baby.

After the thickening of the womb and the hormonal changes that take place in the body of a pregnant woman, there is a third change that takes place. Nutrients from all over her body begin to flow toward the life that is growing inside of her. Nourishment first goes to the baby and then to the mother. Let's look at this from a spiritual viewpoint. Let's say that a woman has a crisis of some kind that she needs to overcome. Just like those nutrients in the body of a pregnant woman, all of her thoughts, emotions, and energies begin to flow toward that situation. She is endeavoring to bring something forth. Then she sees the answer in her mind's eye and in her heart, and begins to prepare for the manifestation of the answer.

Another interesting thing happens in a woman's body during pregnancy - her center of gravity changes. In case you haven't noticed, a woman sits, stands, and walks a little differently when she is nine months pregnant than when she is only three months pregnant. As the baby grows, her stance becomes stronger and more balanced. Similarly, when we are holding fast to God's Word in our hearts, we, too, must stand fast so that we will not be shaken or moved from our position or place. No matter what the circumstances, we will not back up or back off. We are determined to give birth to the dream that God has placed in our heart.

I have shared this analogy so you can see that women, by design, are keepers of words. They hold words spoken to them until those words produce something. If only husbands would grasp this important truth! It would change their life and their marriage. So much of a husband's success or failure—his enjoyment or his "just enduring"—is determined by the seeds that he sows into his marriage. A woman, by nature, will produce what a husband sows into her life.

Another unique facet of a woman's design that goes along with this is her persistence. I will illustrate this from the following well-known passage.

"...There was in a certain city a judge who did not fear God nor regard man. Now there was a widow in that city; and she came to him, saying, 'Get justice for me from my adversary.' And he would not for a while; but

afterward he said within himself, 'Though I do not fear God nor regard man, yet because this widow troubles me I will avenge her, lest by her continual coming she weary me.'"

Luke 18:2-5 NKJV

The judge in this story just didn't care. But notice, that did not stop this woman—she came to get something, and she was not leaving without it!

Just as a pregnant woman will not let go of the life that's developing within her, a woman will stick with the program, so to speak, until the job is done. A woman is persistent and enduring by design. This God-given design should teach all of us that once we have conceived the Word of God in our heart, we must never let it go. We must stay with it until there is a birth. Whether it takes six months, nine months, or even years, if you know that Word has been conceived in your heart, you must persist and never change your mind about the outcome. Very simply, a woman who is pregnant knows she has a baby coming. She can't see the baby yet, but you cannot talk her out of her belief that a baby is on the way! We all can learn something from that.

Women are not only great incubators of life—they are also gifted at bringing forth that life. They are "meditators" and "communicators" of life! Do you know why Jesus waited for a woman to come by the tomb after His resurrection? He knew that if He told a woman that He had risen from the dead, she would recognize the significance and would not forget it! She would communicate it immediately to everyone she knew. That's not her fault or weakness; it's her design. Many have seen this strength as a flaw and have not valued it properly or as God intended. Think about it. John and Peter were both at the tomb, but after they discovered that it was empty, there was no record of them telling anyone about it. It was as if one turned to the other and said, "Hey, you wanna go fishing?"

Jesus trusted a woman with the revelation of His ascension from death and the grave. He knew that she would carry that Gospel to every person who would listen. She would disseminate and communicate life. That's part of her design—and it's a strength not a weakness. If you, as a husband, will recognize the design, purpose, and value of your wife and sow the right things into her and into your marriage, you will reap a marriage that's "Heaven on earth." If you sow peace, you will reap peace. If you sow gentleness, you will get gentleness. If you sow love, you will get love—and you will always get a multiplied harvest on your seed. If you get hold of this secret, then you have gotten hold of the secret of life, because your wife will bring forth life from what you have planted in her and she will do it by the design and purpose of God.

2

THE MOTIVATED MARRIAGE: WHAT MAKES YOU 'TICK'?

Dr. Maureen Anderson

Every person has a basic need to feel loved, and marriage is a relationship in which both parties especially need to experience feelings of love, contentment, and well-being. When a husband and wife feel happy and loved in their marriage, they create a happy home environment in which their children are raised experiencing those same feelings. Children's basic need for love is met in an atmosphere where their parents' marriage is healthy and thriving.

To be loved unconditionally is the cry of each person's heart, but everyone receives love differently. There are three components to a great marriage: (1) sex, or the physical aspect of marriage; (2) friendship, or the relational aspect; and (3) commitment, or the familial aspect of marriage. Although all three of these elements must be present to have a successful marriage, the importance placed on each will vary with each person. In other words, each person will feel the happiest in the marriage relationship, when he or she is being fulfilled in one of these areas— physical intimacy, relational intimacy, or familial intimacy. This is why it is so important to find out what pleases your spouse and what makes him or her feel the most loved. Both parties in a marriage must derive happiness and fulfillment from the relationship, in order for that marriage to be completely successful.

I liken these three elements—physical intimacy, relational intimacy, and familial intimacy—to the main ingredients in a recipe. All three of them are neccesary to make the recipe work, because if just one ingredient is missing, it will cause the dish to flop. You might have a favorite ingredient, but that does not mean that ingredient is more important than the others; it simply means that it is the most important one to you.

Do you know your favorite "ingredient"? Equally important, do you know your spouse's favorite ingredient? If you don't know which element is most important to you, ask yourself the question, *What says love to me like nothing else?* Is it physical intimacy and closeness? Is it emotional intimacy—long conversations and time spent together doing everyday activities? Is it repeated expressions of long-term commitment in every season of life ? Is it feelings of warmth that you feel when family is near?

To be loved unconditionally is the cry of each person's heart.

Once you know what makes you "tick" in marriage, it's important to communicate that to your spouse, and then find out which of these three elements he or she favors most. Even if it is not the thing that touches your heart the most, your willingness to meet your spouse's needs will make your marriage complete. Great marriages are kept fresh and alive by remaining in a constant mode of discovery concerning your spouse's likes and dislikes.

People's needs can change over time, so it's important not to paint your spouse into a corner, so to speak, concerning his or her needs and desires in marriage. For example, sex and physical intimacy may be of foremost importance to you at one point in your marriage—yet later, commitment and family become more important to you. Never assume that you know everything about your spouse! Stay interested in learning his or her changing priorities and desires through every season of your lives together. Now let's look in greater detail at the three elements that motivate people in marriage.

Physical Intimacy in Marriage

A person whose priority is physical intimacy, ranks sex and romance as the most important element in their relationship with their spouse. God created sex for marriage. Sex is a gift from God that was meant to be enjoyed by a man and woman in the context of marriage. God intended sex for pleasure and pro-creation, but it is also a symbol of the covenant between a husband and wife to remain through life as "one flesh" (Genesis 2:24; Ephesians 5:31).

Individuals who are in a highly physical relationship usually have a lot of energy or chemistry between one another. They feel just as much in love with their spouse as the day they got married, because they have kept the thoughts and emotions of physical intimacy alive. As a result, the sexual attraction between them continues to grow through the years —not because of what's happening on the outside, but because of what's happening on the inside in their hearts and emotions.

Sexually motivated individuals place a strong emphasis on great sex, and the act of lovemaking helps them keep a close relationship. They feel emotionally connected through sexual intercourse. Generally in marriage, sex tends to deepen the bond of love between a husband and wife. Outside of the bedroom, a

The act of sex can actually "wipe out" negative memories and provide us with a clean slate.

physical couple will often flirt with and tease each other.

Due to the various brain chemicals that are released during sexual intercourse, a person will feel almost "high" from the feelings of intimacy that are derived from a healthy, satisfying sex life. Sex is very important to them *(and it should be important to every married couple)*. They are fulfilled by the feelings of love they experience when they enjoy physical intimacy with their spouse. This is a result of certain chemicals that are released by the brain during sex. One of these chemicals is known as *peptide oxytocin*, which causes a person to feel good about their relationship, themselves, and life in general. This chemical promotes deep bonding and encourages more affectionate behavior. Studies have also shown that oxytocin actually blocks unpleasant memories in the brain. This sheds some light on why make-up sex is so popular! This chemical causes us to "forgive and forget" whatever we were so upset with our spouse about!

The body also releases endorphins when a person engages in affectionate behavior. Endorphins produce energy and promote healing. They have also been proven to act as natural pain-relievers in the body. That's why affection promotes feelings of well-being. During sex, the chemicals that flood our body bring a deep sense of peace, calm, and well-being.

The body is absolutely amazingly put together by God, and science is catching up in understanding how it works. Just as our body releases chemicals during sex, it also releases chemicals when we argue or fight that can be detrimental to our health and well-being. That's one of the reasons why God commands us, "'Be angry, and do not sin': do not let the sun go down on your wrath" (Ephesians 4:26 NKJV). It's crucial that we learn to forgive our spouse quickly and refuse to allow strife to interfere with our physical intimacy. If we have had an argument or disagreement, the act of sex can actually "wipe out" negative memories and provide us with a clean slate, so emotional intimacy and bonding can continue in the relationship.

Potential Problems in the Physical Marriage

Physically oriented people always feel "in love" because whether they are consciously aware of it or not, they crave the emotional high that comes from the release of those feel-good chemicals during sex with their spouse. No matter where they are, when they think of their spouse, they are flooded with that desire for intimacy with him or her. However, people who are motivated this way can confuse their emotions for true love—their emotions can bounce around from high to low. They need the stability that comes from the knowledge of God and His Word so when their emotions try to confuse them, they can stand firm in the godly character that is produced by a genuine relationship with God.

Friendship in Marriage

People who favor this aspect of marriage place emphasis on personality, as well as emotional and intellectual compatibility. They tend to view their spouse as their best friend, and thrive on participating in hobbies and activities that they can enjoy together. They feel most loved when they are spending quality time with their spouse—having long talks together, sharing their dreams, goals, and desires, or just being together.

"My dove in the clefts of the rock, in the hiding places on the mountainside, show me your face, let me hear your voice; for your voice is sweet, and your face is lovely…. His mouth is sweetness itself; he is altogether lovely. This is my lover, this my friend, O daughters of Jerusalem" (Song of Solomon 2:14, 5:16). In these two verses, we have the perspective of the husband and his attitude toward his wife, as well as the wife's perspective of her husband and her attitude toward him. They have a friendship relationship that is based on true love. Each highly values the time spent together, just noticing and admiring one another.

People who prize the relational facet of marriage like to regularly spend time alone with their spouse, free from the distractions of everyday life. They enjoy focusing on activities they can do together, but they especially crave spending quality time focusing on each other. Just as those who value physical intimacy and need a fulfilling sex life to feel connected to their spouse, a relational person needs intimate, heartfelt conversation to feel connected to their loved one.

Certainly, relational or friendship relationships are not limited to marriage. However, friendships tend to provide the model for the behavior in marriage that a relational person desires.

This same principle of relational intimacy can be found at work in Moses' friendship with God. "As Moses went into the tent, the pillar of cloud would come down and stay at the entrance, while the Lord spoke with Moses…. The Lord would speak to Moses face to face, as a man speaks with his friend…" (Exodus 33:9,11). Moses enjoyed face-to-face fellowship with God. Moses' relationship with God was anything but casual; it was an intimate friendship that became the focus of Moses' life. Moses wanted to be God's friend, so he built a tent to shield himself from distractions so He could commune with the Lord. Moses went to the tent to meet with God face-to-face. Moses honored God in friendship, longing for God's companionship and giving God his undivided attention on a consistent basis. In return, Moses had great favor with God.

It has been said that the lifeline of true love is friendship. Friendship connects you to your spouse because there are so many emotions involved in sharing thoughts and feelings while communicating your dreams, goals, desires, ideas, and love for each other, as well as the things you care about and need. The way you connect with and develop your relationship with your spouse is very similar to the way you develop your relationship with God.

When you read God's Word, you hear His heart and you gain a better understanding of His character and nature. Of course, God knows everything about you, but when you talk to Him and commune with Him from your heart, you form a greater bond. This bond affects how you view others and how you react to situations in life. You will be more conscious and aware of His loving presence in your life and His great love for you. Your friendship with God will have a positive effect on your whole outlook on life. You will become more confident and assured of your future when you are in close fellowship with God.

You can have many wonderful friendships in life with fellow church members, co-workers, or even extended family. But intimate friendships, such as the one you have with God and your spouse, are different. Those friendships go beyond the level of small talk and "acquaintanceship." People in these kinds of relationships are very close. They share things with one another that they would not share with anyone else. Trust and loyalty have been established; therefore, the connection is easy, not forced. Proverbs 18:24 says that a true friend sticks closer than a brother. In other words, intimate friendships take you to another level. When other friendships have come and gone, a true, intimate friendship will remain. This is the kind of friendship the relational-oriented person desires to have in marriage with his or her spouse.

Friendship Is About Connecting

In John chapter 15, Jesus talks about friendship and love. He addresses us as the "branches" and calls Himself the "Vine." Then He says, "Apart from me, you can do nothing" (John 15:5). What was Jesus talking about? He was talking about "vital connection" and "union."

After He talked about the connection that happens between the Vine and the branch, Jesus goes on to call us His friends. "Greater love has no one than this, than to lay down one's life for his friends. You are My friends if you do whatever I command you. No longer do I call you servants, for a servant does not know what his master is doing; but I have called you friends, for all things that I heard from My Father I have made known to you" (John 15:13-15 NKJV). Isn't that how Christ loved us? He loved us by laying down His life, by giving it up for us. Ephesians 5:25 says that men should love their wives in the same way Jesus loved us—by laying down his own life for his wife. "Husbands, love your wives, just as Christ loved the church and gave himself up for her" (Ephesians 5:25).

God has called husbands to befriend their wives! This may not come naturally to some men, but if they are married, it is their calling as a husband. In fact, if you are a husband, you need to know that your wife is supposed to be your very best friend, next to Jesus! God has called you to an intimate friendship with the wife whom He has given you, and you should be closer to each other than to your friends, co-workers, parents, children, or grandchildren. A relationship like this must be cultivated. It will grow over time as trust is built—trust in the other person's character and in the love you consistently show toward one another.

Tearing Down the Walls of Fear

Friendship in marriage also means confiding in each other. As husband and wife, you shouldn't keep secrets from one another. Friendship is a relationship in which you can make yourself vulnerable. You can be yourself and let the other person know who you are without fear. You can also be trusted with what your spouse shares with you and always believe in him or her.

When the relational aspect of your marriage is being nurtured, there is transparency that results when each feels safe and secure in the relationship. In the Garden of Eden before the fall of man, Adam and Eve were naked and not ashamed (see Genesis 2:25). Similarly, in marriage today, we must be able to bare our thoughts and feelings with each other and not feel ashamed or threatened. Yet so many feel intimidated about sharing their true feelings with their spouse. They are unwilling to make themselves vulnerable, because trust has been broken, or trust had never been established to begin with.

Some people put up walls of separation to avoid being hurt by their spouse—the person they became "one flesh" with in marriage. These walls are built on the foundation of fear and must come down in order for a new foundation of love to be established and their marriage to be successful. Marriage should be a safe haven of trust, warmth, acceptance, and love. It should not be a place where one feels as though he or she must hide from their spouse!

'Talk to Me'

Communication is essential in a friendship relationship, especially in marriage. A couple must share with each other their dreams, desires, needs, and the things that are important to them. This is how this type of relationship develops and grows. When Tom and I were first married, he was the tall, dark, handsome, silent type—a man of very few words. On the other hand, I was a communicator. Tom immediately saw my need for friendship, so he began to study the subject of friendship and marriage. He literally studied to change. He fasted and prayed and was seeking God to find out how to communicate and connect with me effectively on a personal level. He knew that if he was going to be in my world, we needed to be friends!

Marriage should be a safe haven of trust, warmth, acceptance, and love. Developing an intimate relationship with your spouse shouldn't take away from your individuality.

Some people have trouble communicating on a personal level with others because they don't feel connected to themselves. If they are not connected to themselves, they cannot be connected to others. Someone who is disconnected is not in touch with himself. You might ask him how he feels about something and he often answers, "I dunno." And he really doesn't! He is disconnected and basically out of touch with his own emotions, desires, and needs. This person must reconnect with himself before he can enjoy a close relationship with his spouse.

Sometimes people disconnect from themselves because it is too painful or unpleasant for them to be in touch with their feelings. Perhaps they were raised in a home where communication was discouraged. Some children are punished for expressing their likes or dislikes. This practice teaches them the lie that what they feel is not important, so early in life they subconsciously begin the process of withdrawing into their own emotional "shell," where it is safe.

Some people are disconnected simply because no one connected with them in their childhood, even in their own family. They were raised in a family in which connection was not valued. Consequently, they grew up knowing very little about the people in their own home. As adults, they are not usually the type of individuals who seek out emotional connection in marriage. In fact, connecting emotionally in marriage is a foreign concept to them. Nevertheless, friendship and emotional intimacy are a vital part of marriage.

If emotional and relational intimacy challenges you, don't give up! The Holy Spirit can help you connect with your spouse on an emotional level, and enable you to experience joy and fulfillment in your marriage relationship in ways that you never thought possible. When you need to confide in someone, need to be consoled, or have some really exciting news to tell who is the first person you turn to? If you can't honestly answer, "My spouse," then you and your spouse need to make this a matter of heartfelt prayer to God.

Potential Problems in the Relational Marriage

A person who values the relational aspect, can sometimes exhibit extreme behavior that is counter-productive or unhealthy to a relational marriage. For example, in a relational marriage that's based on friendship, the couple might enjoy each other's company so much that they may neglect other relationships. They don't spend adequate time developing friendships with other couples, or even with their own children. When this happens, the strength in their marriage can become a weakness—so extremes must be guarded against.

Developing an intimate friendship with your spouse should never take away from your individuality. A husband and wife are one flesh in marriage, but they are still two individuals with unique gifts and talents placed within them by God. Connecting with your spouse in a relational marriage can be compared to a precious jewel—a bright, sparkling gem with many facets. Since, all of these unique facets make up the whole gem, each one must be valued and esteemed. Similarly, a person's individual "brilliance" should not be shrouded or diminished in his or her marriage relationship, but rather valued and esteemed by their spouse.

Familial Intimacy

For some, commitment and unconditional love are the lifeblood of their marriage. Although marriage is a "forever-after" commitment, some people place pre-eminence on that feeling of deep commitment from their spouse. They derive great fulfillment in the assurance that no matter what, there's no turning back in their commitment to each other. Commitment is crucial in any marriage, because during the hard times when you might be tempted to throw in the towel, commitment will keep you in the marriage. It will enable you to fulfill the vow, or commitment, that you made to God and your spouse. Your commitment will override any temporary feelings of discouragement, frustration, or disillusionment. Consequently, it will also hold you steady and stable, so you can "stay the course" in your marriage.

Although this should hold true in the lives of any married couple, this understanding of commitment makes a familial person truly excited! A commitment-oriented person loves the institution of marriage. They are thrilled with the idea of having one partner for the rest of their life.

People who value this element the most like being married because they love the institution of marriage. In other words, they don't like the idea of being single at all!

A familial person craves affirmation of commitment on a regular basis, as well as feelings of security that family brings. They simply must have children, because their lives are all about "family" and a sense of "community." Of course, every good parent will acknowledge that their children are gifts from God (see Psalm 127:3), but "commitment" people take this to heart more than anyone! They are extremely family-oriented and everything revolves around their children and family activities. They also have a broad social circle and are usually very involved in their community—as long as their involvement pertains to family and family-related activities. In addition, they tend to have extended family living nearby, because they highly value having family close to them at all times. In familial intimacy, family equals security.

Potential Problems in the Familial Marriage

What are the potential weaknesses with familial people? Well for one thing, they can be highly committed to the institution of marriage, but not to the actual marriage relationship! In other words, they like the idea of having someone so they are not alone, but they can be insensitive or clueless about the quality of their marriage. They don't always nurture the relationship, but rather neglect the other two aspects—the physical and relational aspects.

Commitment-oriented people are all about family, but not necessarily the relationships in that family. As a rule, they don't like change, so they can be resistant to notions that their marriage might be lacking. They must learn to differentiate between commitment to the institution of marriage and commitment to their spouse, marriage, and the life that they are building together. God desires that a couple be committed to making the marriage what He intends—not just to have an "ever-after" marriage in which the husband or wife is neglected or not fulfilled.

First Things First

Before we can work on our marriage, we need to work on our relationship with God. Certainly, our relationship with God is secure through the finished work of Christ. Besides just being saved, we need to desire God's matchless and unbroken fellowship and companionship. We must be wholeheartedly committed to Him, spending time in His Word—not just casually reading it, but deeply meditating on it. When we draw near to God and abide in Him, then His Word sinks deep into our heart and changes us (see John 15:7).

Another characteristic of being committed to the Lord is the willingness to allow Him to change us. Some believers don't want this kind of commitment. For them, just to be in the family of God is enough; they don't want to go any deeper than that. But just as God is completely committed to us, He requires that we be committed to Him. Concerning the institution of marriage, when we are surrendered to Him, it becomes easy to surrender ourselves to our spouse, and commit to making our marriage what He wants it to be. Meeting our spouse's needs and making his or her priorities in the marriage our own priorities, becomes our greatest joy. Many people feel frustrated in their marriage, and they don't know why. They don't understand that God made them to have certain needs and desires. God wants you be happy and delighted in marriage! You must begin by delighting yourself in Him and His Word, and by daring to believe in His love and goodness toward you. "Delight yourself also in the Lord, And He shall give you the desires of your heart" (Psalm 37:4 NKJV).

Nothing is too hard for God. He wants to give you the marriage of your dreams, and He already has a plan! Be willing to change and understand what motivates your spouse and what makes him or her "tick." The Holy Spirit will not only reveal truth to you, but He will also show you how to walk in the light of truth, so you and your spouse can experience the joy and contentment in marriage that every couple longs for and needs.

3
DIFFERENT IS GOOD!

Drs. Tom and Maureen Anderson

We have already seen that understanding our **differences as men** and women helps us better meet one another's needs in marriage. When a husband and wife's needs are met in a marriage, that marriage will be happy and successful. Yet so often, instead of **seeking to** understand one another's differences and to value the **unique qualities** of the genders, we tend to devalue those differences. In this chapter, we are going to learn that different is good! After all, everything that God created, He "saw that it was good" (Genesis 1:10,12,18,21,25). **Since we** know that He created the genders male and female—separate and distinct in their design, purpose, and value—we know that our differences are good, as well.

Maureen:

Once of the biggest differences between the genders—and, therefore, between a husband and wife—is the way in which they each bond with their spouse. Since male and female are unique, it stands to reason that their needs are unique, too.

One of the greatest ways that I have found to meet **Tom's needs** in our marriage, is to participate in activities and hobbies that he enjoys. Generally, men are physically active and they bond through **physical ac-**

tivity. So it's important that women participate in the sports or hobbies that their husband enjoys, so that bonding can take place.

I play golf with Tom. Of course, I can only play about nine holes before I'm done, but we have a great time playing golf together. Once we played in Jamaica, where the course overlooked the ocean. It was a beautiful day that we will remember forever. In fact, we have made a lot of memories playing golf together. Although I don't enjoy the game as much as Tom does, I wouldn't trade those times together or those memories for anything.

As a woman, you might think, *It's just a game or silly hobby.* But to a man, it's an activity that creates bonding with the woman in his life. I encourage you, as a wife, to look for an activity that your husband likes that you can learn to do and perhaps even really enjoy. I'm not saying that you need to learn to play every sport your husband likes or take up every hobby he enjoys, but you can try to find at least one, because it's important to him.

Maybe your husband doesn't like to play sports, but he likes to watch sports or even old movies. You can find a way to "get into his world" by preparing popcorn, snacks, or finger-foods that he likes, and then enjoy a football game or movie with him. He may not express it to you, but having you engage with him in activities that he enjoys is one of his most basic needs. Your companionship and interest in things that interest him, affirms him at the most basic level and communicates love, security, and trust.

Once you realize how important bonding through activity is to the man in your life, hopefully, you will make the effort to engage in one or more of his favorite activities with him. I learned to play golf and ski as an adult. In fact, I was forty-seven years old when I learned to ski! I did this for Tom, not for me, because I realized the value he placed on enjoy-ing these things with me.

How Women Bond

As a woman, you might not understand bonding through activity, because women generally bond through communication. Obviously, the way men and women bond is different, yet neither is "right" or "wrong." The unique way, in which men and women bond, is part of their individual makeup. Since women bond through communication, men must make the effort to talk! In the early years of our marriage, Tom was not a communicator, and that bothered me a great deal. After we ate dinner, he would get up from the table, but I was just warming up for some after-dinner conversation! He finally made the necessary adjustments to accommodate me, and has since developed into quite a communicator. Today, Tom and I would rather spend time engaged in conversation with each other than with anyone else on the planet.

It's so important to understand the differences between men and women, and to appreciate those differences rather than criticize them. When you do that, you will learn to value and respect your spouse. Then when the two of you have disagreements, you can work them out together instead of fighting and storming off to separate rooms. In addition, your goals will change. Instead of fighting to see who wins and who loses, you will begin to see yourself as a team. You will also desire to help and bless each other and strengthen your marriage, so it can become everything God wants it to be.

Ready-Made or Built Over Time?

Many couples get married with the idea that they married the perfect mate. That's what they were looking for: perfection in marriage. Then when they see imperfections in the other person and in the relationship (and they inevitably will) sadly, they often bolt to a divorce lawyer to dissolve a union that had all the potential of being "Heaven on earth." Where did these couples miss it? They failed to realize that "perfect" or great marriages don't come ready-made, but are built over time. In other words, you don't just get a great marriage; you make a great marriage - and that takes time.

As you know, marriage is a picture of Christ and the Church, Christ's Bride (Ephesians 5:25-32; Revelation 21:9). Well, when we are born again, our new relationship with Christ doesn't just stop there. No, we need to continue to grow in our walk with the Lord. Similarly, the marriage relationship should grow and mature over time. A husband and wife should get married with the idea that they are building something together. It's a process that lasts a lifetime. If more couples took that attitude, there would be less bickering and criticizing going on, and a lot more praying and godly communication!

The groom should love his bride in much the same way that Christ loves the Church, and the bride should adore the groom in much the same way the Church adores Christ. Jesus laid His life down for the Church. He did not come to be served, but to serve others (see Mark 10:45). That is the husband's position in the marriage. He is supposed to be an example to his wife, children, extended family, neighbors, and co-workers of what a godly husband should be. The people in his life should know how much he loves his wife, his bride.

We already read the verse, "Husbands, likewise, dwell with them with understanding, giving honor to the wife..." (1 Peter 3:7 NKJV). Husbands, as well as wives, must understand the differences between the genders and walk in love instead of criticizing each other over these differences. One of the biggest differences in men and women—besides the most obvious physical differences—is in the way they process and communicate information. Men tend to major on majors; women tend to major on everything! A man needs to understand that about his wife, so that when she's majoring on things that he doesn't think are as important, he won't put her down or criticize her. Instead, he will realize that she's not looking for detailed solutions to her problems as much as just a listening, sympathetic ear.

A husband should know that comfort goes a lot further than criticism in the marriage. So instead of criticizing his wife for over-focusing on something, he could very lovingly and gently comfort her and let her know that what she is so focused on at the moment is not a priority, in terms of spending her time and energy thinking about it. In doing that, a husband is helping his wife instead of hurting her, and that goes a long way in building a marriage based on differences, instead of tearing it down because of them.

Men are headliners, while women want the whole story. Women also want to tell the story ten times! A husband needs to exercise patience in this area. When his wife repeats herself she's not trying to annoy him—she's simply being a woman. He married a woman, and the woman in his life is probably going to act like one. He needs to understand and value all the ways in which she is different from him. (The opposite is true too. A wife must value the differences she sees in her husband. He's not a woman, and she shouldn't want him to act like one!)

Logic and Emotions — Seeing Past the Facts and Feelings

When a man processes information, he tends to be motivated more by logic, whereas a woman tends to be more motivated by emotion. As a result, the man represents logic in the marriage relationship, while the woman represents emotion. This is simply the way God created us, and remember, what God creates is good! Some people think that it is wrong to have or show emotions. However, emotions are not wrong unless we allow them to run our lives—or our marriages! We must be moved by the Holy Spirit and the Word of God, not by our feelings.

God has given us the power to take control of our emotions, instead of allowing them to dictate our lives. In itself, logic is not wrong, but it can become wrong if it is exalted over the Word and the Spirit of God. It seems that the world has exalted logic over believing in the existence of God. This is a tragic and costly mistake.

Celebrating the Differences

As I said earlier, in many marriages, instead of celebrating each other's differences, those differences are often criticized or belittled. For example, when a husband criticizes the fact that his wife is emotional, he is, in effect, devaluing her. Similarly, if the wife criticizes a normal male trait in her husband, she is calling into question his worth, too. Marriage is most successful when it's about the other person, instead of you. Marriage is about laying down your life for the your spouse—not being a doormat, but laying down your life in an attitude of love. I'm talking about the unconditional, God-kind of love. If you are a Christian, you can operate in that kind of love. "Now hope does not disappoint, because the love of God has been poured out in our hearts by the Holy Spirit who was given to us" (Romans 5:5 NKJV).

...the unconditional love of God is the foundation for building a great marriage.

We have the outpouring of God's love in our life so we are capable of showing forth that love, but we have to draw on it. Again, that takes effort; it's not something we are always going to automatically want to do. The unconditional love of God is the foundation for building a great marriage. In talking about unconditional love, people often get confused because they confuse love with a feeling. But love is not always a feeling; it is a choice. It may be accompanied by feelings, but often it's not. There are times when you will need to choose to love your spouse. You can't wait for a feeling. If you do, your marriage could be destroyed while you are "waiting."

Love Begins at Home

Every day when I wake up, I embrace love. God is love, and I am His child. So that means I can walk in love. I can love my husband the way he needs to be loved—the way he best receives it. Since that's different for everyone, that means I need to make the effort to understand Tom, and then show him love in the way that he needs it instead of the way that's easiest for me. That's what it means to lay down your life in marriage. Have you ever heard the saying, "Love is not love until you give it away?" It's true. Love is an action, and it is expressed through giving. This can be seen in God's sending His Son, Jesus to the earth as the Savior of mankind and Sacrifice for our sin. "For God so loved the world that He gave His only begotten Son, that whoever believes in Him should not perish but have everlasting life" (John 3:16).

God loved the world—you and me—when we were dead in sin. Since He loved us, He gave of Himself in order to save us. In other words, He showed us His love in the Person of Jesus Christ. "And walk in love, as Christ also has loved us and given Himself for us, an offering and a sacrifice to God for a sweet-smelling aroma" (Ephesians 5:2 NKJV). We are commanded as Christians to walk in love, but walking in love begins in the home. In other words, we should be thinking every day, *How can I show my spouse love?* We need to focus on what our spouse needs. If we don't love our husband or wife the way he or she needs to be loved and go to church and show acts of love and kindness to others, then our love is just "noise" (1 Corinthians 13:1), because love starts in the home.

> *We are commanded as Christians to walk in love, but walking in love begins in the home.*

In his book, *The 5 Love Languages: The Secret to Love that Lasts* (Northfield Publishing: Chicago, IL, 1992), Gary Chapman says that each one of us speaks one love language better than the others. In other words, we each respond best to one of these five love languages: acts of service; quality time; words of affirmation; receiving of gifts; and physical touch. When our spouse fails to "speak" to us in our language, our "love tank" can be drained, and we begin to feel empty and unfulfilled in our marriage relationship. A healthy marriage results when both parties feel loved, cared for, and very secure in the relationship.

In my own words and in no particular order, I will briefly summarize a characteristic of each of these love languages, but I highly recommend that you read Dr. Chapman's book for yourself.

1. **Acts of Service** – Receiving services rendered by a loved one.

2. **Quality Time** – Spending quality, uninterrupted time focused on each other and communicating with each other—talking and listening.

3. **Words of Affirmation** – Receiving words that affirm, express gratitude, and build up.

4. **Receiving of Gifts** – Receiving gifts, big and small, as tokens of thoughtfulness and appreciation. These are simply visual aids that say, "I love you."

5. **Physical Touch and Closeness** – Receiving touch consistently from a loved one, such as a hug, a pat on the back, or a kiss on the cheek—or just being near each other.

My Own Story

When we first got married, Tom was very big into "acts of service." This was the primary love language spoken in his home when he was growing up. His stepmother was from Norway and didn't speak English very well, but she knew how to show love through acts of service. At mealtimes, she hardly ever sat down at the table, because she was constantly waiting on everyone "hand and foot."

Tom enjoyed this expression of love, so you can understand why this was his primary love language. His secondary love language was physical touch. However, neither of those were my main love languages. My primary love language was quality time. I was big on communication, and it takes time, attention, and focus to really communicate with someone else. I came from a large family in which everyone did his own laundry and fended for himself, so there were not a lot of "acts of service" happening at my house. Among a family of seven, however, there was plenty of communication. We were all great communicators, so communication became my primary love language early in life.

When Tom and I visited my family, he was amazed by all the communication that went on there! He was from a quiet home, so when everyone at my house would all talk at once, he could hardly stand it. As you can imagine, when we got married, we both had to make some big adjustments in order to speak the right love language to each other—to show love to each other in the way we each needed to receive it.

It is easy to understand from its simple definition, that "acts of service" are manifested by performing tangible acts to meet someone else's need, such as filling a water glass, doing a chore, or running an errand. Quality time is all about communicating—talking and listening. When you are spending quality time with someone, you are giving him or her your undivided attention. You are not clicking the remote and nodding your head every so often, while your thoughts are somewhere else. When you are speaking the language of quality time, you stop what you are doing and look at that other person, instead of staring at the TV or out into space while he or she is talking.

Now, let me show you, from personal experience, how the two love languages of "acts of service" and "quality time" can collide and leave behind a trail of hurt feelings. Shortly after Tom and I were married, I prepared a meal for us and we were enjoying that meal together. Then

Tom made the statement, "I would like some ketchup." At first, I honestly didn't understand why he would say such a thing! I remember thinking, *Is he asking me for ketchup?* I responded by saying, "It's in the refrigerator." So he got up and got his own ketchup.

Later I learned that this instance, and others like it, affected his feelings of being loved by me. By failing to pick up on his cues that he desired help ("acts of service"), I was not filling his love tank. After Tom ate his dinner that night, he just stood up and walked away. He was ready to go on to the next thing, but his actions left *my* love tank leaking! I was sitting there thinking, *Hey, we're supposed to sit here and talk, not eat and run!*

Early in our marriage, Tom was not a communicator, and I was not a server. In fact, I hated acts of service! When I first learned about the five love languages, I said, "Oh, God, why is he 'acts of service!'" So I had to change my attitude and my behavior, because acts of service was how Tom best received love. I eventually learned to love acts of service, but not before I made a whole-hearted change in my willingness to show my husband love in the way he needed it most.

Since Tom was responsible for our finances during the early years of our marriage, often he would go grocery shopping with me to help me stay within our budget. At first, I didn't know why he wanted to go to the store with me. In fact, the first time he said, "I'd like to go shopping with you," I thought, *If he wants to go grocery shopping, why should I go too? Why waste the energy? I'll just let him do the shopping instead.* Eventually I learned to appreciate his love language. Acts of service was how Tom best received love in those days, but it was also how he showed love. I needed to accompany him to the store, because he wanted me to do acts of service with him.

Since physical touch was also one of Tom's main love languages at this time, I had other adjustments I needed to make in our marriage. Physical touch was not one of my primary love languages during our early days together, so Tom practically had to give me a warning before he hugged me! I eventually got over that, and now we are a very affectionate couple. I began to realize the value Tom placed on physical touch, as well as the importance that affection plays in a marriage. (We will talk about the subject of affection and physical intimacy in another chapter.)

A big part of having a successful marriage is learning to think about what the other person in that marriage needs, and then being willing to meet that person where he or she is. When you meet someone else's "love need," it's amazing how your needs get met, too. On the other hand, when you are running on empty, because you are not being loved the way you desire, you will experience emotional pain, insecurity and feelings of rejection. If these feelings linger over a period of time, the marriage will not thrive. We all need to feel loved in our own unique way.

Love Must Give to Qualify as Love

Some people receive love best by receiving of gifts, or other tangible expressions of love. They need a visual aid that says, "I really do love you." To those who are motivated by this language, you can say, "I love you," but you need to show them you love them, because they are motivated by tangible tokens of love and appreciation, not just by words.

The reason I recommend Gary Chapman's book, *The Five Love Languages: How to Express Heartfelt Commitment to Your Mate,* is that once you know your own love language and the love language of your spouse, you can go to work filling each other's love tank! Many couples go for years on end running on empty. It's no wonder that intimacy has been destroyed in those relationships. The goal of every couple should be to build and maintain intimacy in their marriage. However, you can't do that if you feel unloved as a husband or wife.

Tom and I spent the first years of our life together learning these things about each other. We both came from dysfunctional families. In fact, we were first-generation Christians, so we had a lot to overcome. We were committed to our marriage, and we persisted in our efforts to build a great marriage by understanding, valuing, and even celebrating our many differences. We learned the truth that different is good, and I can honestly say that today our marriage is "Heaven on earth!"

Tom:

Our differences as husband and wife are good, because our gifts and purposes are a result of our uniqueness and design. In other words, who we are inherently as male and female is what we bring to the table in marriage to foster, strengthen, and bless that union. In short, we need each other!

We've established the fact that women, by design, are incubators. They foster words and bring forth life from those words. In fact, the name of the first woman, Eve, means "giver of life." Women tend to think about, meditate, and process in their minds the same thing over and over again—for long periods of time. They should not be criticized or belittled for this, because it's in their nature to do this.

If something goes wrong, I can't lay the blame on her. I can't say "I told you so!"

A godly woman who processes problems in the light of God's Word, can bring forth wisdom and a godly solution to the dilemmas of life. Men tend to make snap decisions when they are faced with a situation that needs their attention. Men have a gift for making decisions, but when those decisions are made in haste, oftentimes, they are not based on the wisdom of God.

I have made certain decisions in the past based on pure, simple logic—and that's a good thing—but at times I've inadvertently excluded the wisdom of God. Maureen has said to me, "I'm not sure we should do it that way," and she would tell me why. After I thought about it, in many cases I concluded that she was right and that I was about to mess up, if I continued with my original assessment. What happened? I had made a snap decision; she had given birth to truth. I'm not saying that a man can't walk in the wisdom of God. He certainly can and should do that, but a wise man will listen to the godly counsel of his wife.

There is another side to this process of decision-making that I want to reiterate. If I make my final decision based on input I received from my wife, the responsibility for that decision is mine, not hers. Ultimately, it is my responsibility to make the decision. So if something goes wrong, I can't lay the blame on her. I can't say, "I told you so! See what you've done!" No, I listen to Maureen, and I glean wisdom from her insight, but the ultimate decision is my responsibility. In other words, I am the one who is responsible for the decision once it has been made.

There has been so much error concerning the subject of a husband's headship in the home. The truth is, marriage is a fifty-fifty partnership. Both parties have the potential to walk in the wisdom of God. If they are saved, both parties possess knowledge, understanding, and the power of God. As they learn to draw on each other and their unique gifts as individuals, then they will collectively meet with more and more success in the marriage. It's true that the husband must accept the ultimate responsibility for making decisions for the family, but that doesn't mean he's a "Lone Ranger," who doesn't value the gift of God in his wife.

A Man Is a Protector and a Provider

In the last chapter, we learned the differences between the genders and the fact that there was a God-ordained purpose in our design and our differences. For example, men were designed to be faster and stronger. Does that mean that there's never been a woman who was faster or stronger than a man? No, of course not. The Bible says that men are to treat their wife as the weaker vessel (1 Peter 3:7). It doesn't say that she is the weaker vessel; it simply says that her husband should treat her as the weaker vessel.

This might sound confusing so let me illustrate what I mean. When I'm with Maureen, I open the door to the car or to a building for her. That doesn't mean that she can't open a door by herself—she does it all the time when I'm not with her! But when I'm with her, I do that because I want to honor her as "the weaker vessel." Have I always opened doors for my wife? No, she trained me to do it. She would just walk up to a door and stand there, cool and collected, until I opened it. So I was trained quickly to perform this act of chivalry for my wife. This simple act of opening the door for my wife makes her feel cared for and protected.

Chivalry has been largely lost to this generation, because parents have not trained their children in this area. I think it's courteous for men, in general, to open doors for women. When I was growing up, we called our elders "ma'am" and "sir." You rarely hear that anymore. That's sad because those words carry with them tones of respect. If we fail to teach our children respect, then when they grow up, they will not respect themselves or others, as they should. We often see this in manifestation in the way young people treat property. If they have no respect for property, they will mishandle it. This is unfortunate, because when a young man is groomed to behave biblically as a man, he creates the right atmosphere for success in his own home life and marriage.

Man is a protector and a provider by nature. These traits were determined by his design. Sometimes these traits are misinterpreted as being "macho." Usually, a man who exhibits these qualities is only being true to his purpose.

I have been accused of being overprotective in my role as a protector. For instance, I don't want Maureen to go shopping at night by herself. If she needs to go out at night, I will offer to go along or even go to the store for her. I am not babying her—I'm simply taking responsibility and being true to my nature.

Just as a woman should not be faulted for her design; a man should not be faulted for his design, either. A part of a man's makeup is to protect and provide.

I'm sure you know men who do not make an effort to provide for their families. They might be selfish or lazy. A lazy man had to learn how to be lazy over time, because work is an integral part of his purpose. Perhaps something in his childhood trained him to be lazy and unmotivated. Maybe some outside influence impacted his life, because when a man is true to his design, he won't be lazy. He will work to provide for his family.

Unfortunately, today many parents are raising their children to be unmotivated. I'm not saying that they are doing this intentionally. Look around and you will find that motivated young workers are few and far between. Maybe as they were growing up, someone just handed them money to buy what they wanted, instead of training them to work for it. Or maybe their home was cleaned by a cleaning service, and they were never required to learn these basic life skills for themselves. Failing to incorporate these basic values in our children while they are young, will cause them to be ill-equipped to thrive in a home of their own later in life.

God knew what He was doing when He created the genders male and female. He created them to look differently, act differently, feel differently, and think differently. We have seen that men are logical thinkers; they tend to think in terms of the bottom line. They don't usually think as thoroughly as women. They are also emotionally disconnected in their thought process. Why? They are built that way so they can, for example, kill a deer, skin it, and provide food for their family. Or on the battlefield, they can kill an attacker when confronted, in order to protect their family's freedom and well-being. For the most part, women are not designed that way. They are both thinkers and feelers. But men make very few connections between the thinking and feeling parts of their brain. They have less connection between the hemispheres that, respectively, influence logic and emotion.

Emotion lives on the right side of the brain; logic lives on the left side. That's the way God created us. We have seen this in the womb. When a male baby receives an infusion of testosterone in his brain, that slows the growth of the emotional, right side of the brain, so that the "logic side" grows a little bit faster. This doesn't mean that males are not emotional; it simply means that they are less emotional than females.

Generally speaking, men cannot do multiple tasks simultaneously. We like to do one thing at a time. So when a man says, "I'm listening dear—I'm just watching the game," he is probably lying about it no matter how good his intentions! He's only listening to one of those things—his wife or the game, but probably not both. On the other hand, women have the ability to do multiple things at once. Maureen can be listening to praise and worship and scriptures on CD at the same time she's doing Sudoku—and while she's doing that, she can even catch something she heard from another room on the evening news!

A Man and His 'Separate' Emotions

Men have difficulty thinking or feeling multiple things at the same time. We can think without feeling, and we can feel without thinking. Conversely, we can't think when we are feeling, and we can't feel when we are thinking! That's why we lose every argument with our wife! A woman can get her husband over into the emotional realm in a conversation, where he can't even think straight. His brain will zero out! An hour later, he might think, *Oh, I should have said this, this, and this.* But at the moment, he couldn't think; he could only feel. That's part of what enables him to protect so well. That's just how he's made.

A man can set focused goals from which he can't be deterred. This is his strength. He has the ability to determine the shortest distance between two points, to gain momentum, and to maximize efficiencies. Changing a man's goals takes reprogramming and time. For example, if Maureen and I are set to go to a particular restaurant, I've already plotted the route that I'm going to drive to get there, and I've already decided what I'm going to order off the menu! If Maureen suddenly says, "Let's go here instead," my brain has to re-program. Suddenly, I'm dazed. *Which way do I turn? What am I going to eat?* Once I re-program, I'm okay, but it takes a little bit of time and effort.

Men are protectors; women are nurturers. That's their design. Men and women can see the exact same thing and have two completely different thoughts about it. A woman can see a tree and think, *How pretty.* A man will see the same tree and think, *I'll cut it down and build a house.* Neither thought is wrong, necessarily. Each is different, because different processes are taking place when the man and the woman look at the tree.

Women are emotional thinkers. They evaluate, incubate, rehearse and review every possible scenario. A woman doesn't like it when a man solves a problem in one sentence, especially after she has thought on the whole picture for so long. Instead of trying to solve it in a sentence, he simply needs to listen to her as she continues to give birth to the answer by talking about it. She probably already knows, or thinks she knows, what she's going to do. The last thing she wants to hear from a man is, "That's easy; just do this."

Women see detail. They see everything going on around them, and they remember what they see and hear better than men do. They can remember who wore what or said what, on what date, time or place. We think back to certain events and have trouble even remembering the year it happened! A woman can change a diaper, talk on the phone, and check homework—all at the same time. She can sense other people's feelings intuitively. She perceives, analyzes, and evaluates the status of relationships. She has insight about things that men don't have a clue about, because she can think and feel at the same time.

In order to separate logic from emotion, a woman must talk about a subject from every angle. Have you ever noticed that a wife can tell the same story over and over again, highlighting every angle—the left, right, middle, top and bottom—while her husband is thinking, *Okay, enough already! I got it! I got it!* (Notice I said that he's only thinking these things. A smart man will never speak those words out loud, because he understands and appreciates his wife's differences.)

We Need Each Other

As different as men and women think, perceive, process thoughts, and behave, the fact remains that men and women need each other. Men need women to help them avoid the potholes of life. For instance, Abigail saved David from inflicting unnecessary harm to her wicked husband Nabal, by intervening and feeding David and his starving troops (see First Samuel 25:2-42). She basically kept David from making a serious mistake—and later, when Nabal died, she became David's wife.

In the New Testament, Pilate's wife tried to influence her husband to have nothing to do with the crucifixion of Jesus. Finally, Pilate said to the Jews who were intent on killing the Savior, "I wash my hands of this Man's innocent blood. I find no fault in Him" (Matthew 27:24; Luke 23:4; John 18:38). A woman needs her husband because of his ability to focus on a goal and make everything go in that direction. She also needs him because he is the responsible party in the relationship. It is his God-ordained design to be the responsible party in the home—not a dominator—but a partner who bears ultimate responsibility. A husband and wife are fifty-fifty partners, but, ultimately, he is the one who is responsible to protect and provide for his wife and children.

4
THREE THINGS THAT DRIVE A SUCCESSFUL MARRIAGE

Drs. Tom and Maureen Anderson

It has been said that knowledge is power, and we know from Scripture that people can be destroyed for a lack of knowledge (see Hosea 4:6). Consequently, many marriages have been destroyed because one or both parties in a marriage, simply did not know what else to do. If they had been equipped with knowledge and understanding from God's Word—or even with practical knowledge that had its basis in God's Word—many of these marriages could have been saved. In this chapter, we are going to share some practical knowledge concerning the driving force behind every successful marriage. Certainly, God and His Word are number one, but connecting God and His Word to marriage requires understanding and effort. This is where prayer and seeking God comes in—to give us the wisdom, understanding, and grace to apply His Word to the circumstances in our lives.

No Longer One, but Two — No Longer Two, but One

"'And the two shall become one flesh'; so then they are no longer two, but one flesh" (Mark 10:8 NKJV). So far, we have addressed husbands and wives, both separately and as couples. It is important to realize that while we each have our individual roles to play in the relationship, marriage is indeed a partnership. We must work out our problems together, even if a particular problem is with only one spouse. If you are married, never allow your spouse to go through a difficult situation or trial that they are facing alone. You are a team, and teams act together—in unison—toward a common goal. It has been said that the happiest marriages consist of two of the best forgivers on earth. So whatever issues you may be facing, the first thing you need to do is to get past your hurt feelings quickly and join forces with your spouse to work through issues that ultimately affect you both.

Maureen:

I've discovered three specific keys that can help you and your spouse achieve "Heaven on earth" in your marriage. In fact, they are the driving forces behind all successful marriages:

1. Desire to please your spouse.

2. Behave in a loving manner.

3. Strive to meet your spouse's needs.

This may sound simple, but these are the elements that make a marriage happy and successful. When husbands and wives buy into the truth that marriage is about giving—not just receiving—they both will be mutually fulfilled in the relationship.

Number One: Desire to Please Your Spouse

The first driving force in a successful marriage is the desire to please your spouse. Do you know what pleases your spouse and makes him or her happy? Do you know the desire of his or her heart? Never allow yourself to become indifferent to your spouse's dreams, but instead take an active interest in those dreams. As a husband or wife, we must know what makes our spouse "tick." We need to know what really makes that person happy and content in life. Whatever it is, we should want that for our spouse and should do whatever we can to please them.

How to Meet Your Spouse's Needs

Many people sincerely desire to meet their spouse's needs, but they don't know where to begin. I have compiled the following list of helpful ways to discover and meet the needs of your spouse.

1. Ask the Holy Spirit for help in discerning your spouse's needs. Sometimes we simply need help to stay sensitive to our spouse's changing needs. And who knows our spouse better than his or her Creator?

2. Spend quality time with your spouse while communicating your needs—talking and listening.

3. Express your needs in love, not in accusing tones.

4. Be flexible and willing to change if necessary.

5. Accept each other's unique qualities and differences. It's difficult for someone to open up when he feels he might be ridiculed for what he shares.

6. Don't pressure the other person with "fairy tale" expectations. Put your faith in God first. Then realistically assess in your heart how your spouse can best meet your needs.

7. Make the needs in your relationship a priority. Make no mistake, many activities will vie for your attention to distract you from the things that are most important: your relationship with God and your spouse.

8. Keep the goal of deeper intimacy ever before you. Remember the truth that meeting another's needs, big and small, creates emotional bonding.

Tom:

As Maureen said, there will always be things that will come to distract you from what's most important in life: especially your relationship with your family and your spouse. Most of these distractions will come in the form of activities and obligations. I encourage you to be alert concerning the things you think you "must" do that take you away from your family, because Satan—the enemy of your soul and of your family—is very subtle in the way he presents some of these things.

The 'Parent Trap'

Even the most well-intentioned parents can interfere in their children's marriages, and cause great damage or even divorce. Although it's sad that many of these parents are blinded to Scripture regarding the type of relationship they should have with their married children, it's up to that married couple—not the parents—to draw the line and set the boundaries where this type of interference is concerned. "Therefore a man shall leave his father and mother and be joined to his wife, and they shall become one flesh" (Genesis 2:24 NKJV).

The desire to please your spouse should be one of the driving forces in a happy marriage. Pleasing your spouse can be a challenge when one or both of your parents are pressuring you to please them, too. In that type of situation, you must focus on your priorities—on God first and your spouse second. When you put the Lord first, His wisdom is going to dictate that you seek to please your spouse and that you say, "No!" to Mom and Dad.

Just Say 'No' to Mom and Dad

When a man and a woman say, "I do" and become joined together in holy matrimony, they become "one flesh" in the sight of God. They are not just making a connection in marriage. We have read Genesis

2:24 and thought it meant that a man physically leaves his family to get married, but it's okay for him and his wife to hang on to a dysfunctional, interfering relationship with their families. We have thought that we could continue to have our families enmeshed in our lives and everything would be okay. It will not be okay! You cannot truly become one flesh in marriage if you still have the tentacles of your family's wishes, opinions, and desires woven into the fabric of your new life with your spouse.

Genesis 2:24 says, that a man shall "leave and cleave" in marriage— that he shall leave his parents and cleave, or be joined to, his wife. The word "leave" in that verse, portrays a married person who is no longer controlled, obedient to, or submitted to his or her parents. With this verse as your standard of truth, it is easy to determine which behaviors from a married person's family are dysfunctional and distorted, and which are normal and healthy.

A married man or woman can still love and respect his or her parents, but that husband or wife must not allow a parent to cross the boundary lines, where God-ordained authority between the husband and wife is concerned. Too often parents try to cross those lines, and one or both parties in the marriage allow those lines to be crossed. Once authority inside a marriage is yielded outside of the marriage—outside of God's will and established order—chaos and confusion will result.

When a man and woman become "one flesh" in marriage, a change must take place in the couple's relationship with their parents, siblings, grandparents, and so forth. Those relatives must take on new roles. They can continue as friends and advisors, but decisions concerning the new couple are ultimately theirs alone to make. That means that parents should not try to control, manipulate, or stick their nose into the couple's business!

I'm not saying, that a son or daughter can't seek and counsel wisdom from his or her parents, and then take that advice back to the marriage.

But that advice should not be taken back as a weapon to be used against his or her spouse! Ultimately, decisions come from inside the marriage, not from outside the marriage. If this principle is violated, it will be impossible to put your spouse first above all others, and this will not be pleasing to God.

Maureen:

From time to time, Tom and I will hear of a couple having marriage problems, and one of them has gone to a parent about the problem, often without talking about it first with his or her spouse. Fortunately, in some cases, a wise, godly parent will encourage them to go back and communicate with his or her spouse concerning the situation. On the other hand, often the parent becomes hurt and angry instead, and lashes out at the other spouse behind his or her back. Consequently, nothing is resolved—in fact, the fires of discord are only fanned until they become a raging inferno!

This reminds me of the sage counsel a respected minister once shared: "In every situation and circumstance, ask yourself, 'What does the Word of God say and what would love do?'" Of course, love is the foundation for a great marriage. But remember, love is an action; it does something. It is a driving force in the success and well-being of a marriage.

Number Two: Behave in a Loving Manner

The first driving force in a happy marriage is the desire to please your spouse. The second driving force is closely connected to the first: We must behave in a loving manner at all times toward our spouse. If we have to address something in the marriage that could cause hurt feelings, we must do it in a loving way. We should never be guilty of treating friends, co-workers, or fellow church members with more tenderness and consideration than we do our own flesh and blood!

Behaving in a loving manner entails having insight into how our spouse best receives love. We talked about the love languages, and we discovered that in a marriage one spouse might receive or respond to love differently than the other. Yet that does not make his or her way less valid or important. We must purpose in our heart to "wake up" to the needs and desires of our spouse—to allow our heart to become awakened to the beauty in that other person.

Real love—the God-kind of love—is about giving. That's the way God's Kingdom operates: in giving, not taking. Jesus came to give; the devil came to take (John 10:10). In so many marriages today, we see people entering the relationship for what they can get out of it, not for what they can contribute to it. Love is thinking of the other person and trusting that he or she is thinking of you. Marriage is two-sided. A marriage that consists of one giver and one taker will not be successful. But a marriage in which both partners behave in a loving manner, will succeed and flourish.

How to Address a Lopsided Marriage

In any teaching on marriage, we invariably hear of situations in which one mate gives and the other simply takes, with little or no regard for the needs of the other person. Well, that must be addressed, but it must be addressed in love! It can't be addressed in an emotional way, because that's usually when accusations begin to fly, and the "guilty" party starts throwing up walls and defenses—all attempts to resolve the problem become futile.

If you must address an issue of "lopsidedness" with your mate, address it first with the Lord. Go to Him in prayer and fasting. Seek His face and humbly and sincerely ask Him what to do. He may lead you to endure a season of sacrificial giving in love, while He works in that other person's heart.

Almost any marriage counselor will tell you to use "I" statements instead of "you" statements, when confronting someone. In other words,

> *We should never be guilty of treating friends, co-workers, or fellow church members with more tenderness and consideration than we do our own flesh and blood!*

instead of accusing the other person— saying things such as, "You always do this" or, "You never do that" —you could say, "I know that you're a kind person. I know you probably don't realize it, but I'm feeling unfulfilled in certain areas, and I'd like to talk about it if it's okay with you." This way you are attesting to your own feelings, not in a whiny, complaining manner, but as a matter of fact. You are being honest, but you are also being loving. Also, you are not getting into strife and saying and doing things that you will regret later.

You Can Be Right and Still Be Wrong

Did you know that you can be right in a situation, and still be wrong? You can be right in your argument, but present it in a wrong manner— outside the confines of God's love. Now your problem has been compounded, because instead of just dealing with the original problem, now you also have to deal with your misbehavior. Most of the time in a "lopsided" marriage, the person whose needs are not being met will just bury his or her feelings instead of communicating, or will communicate in an unloving manner. This can create chaos in the marriage.

The need for change in such a marriage must be communicated, but it must be done with an attitude of prayer and forgiveness, instead of anger and resentment. Even then, things may not turn around completely overnight. If your spouse is open to God's dealings and is honest in his or her estimation of the problem, then you have taken a huge step toward a happy and rewarding marriage.

Number Three:
Strive to Meet Your Spouse's Needs

The third element of a successful marriage is striving to meet your spouse's needs. What are your spouse's needs? Needs can change through the seasons of life. What your spouse needed last month might not be what he or she needs today. For example, if your spouse has been working a lot of overtime, is there something you could do for him or her at home that will make life easier? Maybe you could temporarily double up on some of the responsibilities in the home.

Your spouse's need might be anything from something tangible, to a need for spending some extra quality time with you. You can train yourself to become more sensitive to your spouse's needs, and then strive to meet them. That word "strive" implies expending effort and energy. In other words, it might not always be easy or convenient to meet your spouse's needs. That's why you must strive to do it! The effort you put forth to meet your spouse's needs is so important! It's the investment of a lifetime, and it will mean the difference between feelings of love that grow and flourish, and feelings that weaken and wane over time.

Happiness is found in relationships—relationships with God, your spouse, your children, and your family and friends.

Feelings of love are a response to having your needs met. In other words, when your needs are met, then you feel loved. For example, think of how loved you felt when God met your need for salvation. The moment you asked Jesus into your heart, you felt the weight of the world lift from you. Not only did God save you, but He continues to meet your needs today, because He never changes. He's the same yesterday, today, and forever (Malachi 3:6; Hebrews 13:8). "And my God shall supply all your need according to His riches in glory by Christ Jesus" (Philippians 4:19 NKJV). "Let us therefore come boldly to the throne of grace that we may obtain mercy and find grace to help in time of need" (Hebrews 4:16 NKJV).

Certainly, God does not expect you, as a couple, to take His place in each other's lives that only He can fill. You are not supposed to make your spouse a "god." However, it is scriptural to meet your spouse's needs as much as you possibly can. Even medical science has confirmed that when someone meets another's need, a special bond occurs between them. So a husband and wife should desire to meet each other's needs as much as possible! Feelings of pleasure, peace, and fondness grow in an atmosphere where a person's needs are met. A husband and wife who consistently meet each other's needs, form a greater bond than those who don't.

Also, when your needs are being met, it creates within you a desire to meet the needs of others. Instead of waiting for your husband or wife to meet your needs first, take the initiative to find his or her needs and meet them. True love develops over a lifetime of putting each other first and meeting each other's needs. Science has also proven that when a person's needs consistently go unmet, chemicals that cause negative emotions about the relationship are released in the body. The person becomes overwhelmed by a sense of disappointment, discouragement, frustration, dissatisfaction, and lack of connection or intimacy. If these negative emotions continue, a critical attitude usually begins to develop, along with feelings of deep resentment and contempt. If this pattern is allowed to continue, without acknowledging or addressing these emotions, then the marriage will fall into deep trouble.

How does a marriage get to this place? Often it's the result of our hectic lifestyles—which is usually the result of overvaluing material things and undervaluing our relationships. When we become too busy in our quest to obtain things, we gradually stop valuing our relationships. We stop valuing our marriage, and as a matter of course, we place less and less importance on pleasing our mate, walking in love, and looking for ways to meet our spouse's needs. Slowly and subtly, the marriage begins to erode. Dissatisfaction continues to mount until one day, suddenly, we are unhappy with the relationship. Criticisms start to fly as we begin to devalue our spouse and blame each other for everything that's wrong in our marriage.

Happiness Is Found in People, Not in Things

Does this describe you or someone you know? If your marriage is in trouble, I encourage you to put your desire for material gain on hold, so you can work on your marriage. Perhaps you will need to get rid of some things that have become a "money pit" to maintain. Maybe you will have to drive cars that are less than new for a while. You should do whatever you need to do to cut your budget, so you can focus on what's important—and you should do it as quickly as possible! You don't need more possessions, but you do need a happy marriage and a life of fulfillment, contentment, and effectiveness for the Kingdom of God. Happiness is found in relationships—relationships with God, your spouse, your children, and your family and friends—not in your possessions.

I'm not talking about something I read in a book. I've lived this. Tom and I didn't really begin prospering in life until we were in our forties. Our basic needs were met when we were in our twenties and thirties. Tom worked hard, but we didn't invest all of our time and energy into obtaining more things, or bigger and better things. Instead, we invested in each other and in our relationship, and we were very happy and fulfilled. It has been an investment that has paid off abundantly! Today we have material prosperity and possessions, but we know that these things can never fulfill us. We are happy in life, not because we have wealth, but because we have each other, and a happy, successful marriage that's "Heaven on earth."

How to Make God Happy

God will give you and your spouse material things. He will bless you and increase you when you put Him first—when you are chasing Him and His Kingdom, instead of things. "But seek first the kingdom of God and His righteousness, and all these things shall be added to you" (Matthew 6:33 NKJV). Marriage is an institution created by God, as well as a picture of the relationship between Christ and the Church (Ephesians 5:21-33). When marriages thrive and succeed, God is honored. Part of "seeking first God's Kingdom," is honoring Him and His will in your marriage. When you pay the price to build your marriage according to His Word—and to endeavor to please your spouse—you are pleasing the Lord, too.

5
RESPONSIBILITY BEFORE AUTHORITY— DON'T PUT THE CART BEFORE THE HORSE

Dr. Tom Anderson

The roles and responsibilities in marriage have been greatly misunderstood over the years. There have been many teachings on marriage in the Church that have hurt marriages more than helped them. Since God created the institution of marriage, His Word sheds light on this subject. God has established a divine order for the home. If we follow His design and order for marriage, then He will cause it to prosper and flourish beyond imagination.

Some traditional teachings have placed women in a hyper-submissive role to their husbands that is unreasonable and reaches beyond the bounds of Scripture. In fact, some of it defies sound biblical doctrine! Some things that happen in the home in the name of religion, do nothing more than bind up the spirit of a woman—making her a "shell" of a person—while giving her husband a free pass to do as he pleases, answering to no one.

Running with the Wrong Rule

What are the responsibilities of men in marriage? Are we, as husbands, responsible to just sit on the couch and watch TV, while our wives bring us our favorite cold drink or snack? Very often the picture of a husband is someone who lies on the sofa or recliner and hollers at his wife to toss him the remote, but she can't hear him because she's outside mowing the lawn! Of course I say that jokingly, to make the point that the wife's role in the marriage is not servitude! This is a false concept that needs to be exposed and dealt with, in order to have a happy and thriving marriage.

Many Christian men, and even whole denominations, tout the verses about men ruling over their wives and families (Genesis 3:16; 1 Timothy 3:5). They preach certain verses on "rulership" in the home and want to "run with it." The only problem is, they are running with the wrong rule! Let's look at one of these verses on "ruling." "To the woman He said, 'I will greatly multiply your sorrow and your conception; In pain you shall bring forth children; Your desire shall be for your husband, And he shall rule over you'" (Genesis 3:16 NKJV).

After the Fall of man, God addressed the man and woman and then said to the woman, "Your desire shall be for your husband, and he shall rule over you." There have been so many misconceptions about that statement! What does that mean, "Your desire shall be for your husband"? That phrase actually means, "You'll desire to rule over your husband." We have seen the battle of the sexes occur in every generation, since God made that historic announcement. This struggle for power was not something that God put on Adam and Eve; it was simply the result of sin. In other words, God did not command the husband to rule over his wife; He simply related that a power struggle would ensue as a result of their sin. God said, in effect, "She will want to rule over him, and he will want to rule over her. They will have to deal with it."

The result of the Fall was not a curse from God; it was simply a cause-and-effect outcome. Sin always has an outcome. The Bible says that although it may bring a sense of pleasure and satisfaction for a while, it is only for a while—for a season. Then the "wages" of sin are always some form of death. (See Hebrew 11:25; Romans 6:23.) Christ has redeemed us from the curse of the Law (Galatians 3:13), and restored our position with the Father. It's a grace position. Under the New Testament in this era of grace, we are supposed to operate under the law of love. We are commanded to love one another, even as Christ has loved us (John 13:34)—not vie for positions of authority and control!

In many marriages today, the wife tries to run the home, and there are several reasons for this. Perhaps the husband is lazy. Maybe he's passive or just ignorant and doesn't know what to do, so he does nothing. Maybe he just doesn't want to do it, or becomes indifferent. There's some selfishness on his part, and he simply does not want the responsibility that's involved in leading a family.

On the other hand, the wife may have some trust issues where men are concerned. Perhaps her own father wasn't responsible in her home when she was growing up. Or at the other extreme, a woman finds herself in an abusive situation with an aggressive husband, who has taken the "submission" verses out of context and is using them for his own ends. "Submitting to one another in the fear of God. Wives, submit to your own husbands, as to the Lord" (Ephesians 5:21-22 NKJV). The husband who uses this verse to rule over his wife with an iron hand, has missed the part of the verse that says "as to the Lord." The Lord Jesus is not abusive, harsh, cruel, or demanding. So these husbands are definitely missing the point!

Something Every Woman Must Know About God Before Submitting to Her Husband

Ephesians 5:22 says, "Wives, submit to your own husbands, as to the Lord." Let's look at that phrase, "as to the Lord," because this is where many people miss it concerning this verse. They either skip over it altogether, or they misunderstand what it's actually saying. For example, if you have a wrong idea about God, you're going to misread this phrase. If you think God is the One who's making you sick, keeping you broke, and making your life miserable, you have the wrong attitude toward God. So consequently, whether consciously or subconsciously, you believe that He is abusive.

Some people view God as a hard, cold judge who is just waiting for them to step out of line so He can rain judgment down on them. That's very sad, because if you don't see God as He really is—as a good God—you are probably going to submit to abuse in relationships (I'm especially talking about women, although men can be abused, too). But if you see God as loving and good, and you understand that He has a good plan for your life, you will recognize abuse for what it is, and you will not accept it. You will never accept that kind of behavior as normal, because you know that the enemy, Satan, is the one who steals, kills, and destroys. You are vitally aware that Jesus came to bring you life "more abundantly" (see John 10:10).

In marriage, it's critical that a woman does not submit to anything that trespasses the boundaries of God's love. Instead, she must encourage her husband to rise to the occasion and become the loving leader that God intends him to be. He should portray the image or picture of Christ in the home—not the image of a harsh, tyrannical taskmaster.

Responsibility Before Authority

The husband and wife have the same value in the marriage, and neither one is supposed to "rule over" the other. The husband has certain responsibilities in regard to authority. His authority in the home extends only to the degree that he is willing to take responsibility for his family. He should wield that authority in an attitude of love.

When a husband and wife are functioning in a marriage with an attitude of love and cooperation, it is amazing how problems get resolved, goals are reached, and the marriage is strengthened. When a husband and wife are submitting to each other "in the fear of God" (Ephesians 5:21), it transforms and blesses them, their marriage, and their children.

Working Together

Ephesians 5:21 says, "Submit to one another out of reverence for Christ." It is important that husbands and wives submit to each other. In other words, they should work together. Yet much of the church world preaches, "Wives, submit to your husbands." This conveys the attitude that the wife is supposed to do any and every thing that the husband says without questioning him. He's the king of his castle, but he doesn't have a queen! This mindset ignores the synergy that should, and must exist, between a husband and wife in marriage. They are much more powerful when they work together, than when they are working separately. In fact, two people in agreement can do almost anything they set their hearts and minds to do!

If a husband and wife are in agreement and pulling together, they will be more successful and effective in every area of life. On the other hand, when a husband and wife are not in agreement, everything in life becomes more difficult. If a husband has one idea about how to raise children, and his wife has a completely different idea, this can have a negative effect on the children. These differences need to be discussed and resolved, so they can work together as a team to successfully raise their children.

A Side-by-Side Partnership

You have probably heard the saying, "**Behind** every great man is a great woman." But I will take this a step further and say, "**Beside** every great man is a great woman." The wife should not be walking behind her husband through life; she should be walking beside him. I will also go so far as to say that every successful man on earth has been influenced by a woman who did not put up with the things in his life that were unsavory or lacking in character. Instead, she submitted to God, prayed for her husband, and encouraged and helped him to grow and change.

I can honestly say that I am successful today because of God and my wife! Proverbs 27:17 says, "As iron sharpens iron, so one man sharpens another." I am "sharp" today, because of my wife. She is my equal and my partner in life. She has played a vital role in my growth and development as a man, husband, father, and minister.

So much can be accomplished when a husband and wife work together, side by side, to build a marriage, a family, and a life together, that will affect and bless future generations. Let me illustrate the power of this kind of unity from something I learned on my job as a young man. In those days, I cut timber for a living. I quickly discovered that if you had one horse, it could pull one ton of logs out of the woods. It would logically stand to reason, then, that two horses could pull at least twice that amount of weight. Yet I discovered that if those two horses were not in stride together—working side by side—they could only pull half the amount of weight, or about half a ton—even though there were two horses. But together in unison, two horses could pull not just two tons, but as much as four tons of timber!

Similarly, if a husband and wife are not in unison, they shoot themselves in the foot, so to speak. Anything they try to accomplish is almost counterproductive. They are not functioning at their optimum or highest potential, because they are not functioning side by side, in harmony and agreement.

Jesus said, "Take My yoke upon you and learn from Me..." (Matthew 11:29 NKJV). Then He says, "For My yoke is easy and My burden is light" (v. 30 NKJV). Jesus' yoke is easy, but the world's yoke is very heavy and difficult to carry; it's burdensome and wearisome. If your family is in a situation in which you, as the husband, are being overbearing in the way you lead your family—or your wife is leading the family for some reason—then you are wearing the world's yoke. Everything you do will take longer and be less than ideal. In other words, you will have to work harder for fewer results.

I'm not saying this to condemn anyone whose marriage has slipped into a situation like this. I'm simply saying that when the yoke of responsibility in a marriage is taken up by both parties and they walk side by side with that yoke they can accomplish the miraculous! "Again, I tell you that if two of you on earth agree about anything you ask for, it will be done for you by my Father in heaven" (Matthew 18:19 NIV). Sadly, the opposite is true, too. Prayers can be hindered, and dreams and goals can die on the vine, when a husband and wife disconnect by going separate directions in their marriage. Often one spouse has a vision for change, but the other does not. This can create a lot of tension, because one is trying to pull for two, yet accomplishing only half the task!

If a husband and wife are in agreement, pulling together, they will be more successful and effective in every area of life.

A Scriptural Portrayal of the 'Ruling Male'

Too often in marriages, we see the self-centered attitude of the "ruling" man. God did not design man to be an egotistical dominator of his wife! Yes, God gave him dominion, but it's the same kind of dominion and spiritual authority that He gave to the woman. They were both created in the image and likeness of God (Genesis 1:26-27). "For the husband is head of the wife, as also Christ is head of the church; and He is the Savior of the body. Therefore, just as the church subject to Christ, so let the wives be to their own husbands in everything" (Ephesians 5:23-24 NKJV).

The man has been given "headship" in marriage. That's not the same as dominion as we know it, or as it's been taught in some circles. As I said earlier, so many men have confused authority with responsibility. They readily accept the idea of authority, but they are not nearly as willing to take actual responsibility for the affairs of their home and family.

...he must prayerfully make the call based on what he senses the Lord leading him to do and on what he feels is best for his family, not what's best for him.

The man has been given some weighty responsibilities in marriage, such as making final decisions for the household. A wise man will consult and confer with his wife, his partner given to him by God. Then he must prayerfully make the call based on what he senses the Lord leading him to do and on what he feels is best for his family, not what's best for him. Now let's take a look at the husband's responsibilities in marriage.

Number One:
A Man Is Responsible to Know God

A man is responsible to seek out and discover the many facets of God's goodness and character, and then duplicate those characteristics in his own life and display them toward his family. Well, how does God deal with things? Doesn't the Word say that it's His kindness that leads us to repentance (Romans 2:4), and that we should be gentle and speak the truth in love (Ephesians 4:15)? Also, as a man, you must ask yourself, *What is my process for making decisions? Am I willing to gamble or compromise the future success and prosperity of my family on my own intelligence and abilities or am I willing to pray and seek the face of God?*

"If any of you lacks wisdom, let him ask of God, who gives to all liberally and without reproach, and it will be given to him" (James 1:5 NKJV). When a husband makes a decision, he must live conscious and aware of the fact that he is not making it just for himself, but for his family, too. When he lives his life focused on God and his family instead of himself, then he builds his wife's trust in him as a godly leader—someone she can feel safe and secure in submitting to "as unto the Lord." When a family, especially the children, looks to the man as the head of the family, they are looking to see a picture of God. In fact, at a very young age, a child's entire perception of God comes from what he or she sees in their earthly father. So a husband and father must constantly ask himself, *What characteristics of the Heavenly Father am I displaying toward my loved ones? Do they see the Father in me? Do they see Christ?*

God is completely faithful as a Husband and Father. He will never leave us, nor forsake us. We never need to worry about Him betraying us or breaking our trust and confidence in Him and His Word. Does your family have this same unshakable trust in you as a husband and father? Broken trust is devastating to a family and is very difficult to restore.

To illustrate how broken trust affects relationships, I'll use the example of a man's relationship with his stockbroker or financial advisor. Let's suppose, for example, that you had a financial advisor to whom you had entrusted your hard-earned money. That money represented your life, because of the time you invested in earning it. Yet over time, you never earned a profit and sometimes you even lost money, because that advisor was making decisions based on what was best for him, instead of for you. How long would it take you before you stopped giving that advisor your money? How long before you stopped trusting him completely? His selfish actions and disregard for your future welfare, led to a broken relationship of trust.

This is exactly what happens when a man puts himself and his own interests above those of his family. No one wants to submit to a man like that because there's so much distrust and misgiving. Most women have no problem submitting themselves to their husbands, if they are living in an attitude of love. When a husband loves his wife and family as Christ loves the Church (Ephesians 5:25), submission becomes almost an automatic response, because it's easy to trust someone you know won't ever hurt you or who has your best interest at heart.

Another way that some men miss it is by refusing to even listen to their wives. So when they make a decision, she doesn't wholly support it. When he neglects her ideas and her counsel, he sabotages his own success. Consequently, he forfeits the support of his wife through his foolish behavior. A wife who is required to submit to her husband's every decision without the ability to provide any input, is in a "dictatorship" type of relationship, instead of a godly marriage.

Number Two:
A Man Is Responsible to Provide and Protect

"For the husband is head of the wife, as also Christ is head of the church; and He is the Savior of the body" (Ephesians 5:23 NKJV). As I said, many people read, "For the husband is head of the wife…" and just stop there. They don't say much about the rest of the verse: "…as also Christ is head of the church; and He is the Savior of the body." It is a man's responsibility to be the head of his wife, as a covering for her. In other words, she is to come under the covering of her husband. That's his duty, not just his privilege. This responsibility gives him orders from the throne room of Heaven to provide for her and protect her, not to boss her around!

Now, I understand that there are women, even some Christian women, who do not like the fact that their husband is a covering for them. They see it as an indication that they are somehow inferior beings. However, this does not imply that she is less than the man, it's simply the way God set up the marriage relationship. He is a God of order, and everything He designs is created on a system of order. Marriage was set up by God as a 50-50 partnership, with the husband as the head—the covering, or protector, and provider—for his wife.

'I've Got You Covered'

"And the Lord God commanded the man, saying, 'Of every tree of the garden you may freely eat; but of the tree of the knowledge of good and evil you shall not eat, for in the day that you eat of it you shall surely die'" (Genesis 2:16-17 NKJV). Before Eve ever arrived on the scene, God had given Adam responsibilities and instructions. The Lord had ordered Adam to take care of the Garden, and then commanded him concerning the tree of the knowledge of good and evil.

This is a picture of stewardship and man's responsibility to act as the covering in the home. The man covers his home by making sure that his family is headed in the right direction spiritually. Satan does not have the power to harm anyone. The only weapon he has is deception, and he uses this to trick people into giving him a place in their lives, so he can work destruction in them. The enemy repeatedly spoke deception into Eve's life, until deception finally took place in her heart (see Genesis 3:1-13). The deception occurred when, although she knew she shouldn't eat from the tree, she did it anyway. However, Adam was just as much at fault. His passivity in allowing her to eat as he stood by her side, gave strength to her deception. Eve stepped out from underneath Adam's covering, and he allowed it, without any apparent resistance on his part. By the time they realized there was a problem, it was too late.

Responsibility in the Fall seems to weigh very heavily upon Adam. As the authority figure and the one to whom God gave the initial instruction and warning, Adam could have and should have intervened. Notice that nothing happened after Eve ate of the forbidden tree. It was only after he ate that their nakedness was revealed. I wonder what would have happened if after she ate, Adam simply said, "Eve, ask God to forgive you and come on back under my covering"?

After the Fall of man when God revealed that there would be enmity between the devil's seed and the woman's seed, the husband's covering over his wife was still very important. When a husband is functioning properly in his role as head of his home, and his wife comes under that spiritual covering, then the enemy is unable to get to her emotions and wreak havoc in her thought life. The enemy has continually attacked women in the area of the emotions. In fact, that's the tactic he used in the Garden to tempt Eve. In order for him to get to the wife, he must first go through the husband.

The husband's duty to act as a covering for his family is not a light responsibility. However, some men find this daunting and intimidating, because their wives know more scriptures than they do. Regardless of whether he knows one verse from the Bible or not, when a man is born again and is willing to accept his role and responsibilities in the home as husband and father, he is anointed to do that job!

The Covering Extends to Your Children

An elderly friend of mine who founded counseling clinics all over the world, had a great impact on my life in this area of covering. He often related the story of a time when both of his daughters lived away from home at two different college campuses. On one particular week-end, my friend's daughters, who were both engaged to be married, were planning to visit their parents. On the Friday night before his daughters were planning to come, my friend was awakened in the middle of the night and began experiencing lustful thoughts that attacked his mind. He jumped out of bed, got on his knees, and began to pray until all those thoughts left him.

The following day his daughters arrived with their fiancés. Both daughters had always enjoyed a very open and accepting relationship with their dad. During that visit, each one shared with him separately how she and her fiancé had gotten involved in some heavy petting the previous night and had gone "a little too far." Both shared independently that as this was happening, suddenly, their attention was arrested, and they abruptly stopped what they were doing.

What happened? The enemy was looking for an open door to gain an entrance into those girls' lives and their relationships, but because they were still submitted to their father as their covering, the enemy had to go through their father first. My friend upheld the shield of his covering over his daughter's in prayer, and he prayed the power of God into those situations before they had a chance to turn really bad.

Husbands and fathers have the responsibility to cover their family. Yes, the husband and wife have a 50-50 relationship. They were created equal in God's sight and when they come together in marriage, they become one but someone has to bear the responsibility in the partnership. Otherwise, there will not be any leadership or forward progress, only wasted motion.

'The Buck Stops Here'

Acting as a leader in the home is not about authority, as much as it is about responsibility. This means, that "the buck stops here" with you, the husband. So when you have to make a tough decision, you can't go back in retrospect and blame your wife if you missed it and made the wrong decision. Even if you sought your wife's input and made a wrong decision based on her counsel, you have to own the mistake and bear responsibility for it. In other words, you can't go back to your wife and say, "I knew you were wrong. I knew we shouldn't have bought that. I had a feeling you were wrong. What's the matter with you?" No, you are the covering. You are the head; therefore, you have to accept responsibility for the mistake and learn from it, instead of blaming your wife and trying to make her the scapegoat.

And Speaking of Money...

Another aspect of the covering that a husband provides for his wife and family has to do with providing for them materially and financially. Some husbands allow their wife to bear the responsibility of the finances in the home. They kick back without a care in the world, while the wife takes care of balancing the checkbook and paying the bills. Then she becomes the one who is responsible for determining whether there will be enough money to pay the bills. From an emotional standpoint, women weren't designed for that responsibility, as long as there's a husband in the house.

The husband was designed by God to be the responsible party in the area of finances. Remember, he is the protector and provider, so he's the one who should make sure there's enough money to pay the bills. He needs to be the one who ultimately decides what the family should and should not spend—not so he can be a control freak, but in order to provide his wife with emotional and financial security. She should know that everything is going to be all right and that the future is bright. (We'll talk more about the subject of "men and money" in another chapter.)

Number Three:
A Man Is Responsible to Lay Down His Life

Jesus made the first move toward the Church—"the joy set before Him" (Hebrews 12:2)—in His ultimate act of sacrifice on the Cross. He loved the Church, His Bride—the Body of Christ—not for what the Church could do for Him, but for what He could do for the Church. Christ was a Servant-Leader. He spoke truth in love always. He knew God in Glory and, in fact, had been seated with Him. Yet He left all of that for us; He gave it all up. He lived a sinless life as a mortal human and yet very much God. In taking our place, He took responsibility for that which He was not responsible—the sin of mankind.

How do we apply that to a man's responsibility in the home? For one, he must "crucify" his own flesh and his own desires for the good of his family. For instance, after a long day at work, he may want to come home and be left alone to sit in front of the TV. His flesh is crying out for food, sex, and sleep, but his wife wants to talk! So what does this husband, who's laying down his life, do? He denies his own flesh and gives himself up for her. He dies to what his flesh wants, in order to spend some quality time with his wife and children. No matter how difficult work was, or how bad the traffic was on the way home, he must do what's best for everyone, not what he thinks is best for him.

In an environment like that, a man's family feels loved, protected, and safe. They feel secure, knowing that the head of that home will do everything necessary to provide for their needs financially, emotionally, and so forth. I have a saying that when you are single, you have your whole "self" (submitted to the Lord, of course), and when you get married, you lose half of your "self." When you have kids, you lose the other half. Later, when your kids are grown, you get half back! Yet the fact remains that when you are married, you are not your own; you do not belong to yourself —you belong to your spouse.

Don't Be a Backslidden Romantic

If you're a married man, think back to your dating relationship with your wife. In that phase of the relationship, you were actually engaging in the process of giving up your life. You were experiencing those overwhelming feelings of love, and you felt in your heart that you were going to do this for the rest of your life!

Then you got married, and the demands of work and family relationships hit you hard. You became busy and began reacting to life, instead of taking life by the horns. After awhile, you wondered where that "loving feeling" had gone.

When you were dating your wife, you used to spend hours on end talking about everything. In fact, did you ever call her and say, "What are you doing?" and she answered, "Thinking about you." Have you ever talked on the phone for hours while watching TV together—you at your house and her at hers? What were you doing? Laying down your life. You probably weren't making nearly the amount of money that you are earning now, yet you found the money to take her out as often as you could. You planned ahead; taking her out wasn't an afterthought, but a carefully planned outing or event.

All of that took time, effort, and some creativity. But you gave yourself to it. You were walking out biblical principles whether you realized it or not! Then in marriage, after you won her, perhaps you started to backslide and let those principles slip. You started thinking more about your needs and what you could get out of the relationship. You began doing more taking than giving. Then you wondered where the romance went. If you will go back to doing those "first works" (see Revelation 2:5), you will find that the romance between you and your wife is right where you left it—at the exact place in the road where you ditched those acts of love.

Number Four:
A Man Is Responsible to Value His Wife

Many young men pride themselves in working hard to make the best life possible for their family. They are ambitious; they go in to work early and stay late. They are trying to provide the "dream" for their wife and family. Given your responsibility as provider and protector, you can relate to that as a husband. But have you ever felt conflicted, because your wife wants you to leave work at the earliest possible moment so you can spend every possible moment at home with her? That can create some tension. Your wife wants you to be great, but she also wants to know that you would give it all up for her.

Most women are romantics at heart, and they have a deep need to know that their husbands are willing to sacrifice for them. They need to know that they are the most important person in their husband's life, next to the Lord. Women may like nice things, but, ultimately—if they had to choose—the kind of house or the neighborhood they live in, the kind of car they drive, and their dreams for material blessings, would not matter more to them than their relationship with their husband. What matters most in comparison to those things is their marriage, because if everything you have was gone tomorrow—but you still had a loving relationship that had been nurtured and cared for—you could still be happy, because you have each other. You would still have what you valued the most.

I believe God put it in a woman to highly value relationships. A wife needs to know that you value what she values, and that you would sacrifice everything for her. Once you prove that you would, she will be content and rest in her relationship with her husband. Often there is tension when a husband has a sports night or a poker night once a week with the guys. His wife constantly nags him to stay at home to be with her instead. He's at home six nights a week, so he's wondering why there's a struggle. The real issue is that she wants him to prove to her that she means more to him than his friends, and that he would give up his night out for her.

If this is your situation, instead of struggling with your wife, let her know that if you didn't have a single friend in the world but her and God, you would still be happy. She really needs to know that you are willing to lay down your life because you value her. Once she is convinced of her value in your eyes, she will probably be very gracious about you having time with your buddies. You have placed her in the position of honor, esteem, and value where she rightfully belongs.

There can also be tension in a marriage with in-laws, especially if your wife doesn't feel more valuable or important to you than your parents. (Do I need to say here, that it's never a good idea to side against her in favor of your parents?) "...a man shall leave his father and mother and be joined to his wife, and they shall become one flesh" (Genesis 2:24 NKJV). "...a man shall leave his father and mother and be joined to his wife, and the two shall become one flesh" (Ephesians 5:31 NKJV).

"Cleaving" is all about becoming one flesh. When you look at the original Hebrew translation of Genesis 2:24, it means that both the wife and the husband are to *leave and cleave*. We can see the wisdom and logic in obeying that, by not living with your parents as a young married couple! What about cleaving to your spouse in other ways? Did you know that you can drag your parents into your marriage, without living in the same house with them?

If you talk to your parents about every problem that comes up between you and your spouse, you are not "leaving and cleaving." Instead, you are creating discord between your spouse and your parents. You are going against God's design and order. Your spouse now has in-law troubles—and you caused it! Also, it's not wise to discuss with your spouse, any issues you have with your own parents—not if you want your spouse to love and honor your parents as he or she should.

Whatever you share with your spouse may cause him or her to become offended at your parents. Then you create a situation in which your spouse is having problems letting go of that offense. You may get over your issue with your parents, but your spouse may never get over it. Never, ever get angry with your in-laws to your spouse. After all, your spouse is a direct "product" of his or her parents, just as you are of yours. So if you dislike or disapprove of your spouse's parents—even if they're wrong about a particular thing—your spouse is subconsciously hearing that you dislike him or her.

You Can 'Leave' and Love

You can "leave and cleave"—leave your parents and cleave to your spouse—and still love your parents and your spouse's parents. In fact, one of the greatest things you can do for your marriage is to love your spouse's parents unconditionally, and show acts of love toward them every chance you get. For example, take your mother-in-law out for Mother's Day. For Father's Day, take your father-in-law on a short outing. Go overboard for your in-laws. Doing so will pay great dividends in your family relationships.

I'm not saying that loving your parents means you have to allow them to interfere in the affairs of your life, or manipulate the decisions you and your spouse make for your own family. But you must show the God-kind of love toward them.

As a man, you have the responsibility of showing value and honor to your wife, guiding the affairs of your home, protecting it from outside interference, and keeping peace within the borders of your home and family. That doesn't have to be a balancing act, if you understand your responsibilities and priorities and put first things first.

A part of your job of keeping peace is to protect your home from strife, including where parents and in-laws are concerned. If your wife becomes upset with her parents about something, you need to point her back to them, not side against them. It may be okay for your wife to spout off something about her parents in frustration, but it's not okay for you to say it! If you say it, you are creating separation, instead of making peace.

No matter how legitimate your wife's complaint may be, you should continually point her to the good things about her parents and yours, and encourage her to think on things that are "lovely" (see Philippians 4:8). Even bad parents do a lot of good things, so don't only focus on the bad, or you will have bad seeds that will eventually produce a harvest. That harvest is intended to spring up and trouble you and your house (Hebrews 12:15). It could spring up and be in full blossom when you least expect it, such as at a holiday party or other family gathering. You must not allow this; you must encourage peace. You must do it in love, instead of criticizing and condemning your wife for her negative feelings. Remember, she must know that you value your relationship with her the most.

There's No Room for God's Best on the Path of Selfishness

A married man must lay down his life for his wife. He can either take the attitude that "this is not what I bought into when I committed to marriage," or he can dig in by the grace of God, and commit himself to make the best life possible for his family. Then as he lays down his life—his will and desires—for the good of those he is now responsible for, he will reap so much more joy than if he had followed a selfish path. Think about it. Jesus laid everything down to come to earth as a man. Then He laid it all down again when He gave up His life—spirit, soul, and body—for His Bride, the Church. But look at what He reaped! God raised Him up in glory, and Christ is still reaping a harvest each time a person gets saved. Remember, we identified the woman as a "wombed" man, who will incubate, nurture, and produce based on what her husband sows into her life. If he lays down his life for her, she will give life back to him. In fact, the only way for a husband to be truly happy and fulfilled in life and in marriage, is by giving his life wholly to his wife. He will reap infinitely more than he could ever receive by holding back and hanging on to his life.

Jesus said, "He who finds his life will lose it, and he who loses his life for My sake will find it" (Matthew 10:39 NKJV). Jesus was saying that the one who gives up his life gains life, but the one who holds on to his life loses out. In other words, if you give up your low life, you will gain the high life. But if you hold on to your low life, you will lose the high life. If you hold on to your poker parties and your buddies, you will do so at the expense of your marriage. You will cheat the marriage and yourself, and lose out on building the "Heaven-on-earth" marriage that God wants you to enjoy.

Number Five:
A Man Is Responsible
to Have a Vision for the Future

Many men lose out with their wife because they are shortsighted. They don't see "the joy set before them" in marriage. Instead of thinking ahead about what they want to ultimately reap in life, they think only about what they want and need at the moment. Years from now, what kind of memories do you want to have as a husband and father? Sometimes the future is

If he lays down his life for her, she will give life back to him.

difficult for us to wrap our minds around. But can you think about next month? For example, if you spend hours at a time in the front of the TV this next month, watching sports and channel-surfing instead of spending time with your wife, what do you hope to gain at the end of the month? Will you remember any of the scores of the games you watched? You may remember some things, but years from now, the things you saw on TV that month will be a vague memory at best.

I didn't ask this question to condemn you, but to make a point. One evening alone with just you and your wife, can create memories that will last a lifetime. One evening of giving your children your undivided attention can produce priceless memories that will shape their lives for years to come. You must decide what is most valuable to you in the long run and sow your time wisely into those things—into things that last.

Fulfill Your Dying Wish Today

Perspective plays a part in being a great husband and father, as well as taking responsibility for leadership in the home. At the end of your life, the memories that you have with your family will be your most important possessions. The life you have built with your wife will help lay the foundation for your children to build their own families on. The happiness you all share as a family—not just your own happiness—will be your crowning reward and delight in life. Yet how many men lack this perspective when they are young? Then when they are old, their lives are so empty and filled with regret.

The saying is true that no one says on his deathbed, "Oh, how I wish I'd watched more TV or gotten drunk more often with my friends." No, unfortunately, the last thoughts of many men turn to the shortsightedness of their youth, and to the deep regret they feel for not investing more in the things of priceless value: their own family.

Get on the Same Page with God

Anytime you undervalue something that God deems as valuable, you are going to end up with regrets. He created marriage and family; therefore, He values and loves it. He desires that you show the same care for it; nurturing these valuable relationships in your life instead of neglecting them. Yes, man has a certain authority in his home. It was given to Him by God to bless his family, not to hurt or destroy them. Before authority, a man must take responsibility, and that is no small undertaking!

Putting the cart before the horse and emphasizing a man's authority without teaching him his responsibility, is a recipe for disorder and chaos in the home. As a man faithfully fulfills his duties as a husband and father—and does it as unto the Lord—his rewards will be great. The blessing he sets in motion for his family will last and be perpetuated for generations to come.

6
'WHERE ART THOU,' O MAN — AND WHY AREN'T YOU TAKING OUT THE TRASH!

Dr. Tom Anderson

"And the Lord God called unto Adam, and said unto him, 'Where art thou?'" (Genesis 3:9 KJV). The Bible is clear that although the husband is the head of his wife in marriage (Ephesians 5:23), that position of leadership is one of responsibility, as much as authority. It was designed as part of God's divine order for the home, to bring blessing to him and his family. However, far too often in marriage, the husband abandons this position of responsibility and is "missing in action" as far as real leadership in the home is concerned. God is calling Christian husbands to fulfill, not neglect, their God-given roles of leadership in marriage.

'Husband, Come Forth!'

This reminds me of the situation in the Garden of Eden, after Adam and Eve had sinned and hid from the Lord. God called to Adam, "…Where art thou?" (Genesis 3:9 KJV). Of course, God knew Adam's precise whereabouts, so He wasn't trying to locate Adam. Instead, God was calling on Adam to come out and be accountable. The same is true today. God is calling husbands everywhere, to lay aside the things that have held them and their families back from experiencing His best. It's time to remove these hindrances—to take out the trash—and take your place "front and center," as the head of your home.

Hang Up on Your Hang-Ups

Ephesians 5:25 makes it very clear that the husband has a responsibility to give up his flesh—his selfish desires—for his wife and family. There's only one small problem with that—the flesh does not like giving itself up! The flesh has a lot of hang-ups; it wants to do what it wants to do, when it wants to do it. That means that when the Bible says a husband should act like Christ and wash his wife with "the water of the Word" (Ephesians 5:26), the flesh will not enjoy obeying that! The flesh doesn't want to sow into anyone but itself. However, sowing to the flesh will only reap corruption, not life (Galatians 6:8)."Husbands, love your wives, just as Christ also loved the church and gave Himself for her, that He might sanctify and cleanse her with the washing of water by the word" (Ephesians 5:25-26).

Responsibility has been given to the man to sow good words into his wife—not just in public, but in private as well. It is one thing to be a man of principles at church or in public, but we need to be men of integrity and love behind closed doors, when we are at home with our family. No one knows what goes on in the privacy of a man's home, except his family. As husbands and fathers, we need to regularly ask ourselves, *What does my family see in me?*

For example, does your family see you gossiping about and slandering your boss or co-workers? You may drive home from church bashing your pastor's sermon and think nothing of it—but what is your family taking away from that experience? In talking against your pastor, you are teaching your children, by your actions, that you don't live under authority and that it's okay for them not to live under authority, either.

As I have said before, establishing yourself as a godly leader in your home is really about establishing relationships of trust in your family. Your family will not be able to trust that you can lead them successfully, if they don't believe that you know what you're doing. Your loved ones need to see your love for God, and your dependence on the Word of God, demonstrated consistently on a daily basis. There are many ways that you can show them your love and deep reverence for God and His Word. Just spending a couple of minutes with your children over breakfast, sharing the Word of God with them, will send them the message that God's Word is a priority in your life and that you're not just a Sunday morning Christian. Also, when you share testimonies of answered prayer, your family will be encouraged and feel safe and secure, knowing that you are trusting God and that your faith is bearing fruit.

Your wife and children must trust you, no matter what. You need to keep your word with them before you keep it with anyone else. Even if you do that —yet they see you lying to others—it's going to affect their trust in you. Do your children hear you make up excuses to others when you don't want to accept an invitation? If they perceive you as dishonest, then when you tell them you want to spend time with them, hear what they have to say, or even that you love them, they may question your sincerity. What about your wife? If you stretch the truth with others, and then you get home late from work and tell her that traffic on the expressway was horrific—that may well be the truth, but she's thinking, *Well, he lies to everyone else; maybe he's lying to me, too.*

Make It Count

The power of the man's responsibility in the home is absolutely amazing. The example you set before your family, especially your children, is so critical to their emotional well-being, as well as their own character. Children follow exactly what they see their dad doing, more so than their mom. Everything a father does and says is constantly on display. Little eyes are watching, and little hearts are forming belief systems based on what those eyes behold. So much is happening just by the husband and father's presence in the home. It is his God-ordained assignment to make his presence count!

As a man, your responsibility is to die to your flesh and to what your flesh wants to do. You won't always be able to say everything you are thinking or do everything you'd like to do, because this could prove harmful to your children and their well-being. For example, you may want to enjoy an occasional beer or glass of wine or smoke a cigarette or puff on a cigar but if this is going to harm your family, you need to give it up! Do you see the gravity of your responsibility as the head of your house? This responsibility calls for the dying of your flesh, to those desires that are not profitable and could be harmful to you or those you love.

Setting the right example is not always the easiest task, but it is a powerful one. It is critical that you, as a man, accept that responsibility. In fact, if you're single and you don't want that responsibility, I recommend that you don't get married. Men who get married and refuse to give up their "me-centered" lifestyle, end up hurting others, as well as themselves in the long run.

A Man's Greatest Gift to His Children

It's been said that the greatest thing a man can do for his children is to love their mother. This is so true! By loving your wife, you are showing your children a picture of Christ and the Church in your marriage. Not only will your happy marriage produce feelings of security and well-being within your children, but it will also contribute to them building a happy home life of their own one day.

Children live what they see. So if you treat your wife right, your sons will likely treat their wives right when they grow up and get married. Also, your daughters will quickly perceive the difference between a man "who talks a good game" and one who demonstrates godly character consistently, over the long haul. Since children live what they see, if you maintain a devoted relationship with God, they will also grow up having a relationship with Him for themselves. When they see what you have with God is real, then they will want to cultivate that kind of relationship with the Lord for themselves.

Demonstrating Honor

As I said, a man is responsible to his wife to "wash" her with the water of the Word (Ephesians 5:26). He must invest his faith, love, time, and prayers in her. He should build her up consistently, and value her uniqueness and her calling. He must esteem her as the 'queen' of his house—and then ensure that the children in his house properly esteem her as 'Mom.' He must teach them to show honor to their mother. This is primarily done by demonstrating honor toward her. When our children were growing up, I took responsibility for teaching them to honor Maureen. They always remembered her in a special way on her birthday, Mother's Day, and holidays. I never allowed them to speak disrespectfully to their mother. That kind of behavior was simply not tolerated, and I took responsibility for enforcing that. (This was a well-understood rule in our house!)

It's important for a husband to honor his wife, but he must also instill honor for her in the lives of their children. By his actions, he needs to show them—not just tell them—that she is "queen" of the castle! She is the most important woman in his children's lives, so it's important that he, as a Dad, treats her in a loving, respectful manner at all times and teaches them to do the same.

Very often we see fathers allow their kids to speak any way they want toward their mother. He knows what's going on, but he just kicks back in front of the TV, like nothing's happening. But God forbid that the child who's 'sassing' his mother, messes with Dad's remote control! Ironically, as soon as he discovers that his remote is missing, he will immediately jump up and deal with that!

If the children are not honoring their mom in the home, it's because the dad has not trained them to do that. In teaching them to show the proper honor and respect in the home, a father is setting his children up for success in their own families one day. Ultimately, he is positioning them to receive a blessing promised to them by God. "Children, obey your parents in the Lord, for this is right. 'Honour your father and mother'—which is the first commandment with a promise—'that it may go well with you and that you may enjoy long life on the earth'" (Ephesians 6:1-3).

Children will grow up doing what we do, not what we say. A man's children are watching the way he treats their mother—as well as the way she shows respect toward their father. They take to heart, how both Dad and Mom respond to and interact with them. Children are extremely sensitive to their parents' feelings and emotions. Whatever the kids witness in their home, will directly affect their own behavior in marriage one day.

You Will Gravitate in the Direction of Your Choices

Perhaps you grew up in a very godly, Christian home, so taking your place as a great husband and father is natural to you. Or maybe you grew up in a dysfunctional home, and you realize as an adult, that you don't have a clue about what it means to be a great husband and father. Have you ever found yourself doing or saying something unseemly and you thought, *Oh, no! I'm just like my father!* Actually, you probably have traits— both positive and negative—that you saw in your dad when you were a child, and now those traits are being demonstrated in your own house. However, if you are a Christian, you can lay an axe to the root of every negative, harmful, dysfunctional trait that you have acquired from your childhood, and you can refuse to pass these on to another generation.

Regardless of your upbringing, being a great husband and father is not a choice that you make only once—and sometimes it's not even a choice you make once every day. Sometimes it's a choice that you make several times in one day! There is a natural struggle that takes place with "dying to self." I believe that most men desire to be good husbands and fathers—but their flesh just keeps winning over them.

The key is this: *If you choose, as though you were what you want to be, you will become what you want to be.* After a period of making the right choices, you will form the habits necessary to be a good husband and father. In other words, you will gravitate in the direction of your choices, whether they are good or bad.

An Exercise to Help You

Allow me help you start this process in a positive direction. If you haven't done so already, the next time you are driving home from work, begin to work through this out loud: *If I were a great husband, what would I choose to do when I get home? Would I turn on the TV right away, or would I sit down and talk to my wife about her day? After that, if I were a great father, I would help my children with their homework or class project and spend time talking to them about their day.*

What kids witness in the home will directly affect their own behavior in marriage one day.

You don't have to wait until you are driving home from work to begin practicing this. If you feel like you are not where you want to be, in terms of being a good husband and father, you can practice these "if" scenarios anytime. *If I were a good husband, I would take my wife out tonight. She's been working hard lately without a break. I don't want her to have to cook tonight. If I were a good father, I wouldn't yell at my family. I would be patient with my children and teach them how to do what I want them to do. I would discipline them in love, instead of anger, so they would always be secure in my love for them.*

As you practice doing this, after awhile, you won't have to ask or think about it anymore. You will form the habits that help you become a great husband and father. It may not happen overnight, but if you stay with it, with God's help you will change for the better, your wife will change for the better, and your family life will never be the same again!

When our children were growing up, I decided that when I got home from work each evening, the very first part of my time at home would

A person doesn't become great at anything by making excuses and refusing to work.

go to Maureen. I made certain to show my kids how much I valued her. Then I made sure that I chose them over television time. I made the choice to spend some quality time with my children every single night, even if I was exhausted and just wanted to go to another room and shut myself off from everyone.

Early on, I had to consciously think about that—and those decisions were not always easy to make. My "flesh" fought me hard. But I made no excuses and no provision for my flesh, because I had a committed, made-up mind, that I was going to be a great husband and father and have the happiest family life possible, for my sake, for my wife's sake, and for the sake of my children and their own families one day.

Excuses, Excuses —
How to Stop Growth and Progress in Its Tracks

"The lazy man says, 'There is a lion in the road! A fierce lion is in the streets!'" (Proverbs 26:13 NKJV). A person doesn't become great at some sport, profession, or trade by making excuses and refusing to work at it and invest time to get better. Yet how often in marriage do we see people making excuses for why their home life is in shambles, and why it doesn't model anything remotely close to the relationship of Christ and His Church? I have actually heard men say, "I am who I am. My wife's just going to have to deal with it." Often, men make those kinds of statements as an excuse for not changing. In other words, they have no intention of changing for anyone.

Many people take a very hardened approach to marriage and to life. They act like the clay pot has already been fired, and is now eternally unchangeable! But God wants us to be pliable and yielded. He wants to mold us into Christ's image (see Romans 8:29). In order for clay to be molded, naturally speaking, it must be kept wet. Spiritually, we are kept wet by "the washing of water by the word" (Ephesians 5:26). When we continually read, study, pray, and meditate on the Word of God, we keep ourselves from becoming selfish and hardened.

Crucify Your Flesh, Fulfill Your Purpose

Have you ever read some of the things Jesus said in the Gospels and thought, *That's just too hard?* For instance, some people read in Matthew and the other Gospels, "…'If anyone desires to come after Me, let him deny himself, and take up his cross, and follow Me" (Matthew 16:24 NKJV), and they say, "That's asking too much." But that verse doesn't mean we have to take up a physical cross and be crucified. This simply means that we should crucify our flesh, or deny our flesh its desires, in order to take up and fulfill our God-ordained purpose. Our "cross" symbolizes our purpose.

When men get married, part of our purpose is to become great husbands. Well, how are you going to fulfill that? How are you going to become great at being a husband? The same way you became great at baseball, golf, accounting, plumbing, or whatever it is that you are good at. You simply have to apply yourself to your purpose as "husband," and that means you are going to have to change.

Suppose you played baseball and your baseball coach told you that you really needed to practice batting. Then what if you said to him,

"Hey, this is just the way I am. You knew how I batted when you put me on the team. Sorry, I'm just not the best batter. That's all there is to it." Sound ridiculous? Of course it does! You would never say that. Instead, you would probably go to the batting cages and work on improving your skills. You would put in the time and apply yourself in order to become a better batter. Similarly, we must apply ourselves to our marriage. Perhaps you have said this before, "I'm just not a good communicator." Instead of saying that, you need to make the effort to become a better communicator!

You can learn how to communicate. I did, but it was tough! Most of my life, I hardly ever communicated. I just didn't talk much. My wife finally said to me, "Why don't you just say what you're thinking?" I said, "Really?" Now she's trying to figure out how to shut me up, because I'm thinking all the time about a lot of things!

Love Brings Out the Best

"That He might present her to Himself a glorious church, not having spot or wrinkle or any such thing, but that she should be holy and without blemish"(Ephesians 5:27 NKJV). Let's look at that phrase "holy and without blemish." This means, in effect, prepared for the plans and purposes of God. Now let's apply that to the husband loving his wife "as Christ loved the Church" (v. 25). The Word of God has been symbolized as both the 'seed' and 'water.' Just as Christ sowed the Word into the Church and watered it, causing His Body to bear fruit, as husbands we need to plant the Word of God into the life of our wife. Then we must water that Word with more Word, and our wife, like the Church, will grow stronger and become more and more fruitful as a result.

As Christ sows His Word into the Church, the responsible husband also sows into his wife. If a husband is always complaining about his wife and saying things, such as, "My wife is such a nag," he's probably not sowing the seed of the "Word," into her life as he should be. All things being equal, a woman is good soil and whatever her husband plants in her is going to produce a harvest. In other words, if he sows love, he will get love. If he sows romance, he will get romance. If he sows laziness, he will reap laziness. If he sows one seed, he will get a hundred back! So if he sows a little anger, for example, he will get a whole lot more anger in return.

It's been said many times before, but it bears repeating: *If you don't like the harvest you've been getting in life, change the seed you've been sowing!* So if you don't like your marriage, begin to plant some different seeds. When you take a genuine interest in your wife, and in her becoming the best she can be, you will reap the reward of that. However, often a man isn't interested in sowing into his wife's life, because he is too interested in his own needs and what pleases him.

Can you imagine Jesus taking that attitude toward the Church? Can you imagine Him saying, "You don't ever let Me do what I want to do. What about My needs? What about Me? You're not doing enough for Me, and you want what?" No, you never heard the Lord say that, and you never will. He knows that His joy is in His sowing and that His reward will surely be reaped as He fulfills His place and performs His part as the Head of His Body. Why clamor for your own needs, when you have been given the position as head of your house? Why not focus on sowing the right seeds and reaping the fruit of that? Certainly, you can sow the seed of the Word, and you should do that. There are countless different kinds of seeds you can sow into your wife.

What if on your way home from work one day, you spent $15 on some flowers and a card for your wife? Then when you got home, you spent twenty minutes or so, just talking to her? You have just invested less than $20 and about a half hour of your time—just a small seed—but your harvest will be incredible! It's interesting that many husbands don't want to sow anything into their wife or their marriage, yet they want to reap something. However, this can't be done. You simply cannot reap where you have not sown!

The Bible was given to us to help change our thinking, and bring it in line with God's way of thinking. We need God's Word to change our mentality about so many things. For instance, many men have had the mentality that they can just take love, without giving any love in return. No one wins in a relationship like that. If a man will give love, then he will get love, too. In fact, if men want to be truly happy, they must figure out what they want most in life—and then give that! The Bible is very clear on this: 'Whatever you sow, you will reap' (Galatians 6:7).

Love Her First

As we have already seen, husbands are a picture of Christ, and wives are a picture of the Church. By nature, men are initiators; women are responders. A wife will usually respond to what her husband initiates. That's the way God ordered it. Just as we love God because He first loved us (He initiated a relationship with us), a wife loves her husband, because he first loved her. Loving your wife first is the "sowing" process. Eventually you will reap a harvest, because you participated in this process. So if you want to see a harvest in your marriage, you can't just sit around and make excuses. You must be willing to do something to bring that harvest about, and this takes time and effort.

If a farmer plants corn one morning, he doesn't go out the next morning to look for his ears of corn! No, it takes time for the corn to grow. He must plant, and then water and nurture what he has planted. Here's what often happens in marriage. For some reason—through ignorance, stubbornness, or laziness—a husband plants a lot of weeds into his marriage, and those weeds spring up and start taking over the relationship. Then he receives some light and revelation in his heart about marriage, so he decides to plant some good seed into his wife.

If your wife has been overrun with weeds for months and even years by the seeds you have sown into her, then you will not be able to get rid of all this in one day. It will take planting the right seeds for a while, before you will see the harvest of a happy, healthy marriage. In other words, if you have been sowing "weeds" into your marriage, but then you begin bringing home cards and flowers, you might not get an immediate harvest. In fact, your wife may even question your motives. Since you have planted all these bad seeds, distrust has sprung up in the marriage, causing your wife to wonder whether or not you're sincere.

Many men are resistant to the idea of being the initiator and taking responsibility to sow into the marriage. They have the attitude, *As soon as she becomes a great wife, then I'll begin to love her.* A man with this kind of attitude doesn't see that when he begins to love his wife, she will become a great wife. He must act first, then she will respond by becoming what he desires. In other words, when he treats her as an amazing wife, she will become an amazing wife!

Sow Love Into Your Wife and Reap Favor with God

If you are not loving your wife purely for what it will do for her, think about what it will do for you! "Husbands, likewise, dwell with them with understanding, giving honor to the wife, as to the weaker vessel, and as being heirs together of the grace of life, that your prayers may not be hindered" (1 Peter 3:7 NKJV). When you don't treat your wife according to biblical knowledge, your prayers will be hindered. That's how serious this issue is to God. I wonder how many men flounder and fail in life, because they are treating their wives poorly. They might be praying and believing, but their praying and believing are rendered ineffective, because they are mistreating or neglecting their wives.

The Bible has a lot to say about sowing and reaping in the area of finances. Malachi 2:13 talks about sowing and reaping in the area of relationships, in particular, the marriage relationship."...You cover the altar of the Lord with tears, with weeping and crying; So He does not regard the offering anymore, nor receive it with goodwill from your hands. Yet you say, 'For what reason?' Because the Lord has been witness between you and the wife of your youth, with whom you have dealt treacherously; Yet she is your companion and your wife by covenant. But did He not make them one, having a remnant of the Spirit? And why one? He seeks godly offspring. Therefore take heed to your spirit, And let none deal treacherously with the wife of his youth" (Malachi 2:13-15 NKJV).

I tell the men in my church that when they have given offerings but have not reaped a harvest, they need to look at how they are treating their wives. In fact, if my prayers ever seem to be hindered, my relationships are the first place I would look. I would check my heart to make sure I'm walking in love and not holding a grudge against anyone. I would also look at the way that I have been loving and treating my wife.

Study the Love of God and Learn to Love Yourself

In order to love someone else, you must love God first and then yourself. When you realize the great love God has for you, you will begin to value yourself the way He values you. A revelation of the love that God has for you, will equip you to love others. Some people are very selfish in relationships because they don't understand the love of God. Often, they don't love themselves either. They may act as if they love themselves, but it's not real love. They are looking out for "number one" —they are only out to get what they want, regardless of what others want or need. Real love is not selfish (see First Corinthians 13:5). When you really love God and understand His great love for you, you are in a position to really give yourself to someone else and be truly happy in marriage.

Depression and the 'Me' Syndrome —
How to Break Free by Breaking All the Rules

Some people become so steeped in self-thought that they become depressed. In fact, most depression stems from selfishness and self-centeredness. Secular psychology tells you that in order to deal with depression, you need to make it more about you. However, this usually leads to more depression. This is exactly opposite of God's way. God's way is to sow what you want in life. If you want joy and to be free from depression, you are going to have to start breaking some of the "rules" you've learned from the world. You are going to have to sow joy into someone's life who needs it. In other words, get your mind on God and His Word, instead of on yourself. God will meet your needs and the needs of those you are sowing into!

Problems occur in marriage when the husband doesn't love himself. If he doesn't love himself, then he cannot truly love his wife as God intends. The husband who doesn't love himself, can't treat his wife right because he has so much junk in him—in his soul and his thinking—such as rejection, low self-worth, and low self-image. I'm not making excuses for a husband who finds himself in this position. I'm simply explaining why he behaves the way he does toward his wife. He needs to identify the problem and deal with it head-on, instead of burying it and continually struggling with it in his marriage.

Time to Take Out the Trash

If you are in your 30's, 40's, or 50's, and you know you don't love yourself the way you're supposed to and you don't treat your wife right, I have a question for you—*How long have you been aware that you have issues?* No matter what hurtful experiences you have suffered, or how badly you have missed it with your own family, it's time to face those issues head-on. It's time to train yourself to think, act, and live in line with God and His Word. For example, find scriptures that tell you who you are in Christ and who you are to the Father. Ask the Lord to show you which books to read, or which audio or video teachings on the subject you need. Just as you would go to the batting cages to practice batting to improve your skills, you must "practice" understanding the love of God. You must put forth the effort to learn about His love for you, and then start to love your wife as you love yourself.

Unfortunately, our society teaches us to put so much value on our appearance, that many people live very shallow lives on the inside. The Bible teaches us to place value on Christ within us. Being beautiful on the outside does not promise beauty on the inside. A person who is ugly on the inside will eventually show ugly on the outside. Spend time working on the inside, on your own self-worth. Learn about who you are in Christ and how valuable you are to the Father.

What Are You Feeding Your Marriage?

Ephesians 5:28-29 says, "...he who loves his wife loves himself. For no one ever hated his own flesh, but nourishes and cherishes it..." (NKJV). Well, if you are hungry, you feed yourself, right? Similarly, you need to regularly "feed" your marriage relationship. Men sometimes have the attitude that since they fed the marriage last Friday, why should they have to feed it again today! But you need to nourish and cherish your marriage daily. Just as you don't go prolonged periods of time without eating, you shouldn't starve the physical and emotional needs of your wife either.

I'm so glad that Maureen prayed for me in the early days of our lives together, and that I had a teachable and determined heart to win at this thing called marriage! I'm also glad that we received the revelation early on, that biblical submission in marriage meant that I was the head of our marriage with Christ as my model. Both Maureen and I would have suffered for it, if she just submitted to my every whim and had been complacent about the junk I had in my life, as a result of my upbringing. If she had accepted that as the standard in our lives, I would have become a spiritually indifferent and undisciplined man on the road to nowhere. However, she expected the best from me, and I knew God was calling me higher in my walk with Him—in my personal life, as well as my marriage.

I knew it was time to "take out the trash" and take my place as a godly, loving leader in my home. What about you? Is God looking at your home and finding that the leadership position has been neglected or abandoned? When He calls, "Where art thou?" —how will you answer? So much is riding on what you will say to the Lord, in response to His call on your life as husband, father, and leader in your home.

7
'YOU WANT ME TO DO WHAT?' THE WISDOM OF BIBLICAL SUBMISSION

Drs. Tom and Maureen Anderson

To understand the roles and responsibilities of the husband and wife in marriage, we must look to God, who created the institution of marriage and joined the first man and woman together in this holy relationship. Understanding their beginnings at Creation helps us see God's purpose for the unique design of the man and the woman.

> *Then God said, "Let Us make man in Our image, according to Our likeness; let them have dominion over the fish of the sea, over the birds of the air, and over the cattle, over all the earth and over every creeping thing that creeps on the earth." So God created man in His own image; in the image of God He created him; male and female He created them*

Genesis 1:26-27 NKJV

The word "man" here is masculine-feminine. In fact, the word "Adam" in the Bible means mankind or humanity. When God created man, or Adam, He created mankind, and He created mankind in His own image. Notice this verse also says that when God created Adam, He created them, plural. So first—before God ever brought Eve forth in the Creation—God created the human being, Adam, as male and female "in His own image," or with the same attributes that existed in Him (v. 27).

"Then the rib which the Lord God had taken from man He made into a woman, and He brought her to the man" (Genesis 2:22 NKJV). The word "rib" in this verse does not mean rib, as you and I understand anatomy today. Think about it. If God simply took woman from a rib, that act would not have placed a lot of value on her. After all, a man can get by without a rib—but he can't get by in life without his wife. The Hebrew translation of "rib" in creation, portrays half a temple. In other words, God took this masculine-feminine being, Adam, and separated "half a temple," to make two distinct beings, one man and one woman.

"And Adam said: 'This is now bone of my bones and flesh of my flesh; She shall be called Woman, Because she was taken out of Man'" (Genesis 2:23 NKJV). The word "bone" means substance or self-same substance. So Adam was in effect saying, "As I am strong and powerful, so is she strong and powerful." Not only is a husband responsible to protect his wife, as we have seen, but the wife is also responsible to protect her husband—to surround him with faith and love, to help him, and to be a lover, friend, associate, and companion. Woman is the "completion" of man, equal and indispensable.

Let's back up to a time before God brought forth woman from Adam."So Adam gave names to all cattle, to the birds of the air, and to every beast of the field. But for Adam there was not found a helper comparable to him" (Genesis 2:20 NKJV). The word "helper" in this verse means aid, assist, or protect; the completion of man. Adam was able to say, "She is bone of my bone and flesh of my flesh; she's similar and powerful. She completes me."

'You Want Me To Do What?' Putting the Puzzle Pieces Together

Woman was created to complete man in life and to assist him, as a magnificently "created" companion, not as a servant or slave. We have seen that God created man with an innate calling to lead and to take responsibility. Yes, he stands as the ultimate authority figure in the family—under the authority of God Almighty. God conferred more than authority on Adam; He charged him with certain responsibilities where the marriage was concerned. One of Adam's primary responsibilities was to protect and provide (see Genesis 2:15).

Often in marriages today, we find the role of protector and provider being filled by the wife, instead of the husband. This position is vacated because for some reason, the husband is not fulfilling his responsibility; he's taking a passive role in the marriage. Regardless of how he arrived at this place of passivity, it's still in his God-given nature to lead and be responsible for the well-being of his family.

Out of Position, Out of Order

Some wives are viewed as overbearing or domineering. They are seen as women who want to take the lead in the marriage or "wear the pants" in the family. But I believe that because of her own purpose and design, a woman actually wants her husband to take his place as a responsible leader. Yet in some cases, a woman feels like she has to step in and accept the leadership role, because no one else is doing it. Once this shifting of roles takes place, the marriage becomes "lopsided" and out of order. The only way for the situation to be made right, is for the wife to vacate the role and responsibility of leader, because the position must be open in order for her husband to fill it.

A husband is called to be at his wife's side as a leader, protector, provider, and lover. One of his biggest responsibilities that he has in this role is the family's finances. I'm not saying that a husband must handle every aspect of the finances, especially if his wife has better bookkeeping skills, however he must still take the lead in the marriage and be responsible to know the state of his family's financial affairs. (In another chapter, we'll look at the subject of how to handle money wisely.)

I have seen so many women step in to fill this role of financial manager, because the husband had failed to do it. However, a wife must be very careful not to carry this responsibility emotionally, because in her attempt to create order and harmony in the marriage, disorder and disharmony would result instead. She must allow her husband to fulfill his God-given responsibility to manage his household. A wife who is trying to fill her husband's role in the marriage is like a missing piece of a puzzle. Until she fills her own role in the marriage and allows her husband to fill his role, God's picture of an ideal marriage will remain incomplete in their lives. As a husband fulfills his role as leader, protector, provider, and lover, his wife can then "complete" him—because she is the completion of man!

Leading with Love as Your Motivation

As we have seen, a husband's position as leader is one of responsibility, as much as it is of authority. As a leader, he must examine his motives in making decisions concerning his family. In other words, he must ask himself, *Am I acting in the best interest of my wife and children, or am I being selfish, doing only what's best for me?* When a husband proves over time that he makes decisions prayerfully and lovingly—putting his family's interests above his own—his wife and children will feel secure and loved, and they will trust him to lead and guide the family. They will willingly submit to that kind of leadership, because it reflects the type of leadership that Jesus portrayed.

Often we hear about husbands who attempt to force their wife to submit to them. But that's not how submission works. Submission is a voluntary act on the part of the one doing the submitting. Remember, Christ and His Church—His Bride—is the model, and the Bible says that Christ gave Himself for the Church. A woman submits to her husband because he genuinely cares for her and "gives himself" for her, not because he's a dominating ruler. First John 4:19 says, "We love Him because He first loved us." (NKJV). Since Jesus and His relationship with the Church is a picture of the husband and wife in marriage, we can see that the husband should be the initiator in the marriage. In other words, he is the teacher and the example in the marriage. His wife loves him because he loved her first. And from the love he gives to her, she loves him back. If he fails to love her, she will struggle in her effort to complete him (see Ephesians 5:28-29).

Maureen:

The Interdependent Marriage

We know that marriage is a picture of the beautiful relationship between Christ and the Church. God does not want that picture broken. Ephesians 5:21-33 provides wonderful instruction for the way a marriage should operate, based on the model of the Christian's relationship with Jesus. However, there has been so much error and extremism con-

...marriage is a picture of the beautiful relationship between Christ and the Church.

cerning this subject of submission that it has caused havoc in marriages. Let's go to the Word and see what God has to say about the interdependent relationship that should exist between a husband and wife.

> *Submitting to one another in the fear of God. Wives, submit to your own husbands, as to the Lord. For the husband is head of the wife, as also Christ is head of the church; and He is the Savior of the body. Therefore, just as the church is subject to Christ, so let the wives be to their own husbands in everything. Husbands, love your wives, just as Christ also loved the church and gave Himself for her, that He might sanctify and cleanse her with the washing of water by the word, that He might present her to Himself a glorious church, not having spot or wrinkle or any such thing, but that she should be holy and without blemish. So husbands ought to love their own*

wives as their own bodies; he who loves his wife loves himself. For no one ever hated his own flesh, but nourishes and cherishes it, just as the Lord does the church. For we are members of His body, of His flesh and of His bones. For this reason a man shall leave his father and mother and be joined to his wife, and the two shall become one flesh. This is a great mystery, but I speak concerning Christ and the church. Nevertheless let each one of you in particular so love his own wife as himself, and let the wife see that she respects her husband.

Ephesians 5:21-33 NKJV

The first two verses of this passage lay a foundation or springboard for the "rules" and roles of marriage. Verse 21 says, "Submitting to one another in the fear of God." I'm sure you have heard the saying, *There's no 'I' in 'TEAM.*' This simply means that a husband and wife should combine each other's strengths and use them to build a life together as one. In other words, they are a team. They are two, functioning together as one. Each one must assume certain responsibilities and carry part of the load.

Many couples understand this principle—but some of them need help putting this into practice, so they can join forces without killing each other! Verse 22 says, "Wives, submit to your own husbands, as to the Lord." One definition of the word "submit" in this verse, is to 'adapt' or 'yield.' A wife should adapt and yield herself to her husband's leadership, but not be trampled on by a laundry list of unreasonable demands!

Teammate or Slave?
'Who's Rowing the Boat in This Marriage?'

When I became born again, Tom and I were already married. We were members of a very traditional church that taught that the husband was lord over the wife and bore absolute power and rule over her like a dictator. The strong implication was that the wife was nothing; she simply obeyed without questioning whatever her husband told her to do.

Well, Tom wasn't a dictator by any means, but I went along with that teaching, because I loved God and I wanted to please Him. However, after about three or four years in that particular church, I felt completely worthless as a wife and individual. It was like I was being drained of life itself! I had no joy, no peace—I was miserable! I couldn't shake the continual feelings of worthlessness that plagued me.

I knew something was wrong with this church's teaching, but on the other hand, I didn't exactly know the right teaching, either. I simply knew that the fruit wasn't good. Tom recognized what this teaching was doing to me as a person. He wasn't happy, either. So we began to seek the Lord. We learned that when the Scripture says that wives should submit to their husbands, it simply means that a wife is supposed to bond to, participate with, and stand shoulder-to-shoulder with her husband. It means that she should be "in the same boat" with him—she should be a team player!

Have you ever heard the saying, *We're all on the same page*? That means that everyone involved is together in his or her thinking, aim, and mission. They are like a team, in the aspect that they are putting their heads together and pooling their talents and resources to pursue a common goal. In a manner of speaking, they are 'one'—one unit consisting of two or more individuals.

Certainly, a wife should respect her husband's ultimate responsibility in making decisions that guide or provide direction for the whole family. That's his God-given assignment. However, she has a part, too. A wise husband will listen to his wife's input. He may or may not agree, but he should respect her wisdom and insight. Then, ultimately, he must prayerfully do what he feels the Lord is leading him to do, or what he thinks is best. In the Garden of Eden, God created Eve as a "helpmate" for Adam (Genesis 2:18, 20). God intended for them to complement each other and function together. Eve was created to stand side by side with Adam—not under his feet—as a servant or slave.

Contention or Celebration?

Many marriages have fallen short of what God has intended, simply because of ignorance concerning the different roles of a husband and wife—and because they have failed to recognize each other's gifts and strengths in the marriage. When a husband doesn't understand that his wife is a valuable and unique individual, then their differences can become points of contention, instead of celebration. Instead of fighting about our different gifts and strengths, Tom and I have always endeavored to celebrate our differences.

We have worked wonderfully together as a team for all these years. Tom is a visionary. God gives him dreams and plans for our life and ministry. I'm an administrator. In matters pertaining to ministry, almost as soon as Tom shares the plan or vision, I'm "on it" to help bring it to fruition! In fact, as soon as he communicates what he sees in his heart, I usually have staff and volunteers praying and interceding over that vision. I'm not trying to take over. This is my strength, so I am simply taking my place with Tom to assist him in the work God has called us to do.

Tom and I are a team. He needs me and I need him. I'm not a visionary; I'm a builder. I need vision in order to know what to build. Tom is the head of this team, but he's not a builder. He values my strengths to bring forth what he sees as the visionary—and he allows me to operate in those strengths because that's where I function best and am the most effective.

As a pastor, Tom spends long hours praying and seeking God. He studies the Word of God and writes sermons. He has the pulse of the congregation, because it's his job to know what the needs and concerns are of the members of our church. He doesn't have time to organize departments and oversee volunteers. That's an administrator's job. If we both did my job, who would take care of the spiritual oversight of the church? On the other hand, if we both did Tom's job, who would facilitate the vision and the day-to-day operation of the ministry?

My strengths are not Tom's strengths, and his strengths are not my strengths. But together, we complement and strengthen each other, as well as our marriage. We don't feel threatened by each other's gifts, instead we esteem and appreciate these gifts, and that's why we are able to benefit collectively from them. By recognizing each other's gifts, while combining our strengths, we have been able to build a successful family and ministry together.

Progress on the Sea of Life

A wife needs to get on board or "get in the boat" with her husband. She can't have her own separate boat and expect to be truly happy and fulfilled in marriage. A husband and wife must be in the same boat together and combine their strengths, so they can make steady progress and fulfill their destiny on the sea of life. A healthy marriage in which there is unity and solidarity, can accomplish great things in the Kingdom of God.

The enemy has tried to undermine marriages by pitting one spouse against the other. He knows that marriages are strengthened when we complement each other with our differences—but that a marriage is weakened when we use our differences to attack, ridicule, and reject one another. If we give place to the love of God in our hearts and accept one another's gifts and strengths, then the enemy will be defeated in his attempts to hinder our progress or even destroy our marriage.

Sometimes a husband is intimidated by his wife's gift, so he doesn't draw from it properly. In fact, he might try to smother her gift and not permit it to develop and flourish. Similarly, a wife can ill-esteem and demean the gift of God in her husband. She may lack the desire to see that gift grow, and in a case like that, very often the gift never comes to fruition. Everyone loses in this kind of situation—the couple, their family, and the calling that's on their lives as husband and wife.

Tom:

'My Husband Made Me Do It'

"For the husband is head of the wife, as also Christ is head of the church; and He is the Savior of the body. Therefore, just as the church is subject to Christ, so let the wives be to their own husbands in everything" (Ephesians 5:23-24 NKJV). These verses concerning the role of the husband and wife, are often taken out of context and misunderstood. The context is the analogy of Christ and the Church; therefore, the teaching that a wife must submit to her husband "no matter what" is erroneous.

I have actually heard ministers teach that a wife must do whatever her husband says to do, regardless of whether it's legal, moral, ethical or right in the eyes of God! In other words, this teaching purports that if the husband wants to go to a bar and wants his wife to accompany him, she must do it even if this violates her convictions. Or if her husband wants to commit some sin and invites her to participate in that sin, she must do it even if that sin goes cross-grain to her own desires or to the voice of her conscience. If he wants her to commit a crime, she must do it despite the consequences she may face with the law!

To say that a wife must do whatever her husband commands, regardless of the consequences, is a perverted teaching. We are each individually responsible to God for our walk with Him and for whether we obey Him. The excuse "My husband made me do it" won't hold water with God. Colossians 3:18 says, "Wives, submit to your own husbands, as is fitting in the Lord" (NKJV). A wife is supposed to submit to love, because

God is love, but she isn't supposed to submit to abuse or to things that go against her heart or conscience. Now, I'm not saying that a wife should refuse to submit to some decision her husband has made, just because she doesn't agree with it. Certainly, he should hear her out and consider her thoughts about the matter, but, ultimately, it's his responsibility to do what he believes the Lord is leading him to do.

I am aware that there are situations in marriage in which a husband doesn't care about his wife's feelings or value her input in family matters. These husbands are not walking in godly reverence and submission to the Lord. It's also true that some women don't care as much about what the Lord—or their husband—wants as much as they care about what they want! But when two people in a marriage sincerely desire to do what's right according to God's Word—and not fight for their own rights or selfish desires—they are submitting to one another in the fear of God (Ephesians 5:21), and God will bless that kind of attitude and devotion.

To Love as Christ Loves

Husbands, love your wives, just as Christ also loved the church and gave Himself for her, that He might sanctify and cleanse her with the washing of water by the word, that He might present her to Himself a glorious church, not having spot or wrinkle or any such thing, but that she should be holy and without blemish. So husbands ought to love their own wives as their own bodies; he who loves his wife loves himself. For no one ever hated his own flesh, but nourishes and cherishes it, just as the Lord does the church.

Ephesians 5:25-29 NKJV

Again, this passage is talking about husbands and wives and about Christ and the Church. Remember, the relationship between Christ and His Church is a picture of the relationship between a husband and wife. So when Paul writes, "Husbands, love your wives, just as Christ also loved the church and gave...," he's showing a husband how to love his wife—by giving himself to her.

After Paul tells us that husbands are to love their wives in the same manner that Christ loves the church, verse 26 says, "That He might sanctify and cleanse her with the washing of water by the word." A husband loves his wife when he gives himself for her, and when he lays down his life by praying for her and speaking the Word of God over her—spirit, soul, and body. I've seen miracles happen in relationships in which husbands fulfilled their responsibility to speak the Word over their wives.

In many cases, situations of childhood abuse or other negative experiences hindered the wife from becoming what God had designed her to be. The Word of God spoken over her by her husband, "washed and cleansed" her, and those deep-seated issues fell by the wayside! She was released from issues of the past, and her gifts began to flow in the marriage. This added another dimension to her husband's gifts as she "completed" him. When a husband speaks the Word of God over his wife, that Word washes and cleanses her from garbage in the world that tries to bombard her mind. Negative thoughts from the enemy, can be washed away by the power of the Living Word, spoken in faith by her husband.

Maureen:

The Temptation to Quit Just Short of the Prize

The husband has a big responsibility in the marriage relationship. He lays down his life for his wife, and that is not always easy, convenient, or comfortable. As a husband, you may feel as if you're sweating "great drops of blood" as you die to "self" and to your own desires. Just as Jesus said to the Father in the Garden of Gethsemane, "Not My will but Thine be done" (Luke 22:42 NKJV)—you are going to have to voluntarily give up some of your rights for the sake of your wife. You may have to pray to God yourself, saying, "Not my will but Yours be done." You may have to do that more than once!

The other side of this truth is that the potential exists for a husband to cause his wife to become a selfish, self-centered, spoiled brat. In other words, he becomes the giver, and his wife becomes the taker without ever giving back, showing gratitude, or caring for his happiness. We must never forget that we are called to submit ourselves to one another in the fear of God (Ephesians 5:21); and to serve one another in love (Galatians 5:13). Our attitude should be, *What will make my spouse happy? Lord, help me meet his [or her] need.* When we love, give, and serve each other in marriage, we will reap the rewards of a marriage that is truly Heaven-blessed!

Tom:

The Real Purpose for Authority in Marriage

At least four times in the New Testament, God says to the husband, "Love your wife" (Ephesians 5:25,28,33; Colossians 3:19). Remember we said that love is not a feeling, but a choice. In other words, every day a man chooses to show love to his wife. "Husbands, love your wives and do not be harsh with them" (Colossians 3:19).

Women are emotional creatures, that don't respond well to yelling and harsh tones. So when a husband is harsh toward his wife, that doesn't set very well with her. His attitude may be, *Hey, I was just trying to make a point*, but his point was not received, because it wasn't delivered with tenderness or gentleness. God is not being mean or unreasonable when He says to men, "Don't do that." He's simply trying to impart wisdom to a man's heart and blessing to his marriage. "Husbands, likewise, dwell with them with understanding, giving honor to the wife, as to the weaker vessel, and as being heirs together of the grace of life, that your prayers may not be hindered" (1 Peter 3:7 NKJV).

Look at the phrase, "...as being heirs together of the grace of life...." A husband must see his wife as a co-heir. He must be a team player, and he must see her as a member of his team and then dwell with her accordingly. Without this understanding, he risks having his prayers hindered. One of the husband's responsibilities in the marriage is to pray for his wife. Most people have the idea that women are supposed to be the intercessors, and that it's her job to pray for her family.

Certainly, both the husband and wife are responsible for their individual prayer life, as well as their own fellowship and relationship with God. However, as a figure of authority in marriage, the husband has a certain responsibility to "watch and pray," where his wife and children are concerned. He must be spiritually alert and sensitive to God's guidance for his family—as well as to any spiritual attack that may be stirring against them.

Christ is the Intercessor over the Church. "Therefore He is also able to save to the uttermost those who come to God through Him, since He always lives to make intercession for them" (Hebrews 7:25 NKJV). God has called the husband to be the intercessor over his home and family. It is the husband's privilege and responsibility to pray for his wife, and he has the spiritual authority to do it! God will honor and answer the prayers a man prays on behalf of his family.

For example, Maureen grew up dealing with oppression at various times in her life. Her father dealt with mental illness, and I believe this affected her emotions as a child. As a grown woman, she continued to struggle from time to time with oppression. Three different times after we were married, she experienced oppression so dark that it seemed to swallow her and render her helpless and paralyzed. She was so overwhelmed with life that she couldn't even pray for herself.

We didn't know the exact source of this oppression—we just knew it didn't come from God! One night, I stayed up all night "praying in the

Spirit" for Maureen. By morning, that darkness lifted from her, and she never had a problem with oppression from that day on. I'm not sharing this to brag. I just simply took my place of authority in my home and refused to allow the enemy to have a place in my wife. I didn't know exactly what was oppressing Maureen, but I knew it had probably gained some kind of foothold in her life when she was very young. I also knew that I had authority over it, and that it had no place in my home.

I am in no way giving the wife a free pass, so that she can just have her husband do all of her praying for her. As a Christian, she's an intercessor, too. However, ultimately the husband is called to watch over the affairs of his house, and to guard and guide his household. He is the protector naturally, as well as spiritually. He must die to "self," and take his place of authority and responsibility over those in his own house, whom God has entrusted to his care.

Maureen:

Just for Women

We have established the fact that the relationship between Christ and the Church is the picture of the relationship between a husband and wife. So when we read about Christ and His Church, we can see the role a husband should have in his marriage. Similarly, in reading about Christ and His Church—His Bride—a wife can also understand her role in marriage. "...let the wife see that she respects and reverences her husband [that she notices him...venerates,

Marriage was created to reflect God's love—and for the New Testament saint, it should portray the beautiful relationship between Christ and the Church.

and esteems him; and that she defers to him, praises him, and loves and admires him exceedingly]." (Ephesians 5:33 AMP) Think about these words—respect, reverence, esteem, love, and admire. One of our biggest roles we have, as wives, is to set our husband up for success. We are supposed to send him out to "conquer the world," because we believe in him—and we believe that he can do it!

He Can 'Hear' You

As a wife, what you think about your husband affects him. Even when the two of you are apart, your thoughts, words, and emotions affect your husband either positively or negatively. You are "one flesh" with him (Genesis 2:24), so your attitude toward him is vitally important. A husband can sense whether his wife is standing with him in life. Remember, his successes are your successes, too, so I encourage you to stand by your husband, even in your attitudes, and help him believe that he is a success.

'On the Same Page'

To submit to our husband means we are supposed to "be on the same page" with him. We need to pull together with him and add our strength to his. When a husband and wife join forces to accomplish a common goal, they can do great things in life. However, if a wife is constantly pulling against what her husband desires to accomplish, she hurts him, but she hurts herself too. A wife is a helper to her husband, "equal and indispensable." That does not mean that she should not submit to her husband's godly counsel and authority. There have been many times when Tom has discerned that some direction I was about to take wasn't quite right, and I have always respected that. I've backed off those situations to give myself more time to pray about them.

There are also times when the wife will sense direction from the Lord in some area of their lives, and, certainly, her husband should listen to her. Wisdom can be found in her mouth (Proverbs 31:26). If she has been meditating on the Word of God on a regular basis, then the wisdom of God that is needed for a particular situation may come through her.

Recognizing Faith and Fear

It is important to note that just because we as women are "incubators," that doesn't mean we are always going to come up with the answers to the dilemmas of life. In other words, just because we are "meditators" by nature, doesn't mean that we are always meditating on the right thing. Sometimes the "wisdom" on our tongue, that we are speaking forth, is nothing more than fear!

I remember when we first started our church more than twenty years ago. We had a word from God. At that time when we stepped out to obey Him, I still had a lot of fear in me about it. The need to control comes from fear, which can in turn produce fear in others. I wanted to have a lot of control in the church, so I went to Tom day after day and told him what I thought we needed to do. However, my ideas mainly consisted of rules that everyone needed to follow.

After a period of "reasoning" with Tom and presenting my arguments, very gently but firmly, he finally said to me, "We're not going to do that." Then he explained why, saying, "It's not of God, because it's based on fear." I had to take a step back and evaluate my motive for wanting my own way. Tom was right, and I needed to respect his decision. I needed to get free from fear, and the need to control situations as a way of managing fear. Neither Tom nor I wanted a church just based on rules. We wanted people to come to church because they loved God and wanted more of Him, not because they were afraid the pastor (or the pastor's wife) was going to be angry if they didn't attend.

Respect the Lord and the Beautiful Order He Created for Marriage

Some women get upset if their husband overrides their wishes. But we shouldn't want our husband to be passive and just cater to our every whim. A man needs to be able to hear from God and obey Him to the best of his ability, without having to struggle with his wife to do it. He needs to gently, but firmly "stand up to her," so to speak, when she's operating in fear and not in faith. Remember, in the beginning, it was Eve who took Adam down a wrong road. Yet Adam allowed it. A man's passivity or failure to act when something defies his deepest convictions, can spell disaster for his family.

As pastors, Tom and I see that in many marriages today. The husband bows to the wishes of his wife, even though he knows they should go a different direction. He wants peace at any cost, but his compliance ends up being far more costly than "rocking the boat" and standing up to his wife as he should.

In review, Ephesians 5:21-33 tells us how we should treat our spouse. That means that there is a certain way, as defined by God, that husbands are supposed to think, speak, and act toward their wives—and that wives should think, speak, and act toward their husbands. So when it says, "... let the wife see that she respects her husband" (v. 33), it's telling us as wives, how we should be thinking, speaking, and acting toward our husband. The Amplified Bible beautifully expounds on that, "...let the wife see that she respects and reverences her husband [that she notices him, regards him, honors him, prefers him, venerates, and esteems him; and that she defers to him, praises him, and loves and admires him exceedingly]."

Keep Those Big Dreams Alive

These are amazing words for guiding our thoughts, words, and actions where our husband is concerned. In other words, we should be focusing on his positive traits as we "notice" him. We should study him, and know his likes and dislikes, along with his strengths and weaknesses. We should esteem him in our mind as well as in our words and deeds. We should believe the best about him and expect the best. We should expect him to fulfill the dreams that God has put in his heart.

As a wife, you need to have big dreams for your husband, because God has big dreams for him. I encourage you to send your husband off to work each day as a winner. Help him see himself as successful. Also, don't just think about your husband's good traits. Praise him for what you admire about him. In other words, point these things out. This must be your commitment to God and your husband, as a godly wife.

You might be thinking, *I don't feel any of those things for my husband. You don't know the man I'm living with!* If that describes you, I understand your feelings. But I ask you to obey this verse—Ephesians 5:33—by faith, because you love God and desire to be obedient, not because your husband is doing everything perfectly or just right. If you, as a wife, will respect your husband as unto the Lord, because you reverence and respect God, your feelings will eventually change. Who knows what God will do in your husband!

I urge you to say out loud, even if it's by faith: *I admire my husband. God gave him to me. He's a man of God. I respect him. I honor and esteem him. I love my husband!* Say this every chance you get—as you are getting dressed each day, as you are driving your car, and every time a negative thought about your husband comes to your mind. Let your words develop positive thoughts and images in your mind and your spirit. Your thoughts will eventually change your emotions.

Friend, no one gets handed a perfect marriage in life. Great marriages are built over time. Sometimes one or both spouses in the marriage don't even know how to build a happy life together. Many would work at building a better marriage if they understood how, or if they had the right tools. But ignorance has robbed them. Their ignorance of God's Word, has stolen from them the very thing that God intended to be a blessing in their lives—their marriage.

I'm not saying that the responsibility for the success or failure of a marriage belongs to the wife. Since I'm addressing the wife here, I think it's important to emphasize the power of a wife's thoughts, words, and emotions, in setting the tone in her home —and whether they build up, or tear down their marriage (see Proverbs 14:1).

Here's another way that can help you develop the right thoughts and attitudes about your husband. Say, "Thanks! I appreciate you," for every little thing that he does right, or that he does to help you. In other words, prize your husband; value him even if he's not everything that you would like him to be. This way you are not forcing your emotions to go in a certain direction. You are using a powerful tool that will help bring about real changes in your home life, and propel your marriage to the next level.

Earlier, Tom talked about a husband's responsibility to pray for his wife. As a wife, you can pray for your husband, too! In fact, your prayers can make it easier for God to communicate truth to your husband. You must not neglect this important ministry, because through your faith, love, and prayers, God can move mightily in the life of your husband to establish godly order and to bless the entire family.

Marriage was created to reflect God's love—and for the New Testament saints, it should portray the beautiful relationship between Christ and the Church. God has given us His wisdom and instruction for marriage, so let's sift through those erroneous teachings that bring bondage and steal our joy. Instead, let's submit to God and His Word—and then to each other in reverential honor of the Lord. This will be pleasing to God, and we will be blessed in our deeds if we do this.

8

IF IT TAKES TWO TO TANGO, WHOSE TURN IS IT TO LEAD?

Dr. Tom Anderson

"This Book of the Law shall not depart from your mouth, but you shall meditate in it day and night, THAT YOU MAY OBSERVE TO DO according to all that is written in it. For then you will make your way prosperous, and then you will have good success" (Joshua 1:8 NKJV, emphasis mine). While preparing for a marriage seminar that Maureen and I recently taught, I wrote down seven attitudes or "mindsets," that a husband must have if he ever hopes to experience "Heaven on earth" in his marriage. These seven things have become so important in our own marriage. I would like to share them with you, especially if you are a husband, or hope to become one some day.

Each of these seven attitudes is based firmly in Scripture. If you will meditate on these truths, you will become capable of doing them—or practicing them—as the Bible says. Then you will see scriptural results and the blessings of Heaven in your marriage. It won't take long before you and your wife will enter the next level in a "Kingdom" marriage—a marriage relationship as God intends.

These seven attitudes are not difficult or complicated; however, they can be very humbling. I believe they are positive, because they help us, as men, to deal with some of the "macho" mentality that many of us have been raised with. We, as men, will never become just like women—and we don't want to! However, we need to grow in areas that have traditionally been associated with the feminine gender, such as gentleness and kindness. Some men don't consider these characteristics as masculine; however, they are listed among the "fruit of the Spirit" in Galatians 5:22. Since they are characteristics of God, we should exemplify these traits, too.

Are you ready to transform your thoughts and attitudes about marriage? Do you want to take a step up to enjoy the kind of relationship that God desires you to have? If so, let's begin.

Mindset Number 1:
'There Isn't Anything I Wouldn't Do for My Wife'

The first attitude I pondered in preparation for our marriage seminar is this: There isn't anything I wouldn't do for Maureen. The Bible teaches us very clearly that in the marriage relationship, the woman is looked at as the Church, and the husband is looked at as Christ Jesus. Is there anything that Jesus wouldn't have done for His Bride (see Romans 8:32)? No, and there's nothing He wouldn't do for His Bride today. Remember, Jesus said, "I didn't come to be served but, rather, to serve" (see Matthew 20:28; Mark 10:45). Jesus becomes our example in service. As husbands, we have a responsibility to serve our wife. Just think about how far societies—including the Church—have gotten away from this in the past 2,000 years. Overall, marriage is often looked at as the wife primarily serving the husband. This switch in mindset is interesting, but it isn't biblical or workable. Let me say this very plainly. In marriage, we mostly see the husband expecting his wife to serve him. Many husbands believe that if they simply make money and bring it home, then that is enough to maintain a marriage. However, this is not the truth; this is not the way it's supposed to work!

Man Is the Primary Sower of Seed

Woman was designed a specific way by God, to help motivate her husband to "conquer the world"! Man was designed a specific way by God, to lay down his life for his wife. Isn't that contrary to most of what you have seen and heard taught? Is that contrary to the way you have been living? The good news about serving is that when you, as a husband, serve your wife, it is a sowing process, and you will reap a harvest! In other words, service comes back to you. Yet "service" needs to be put in the right order, because as a man, you—not your wife—are the "seed-sower." She is the receiver or incubator, and bearer of the seed you sow. This fact alone should cause you to pause and consider what you are sowing into your marriage. What you sow is so important, because what you sow is what you are going to reap. As I said, there isn't anything I wouldn't do for Maureen. Whatever she asks me to do—short of divorcing her—I will do!

You might be thinking, *That seems like such a tall order!* That's why you need to meditate on these things in light of the Word of God. Let this attitude grow within you. Then you will be enabled to do it—and do it with the right motivation—love for God, love for your wife, and a desire to experience marriage at the level of blessing and fulfillment that God intends.

Meditation, Not Manipulation

Meditating on God's Word will help you get the truth into your heart, and then act on that truth from a heart of love. What happens when a husband and wife do the right things, but for the wrong reasons or with wrong motives? Manipulation is the result. Manipulation is of the flesh, and it will suck the life right out of your marriage. But God's Word will give life to the relationship you have with your spouse.

Maureen and I did not get to where we are in our marriage today, by simply reading a few books or attending a seminar or two. In other words, it didn't happen overnight. Over the years, we have read books, listened to audio teachings, and attended meetings on marriage. Those things are important. We got to this place of fulfillment in our marriage by continually meditating on, and practicing the Word concerning the marriage relationship. We finally got to a place where we could "observe to do it" (Joshua 1:8). After a time, we could put it into practice successfully and experience the rewards of being "doers of the Word" (see James 1:22).

Now, it's nothing for me to get up and make breakfast and do whatever I can to serve my wife. I don't make our breakfast every day, but I am willing to do it as often as possible. I want to do whatever I can to serve Maureen and be a blessing to her. Certainly, I'm not saying that this attitude of service shouldn't work both ways in a marriage. Maureen serves and blesses me, too. However, I discovered years ago that I am the primary "sower" of seed, so I need to take the lead if we are ever going to have the kind of marriage and live the kind of life that God desires for us.

Mindset Number 2:
'I Will Never Cheat on My Wife'

When Maureen and I got married, we made a decision together—an absolute, solid, resolute commitment—that neither one of us would ever cheat. Making that kind of quality commitment takes so much out of the equation, as far as marital problems are concerned. Every marriage faces problems in life that must be resolved and overcome. Why add to those problems with fear, worry, or concern about issues of marital faithfulness and trust? So much is encompassed in that one commitment, or pact, of absolute fidelity in marriage.

My faithfulness to Maureen will never be a concern to her, and her faithfulness to me will never be a concern to me. Unfaithfulness is not on the table, so to speak. It's not a possibility in either one of our lives. Our commitment to marital fidelity is so powerful. Amid all the twists and turns of life, that solid, unwavering, unswerving commitment brings a tremendous level of security to a marriage. Security and trust are the foundation of marriage; they are vital to the success of the marriage.

So many people get married with the attitude, *We'll try it to see if it works*. However, these marriages usually don't work. When we got married, Maureen and I made a commitment to each other for eternity. We vowed that there was no turning back, no giving up, and no possibility of not making it. Our attitude was this: *We're going to do this thing, and that's how it's going to be*. That has been our hearts' determination from the beginning. Divorce was never an option.

I took the initiative in making that firm determination. I didn't leave Maureen to carry the weight of trying to ensure an insulated marriage, safe and free from the outside forces that invariably attempt to work their way into a marriage to destroy it. Adultery is an insidious thing that tries to come into a marriage relationship. Once it is allowed access, it's either impossible or at best, very difficult to get past. The Bible teaches that adultery is a valid cause for divorcing. Can you see why making a commitment to forbid adultery in your marriage can have

When Maureen and I got married, we made a decision together—an absolute, solid, resolute commitment— that neither one of us would ever cheat.

such positive, long-lasting effects on the quality of your marriage? Regardless of your past, if you haven't done so already, now is the time to make this firm commitment to be faithful in your marriage. You need to make this commitment face to face with your wife.

Mindset Number 3:
'My Wife Is a Gift from God to Me'

The third attitude that I have cultivated over the years is that my wife is a gift from God to me. With that mindset uppermost in my thinking, I have made Maureen first place in my life, next to the Lord. No sport or other activity—including my ministry, job, or time with my children or grandchildren—is going to take the place of time with her. She is a gift from God to me. I will not allow anything to occupy a place in my life that would take me from her.

The Bible says, "He who finds a wife finds a good thing, and obtains favor from the Lord" (Proverbs 18:22 NKJV). Your wife is a gift to you from God, and when you meditate on and grasp this truth in your heart, it will change the way you prioritize your time. When you let your wife know that she is number one—that she's second to nothing on earth—it further builds trust and security, and it strengthens your marriage relationship.

Mindset Number 4:
'I Will Give My Wife Everything I Possibly Can'

I have also made the heartfelt commitment over the years, that I will give Maureen everything in life that I possibly can. Today we are doing well financially, but that wasn't always the case. However, I have always been committed to work hard and do everything I possibly could, to provide the best life possible for her. Some husbands seem to have this truth completely turned around! But it's not the wife's job to provide for her husband; it's his job to provide for her. I'm not saying it's wrong for both the husband and wife to earn income, but he is primarily the one responsible for what they have, where they go, and the kind of lifestyle they live. In our marriage, I accept this responsibility. There simply isn't anything that I wouldn't provide for Maureen, if I had the means to. I have always felt this way—whether it meant working one job, two jobs, or even three jobs (and I have done all of those!).

Don't misunderstand me. In the early days of our marriage, we weren't well off so there were times that Maureen went without some of the things she wanted. However, that didn't stop me from working as hard as I could, to get her as much as I could. I'm not talking about a certain set, standard of living that a husband must attain to. I'm talking about doing the very best that he can, with the attitude that there's nothing he would ever withhold from his wife, that he had the means to provide for her.

Some husbands hoard their money or keep a separate account so they can buy their own "toys" and things. However, he should always put his wife first. This may seem like a hard pill to swallow, but if you will embrace this truth, it will change your life and your marriage. Now, a husband's eager desire to provide the best for his wife does not negate her commitment to him if he falls on hard times or is struggling financially.

Maureen is committed to me, and I'm committed to her. If I lost everything tomorrow, we would still have each other, and with God's help, we would rebuild our lives financially. We don't fear abandonment by the other if times get tough. We are secure in our relationship with each other, so we don't fear risk or loss. We have the courage to take a shot at the "next level," because we know that even if all else fails, we will always have each other.

When you make God, and your marriage, foundational to your life, you will not become attached to things. I like material things as much as the next person, but I refuse to allow my life to become so attached to those things, that they become more important than my relationship with God or my wife. I'm attached to God, as well as my wife; therefore, things don't have a hold on me. I am free from the unnatural attachments of the world, because of the priority I have placed on God's Word and my marriage.

Mindset Number 5:
'Everything I Invest in My Wife
Must Have Life or Give Life'

Everything that I invest in Maureen must meet the criteria of 'having life,' or 'giving life.' In other words, I won't steal from her. I won't sow anything destructive into her life. I will support her dreams and goals

When you make God and your marriage foundational to your life, it also keeps you from becoming attached to things.

and what is important to her will always be important to me. I esteem the dreams that God has placed in her heart. I try to do everything I can to help her go wherever she believes that God wants her to. I will never belittle her vision or significance in the Body of Christ or in the plan of God.

When I invest words into Maureen, I make sure that those words are filled with life, not death. If I want to walk in life and not destruction, I have figured out over the years that I must take the initiative to sow life. Therefore, I determine that my words will be filled with love, instead of criticism, anger, or harshness. Have you ever heard the saying, "Happy wife, happy life"? It's so true! Usually, when you hear that saying, you hear it in the context of a wife acting contentious when things don't go her way. That's not what I'm talking about. I'm talking about a harvest of the happy life that a husband will reap, when he purposes to sow into his wife only those things that have, or give life.

Mindset Number 6:
'I Will Infuse My Wife with Seeds of
Praise, Appreciation, and Honor'

The sixth attitude I have cultivated in my marriage is that I will always attempt to infuse Maureen with seeds of praise, appreciation, and honor. I highly value my wife, and I purpose that every word I speak reflects this attitude. I believe with all my heart that a husband's thoughts, words, and actions that are planted in his wife's life will yield fruit and cause her to be what he has planted!

Seeds of Thoughts, Words, and Deeds

Seeds of praise, appreciation, and honor are very powerful things that will produce powerful results. Even the thoughts that you think are seeds, so don't ever allow negative thoughts about your wife to get into your head, because they will eventually produce a harvest of bad words or actions. Don't even go there. Take your thoughts captive (see Second Corinthians 10:5). Think positive thoughts about your wife and discover the power of your thoughts, as you begin to see your marriage in a positive light.

Why would Paul exhort us to take our wrong thoughts captive, if thoughts weren't powerful or capable of causing great damage? You might think, *It's just one small thought.* But think of the power of a small twenty- or forty-watt light bulb in your refrigerator! When you open the door to your fridge in the middle of the night, it could be pitch black in your house, but that very small light will illuminate the inside of the refrigerator so brightly, and even "spill over" into the kitchen. One small light? Yes. But it produces a big result!

I'm not talking about a negative thought that passes through your mind, that you refuse to think on, or allow to remain. I'm talking about little things that are negative (not having or giving life), yet they seem harmless, and you dwell on them. You concentrate on the faults and failures of your wife. In doing this, your "secret" thoughts create a power that's going to vividly manifest in your marriage sooner or later. The lights are going to come on, so to speak, and the effect will be damaging. That's how much power and energy that your concentrated thoughts have on your home environment, including your wife and children. Your thoughts can affect your wife's emotions and demeanor, especially if she's nearby—in the same vicinity or area of the home.

Your Words and Beyond

Face it. The words we speak are either going to build up or tear down. Words are seeds that will produce a harvest, either good or bad. So you need to ask yourself, *Do I want to build my marriage up, or do I want to tear it down?* If you want to build up your marriage, then begin by using the appropriate words. What about your actions or your body language? What about your tone of voice when you speak to your wife? Do these things count? Yes, they count, and they are critical!

Everything you think, say, and do is a seed of praise, appreciation, and honor.

The Bible says, "Do not be harsh with your wife" (Colossians 3:19). Where does harshness come from? Most of the time, it doesn't come from actual words. Harshness is manifested through one's tone of voice. It is also manifested through one's body language. For example, while your wife is talking to you, if you are watching TV or reading the newspaper, that comes across as harsh indifference to her. You are minimizing her importance and significance, and, remember, she is a gift from God to you.

So what should you do? When your wife talks to you, put down the newspaper and focus your attention on her. What you're reading is not more important than her and what you're watching on TV isn't more important, either. If you want to go to the next level in your relationship with your wife and experience a marriage that's like "Heaven on earth," then make certain that everything you think, say, and do, is a seed of praise, appreciation, and honor—a seed of everlasting value to God and your wife.

Mindset Number 7:
'I Give to My Wife in Spirit, in Soul, and in Body'

The seventh attitude I've cultivated, that has taken Maureen and me to the next level in our marriage, is that I give to her in spirit, in soul, and in body. How do you give to your wife in spirit? Well, how often do you pray for your wife in a heartfelt way? In spirit, I give Maureen prayer. In fact, the first thing that I do every morning is pray over her. I don't pray a long prayer—maybe two to four minutes—but I lay my hand on her and pray the blood of Jesus over her. I "cover" her for the day. As her husband, I have that authority and responsibility.

Husbands are a spiritual covering for their wives (Ephesians 5:23). They have a right to pray for their wife, as well as a responsibility to do so. As Maureen's covering, I pray for her divine destiny, as well as the things she is believing for. I pray that no outside influence will ill-affect her emotions, and because she asks me to, I even pray about her ability to maintain her weight. I pray for the things that are important to her life.

Praying for your wife is so important because, first, if it's a believing prayer, you are releasing your faith for God to work in her life. Second, you are accepting spiritual responsibility in your home and establishing God's will and order for your family. God can bless a home and marriage in which the husband is taking his God-ordained place.

God can bless a home and a marriage in which the husband is taking his God-ordained place.

What about giving yourself to your wife in soul? You must practice the last attitude we looked at, sowing only seeds of praise, appreciation, and honor in your thoughts, your words, and your actions. The way I give to Maureen in soul is, I make sure that I keep my thoughts in alignment with what is positive and encouraging. To the best of my ability, I don't let any words come out of my mouth that don't build her up. I'm not perfect at doing this, but because I've practiced it for so many years, I keep getting better, and I'm actually pretty good at it now!

In the realm of the soul, I desire to minister to my wife. For example, I am completely committed to Maureen. Commitment comes from the will. My commitment produces calmness and confidence in her. She is never stressful or anxious about whether or not I'll be faithful to her, or about whether or not we'll always be together. In the area of the mind and emotions, I simply attempt to be sensitive to her at all times.

I will briefly touch on the area of giving to your wife in body, because we're going to talk in greater detail about sex later in this book. In effect, I give to Maureen in body, by giving her the best sex I can. I make it a point to do that by reading and studying wholesome materials that deal with this subject. I also take care of my health, so I can be at my best during our times of physical intimacy.

These seven attitudes or principles from Scripture will ensure the best, happiest, and most fulfilling relationship with your wife that you can imagine. You must practice them as a lifestyle, and doing that takes renewing your mind to these principles. Romans 12:2 says, "And do not be conformed to this world, but be transformed by the renewing of your mind, that you may prove what is that good and acceptable and perfect will of God" (NKJV).

Certainly, it takes two people, both the husband and the wife, to enjoy a happy, successful marriage—just as it takes two people to fail in a marriage. We've heard the phrase, *It takes two to tango,* which refers to the fact that it's usually never just one person's fault when something goes wrong in a particular situation or circumstance. Scripturally, the responsibility for leadership in the marriage points squarely in one direction: to the husband.

If you haven't already done so, as a husband and man of God, it's your turn to take the lead in your marriage. So I ask you, will you take hold of these truths and meditate on them until you are able to lay down your life for your wife, in much the same way that Christ laid down His life for the Church? Will you make the sacrifice necessary to always choose the right thoughts, words, and actions despite your feelings that may lean to the contrary?

There will be a time of "sacrificial" sowing into your marriage. The harvest you will reap will be beyond anything you could imagine. Perhaps you need to "overhaul" your thinking, concerning how you are supposed to treat your wife. Or maybe you simply need to make a few adjustments, as you step up to the next level in your marriage relationship. But one thing is certain: As you meditate on these things and allow them to sink into your heart, you will be empowered to do them. As you do them continually, as a lifestyle, you will never look at marriage the same way again. Your life will be gloriously different, and infinitely better than you ever thought possible!

9
How to Avoid
a Train Wreck
in Your Marriage

Dr. Maureen Anderson

L ove is the foundation of every great marriage. A vital part of having a great marriage involves understanding this love—what it is and what it isn't. Many of us understand that love is not a feeling; it's a choice and a commitment that stands the test of circumstances and time. We have learned to draw on the love of God that has been poured out in our heart by the Holy Spirit. We have also learned that this kind of love is based on giving. The saying is true that, *love isn't love until it's given away.*

Feelings can be involved in love, and in their place these feelings can be beneficial. On the other hand, if they are not in their place, they can be very destructive. In fact, the "feelings" part of love and marriage can either keep a relationship on track over the long haul—or derail it when a couple least expects it. In this chapter, we will study the emotions that often accompany love.

The 'Infatuation' Phase of a Relationship

Many couples date and get married without ever understanding the difference between love and infatuation. In short, true love is about the other person; infatuation is about you. In the following chapters, we are going to look at the subject of love in marriage, but in this chapter, we are going to take a hard look at infatuation—"feelings" of love that are often present in the early stages of courtship and marriage. Infatuation can actually help build a relationship, but the other side of the coin is that it can also destroy a relationship. Like a locomotive at full-throttle, infatuation can act as a means to get you from one place to the next in your relationship. However, if it is misused, it can cause a serious train wreck in your marriage, and bring much pain and sadness to you and those you love.

Infatuation — Physiological in Origin

First, we need to understand infatuation. Although feelings of infatuation can motivate and compel us to do things that are loving and kind, these feelings are not the same as love, as we will see. As I said, infatuation isn't negative or wrong in itself. Infatuation is chemical in nature and physiological in origin. In other words, infatuation has its basis in emotions that are the product of certain chemicals released in the body. God created each of us with a spirit, soul, and body (see First Thessalonians 5:23)—and we know that what God creates is good (Genesis 1:31).

Every cell in our physical body is controlled by our brain, and our brain is controlled largely by our thoughts. This truth is illustrated in Proverbs 23:7, "For as he thinks in his heart, so is he...." It is perfectly normal that our thoughts produce stimuli in our brain and then in response to our thoughts, our brain releases chemicals that can in turn stimulate strong emotions. For example, if you have ever experienced a close call with an oncoming vehicle while driving your car, you have probably felt that involuntary wave of fear sweep over you, as adrenaline coursed through your body in those brief seconds. Of course, these feelings subsided almost as quickly as they came. The medical community has proven that our emotions, over a prolonged period of time, can have drastic effects on our physical health and relationships—whether positively or negatively.

At the Wheel and in Control

Although it's true that feelings and emotions are powerful forces, they do not have to control our lives as believers! Remember, we are a spirit, we have a soul, and we live in a body (1 Thessalonians 5:23). As spirit beings, we can be in complete control of our thoughts and emotions, instead of our thoughts and emotions controlling us. Have you ever

True love is about the other person; infatuation is about you.

heard someone talk about falling in love, as if he or she just couldn't help it? Or have you ever heard someone say, "It was love at first sight"? What that person was referring to probably wasn't love at all. It was simply physical attraction or infatuation. We have control over those feelings of love, as we will see in the following pages.

Medical research has discovered that when we allow ourselves to be attracted to the opposite sex, our brain releases a chemical called *phenylethylamine* (abbreviated PEA), which is also found in certain foods, such as chocolate. This chemical produces positive feelings of happiness, goodwill, and a desire to serve and bless that other person—the object of his or her attraction. When PEA is operating within the confines of God's will and order, it can be a very good thing. Infatuation lays the foundation for a relationship that lasts—a permanent marriage relationship. In other words, the purpose of infatuation and the releasing of PEA by your body is to mentor, train, and develop you, in order to build a healthy relationship with another person in the context of marriage.

PEA stimulates the feelings of optimism and euphoria in the brain. It inclines a person to think positively—on things that are "...true... noble...just...pure...lovely...of good report..." (see Philippians 4:8). In other words, when we are infatuated, all we see is the good, the beautiful, and the praiseworthy things about the other person. Yet it's an unrealistic observation of the situation. We are seeing that person through the rose-colored glasses of infatuation. Don't misunderstand me. I'm not saying that is necessarily wrong. I'm simply saying that we need to understand infatuation—that it's chemically based and not real love at all. Real love is a commitment and a choice that is based on giving. If we fail to grasp the difference between love and infatuation, we will misunderstand our emotions or find ourselves floundering, when these emotions finally subside.

When Infatuation Leads to Sex Before Marriage

Since many people don't understand the purpose of infatuation, they often enter into a sexual relationship with their partner prior to marriage. Since God intended infatuation as a precursor to marriage—and sex to be enjoyed in the confines of marriage—that is a misuse of infatuation that always results in some type of destruction or harm. When we use infatuation for the purpose it was intended, we will focus on blessing that other person, instead of gratifying ourselves. We will be interested in building a long-term relationship with that person, and we will be consumed with his or her happiness, to the point that we constantly think about how we can bless and help that person, and meet his or her needs. Well, that's what love does, doesn't it? Love gives; it isn't selfish or self-seeking. Infatuation is a precursor and stepping stone to love.

Feelings of Love Will Prompt Acts of Love

Have you ever noticed that when two people begin to be attracted to each other and the brain chemical, PEA, begins to flow, they have excessive energy? They don't seem to need much sleep. They think about each other constantly, and all they want to do is bless each other. They want to write notes and give gifts to each other. They want to continually affirm each other. They want to do acts of service for each other. They want to spend as much quality time together as possible, and they definitely want to show affection! They want to do all the love languages!

What motivates a person to do these things? Infatuation and PEA, or the chemical associated with thoughts of attraction. The infatuation phase of the relationship is teaching the person the right way to act in marriage. For example, even if you are not a communicator by nature, when you are infatuated with someone, that PEA is in a sense teaching you to communicate and spend quality time with the other person. You may have grown up never having been taught generosity toward others, but now, suddenly, you desire to continually give to that person who has become the object of your infatuation. You may also want to serve that person by making dinner, baking something, cleaning his or her car, and so forth. Studies indicate that these strong emotions which initially motivated you during the infatuation phase of your relationship, will begin to dissipate within six months and will totally subside within approximately two years. However, this motivation of commitment to love, bless, serve, and meet the needs of your spouse should continue long afterward.

Infatuation—Then What?

When the levels of PEA begin to wane, does that mean that the relationship is over? No! It means that what you learned about blessing your partner, must now be sustained by love that lasts. If you don't allow infatuation to do what it's supposed to do during that period of time, you will revert to the person you were before, and that "training period" will not benefit you, your partner, or your marriage.

Infatuation is a stepping stone to love, but it's not love. Love steps in when infatuation has run its course, and love continues the momentum of loving, giving, and serving. Then it becomes your choice to continue to love, give, and serve in the way that the chemical PEA has motivated and mentored you to do. That's God's plan for building a Kingdom marriage, or a marriage that's "Heaven on earth."

Since so many people don't understand infatuation, when those feelings of infatuation subside, they are either ready to give up on the relationship, or they find themselves unhappy and ill-equipped to sustain a happy, healthy marriage. When that chemical is gone that motivated them, they fail to understand that they are now on their own to continue building a marriage that's "Heaven on earth," by yielding to the love of God that is always motivated to give and serve.

The Power of No!

Problems also arise in a marriage, when people allow themselves to be attracted to someone else other than their spouse. But as I said, they have the power to resist those thoughts and even the strong feelings and emotions that they have already given place to. Yet very often they don't resist, because they don't understand the power of "No!" Your body is not you. Your spirit is the real you. You are a spirit—made in the image and likeness of God (Genesis 1:26). You have a soul, and you live in a physical body. Within your spirit and soul is the ability to exercise freewill and to choose "rightly" or "wrongly." That's where love comes in. God is love (1 John 4:8). So when you are walking in love, you are walking in God and in the light of His Word, and you will be motivated to choose rightly—to do the right things for the right reasons.

So what happens if you feel an attraction for someone other than your spouse? You exercise your power of choice, because you have the power to say, "No, I'm not going there. I plead the blood of Jesus over my life, and I refuse to allow my mind to think about that other person." Merely stopping your thoughts in their tracks can prevent the release of *phenylethylamine* in your brain, before it's ever triggered. But even if you miss it and let your thoughts go in the wrong direction, if you repent and continue exercising your will to do the right thing, your brain will eventually stop producing that chemical, and the feelings you have for that other person will subside.

"Keep [or guard] your heart with all diligence, For out of it spring the issues of life" (Proverbs 4:23 NKJV, explanation mine). We have the power to guard our own heart and mind against thoughts, feelings, and emotions that go against God's will and plan. If we fail to keep our heart concerning relationships, we become dysfunctional, and we won't function in relationships as God intends. Relationships are a blessing from the Lord, especially the marriage relationship. Marriage is a gift from God to believers and also a picture of the relationship between Christ and the Church.

Having a relationship is similar to eating—we can do it correctly or incorrectly. In other words, eating is healthy and, certainly, it's God's will for us to eat. But on the other hand, being a glutton is wrong! Eating the wrong kinds of food over a prolonged period of time will have negative consequences on our body. Sleeping is another good thing when used properly or as God intends. God planned that we require sleep to stay healthy—and He desires that we get the appropriate amount of sleep every day. But if we are lazy, that's wrong. The Bible calls laziness sin.

Infatuation is a stepping-stone to love, but it's not love. Love steps in when infatuation has run its course, and love continues the momentum of loving, giving, and serving.

Similarly, sex is a good thing. God created it to be enjoyed between a husband and wife. However, outside of marriage, it's sin and it becomes harmful and destructive. Just as people get into trouble when they misuse food or other necessities of life, they can also get into trouble because of wrong relationships. Many who become involved in these illicit relationships will claim they "just couldn't help themselves." That kind of reasoning is not biblical or true.

How Reverence for God
Can Keep Your Marriage Safe

How can a married couple keep their marriage safe from the dangers of sin and infidelity? By walking closely with the Lord in holy reverence and fear. When I talk about fearing the Lord, I'm not talking about being afraid of Him like you would be afraid of a dangerous wild animal. I'm talking about having an attitude of reverence toward the Lord. Proverbs 8:13 NKJV says, "The fear of the Lord is to hate evil...." When you fear or reverence the Lord, you love what He loves and hate what He hates. When you hate what He hates, you won't get involved with it, including wrong relationships.

The Bible has much to say about the protective power of fearing God. For example, the Bible says, "The fear of the Lord is the beginning of wisdom, and the knowledge of the Holy One is understanding" (Proverbs 9:10 NKJV). A person who fears the Lord and has a heart to walk in the light of His Word, will be a person of understanding. He will be in a position to be kept from the evil he hates. A part of having understanding is learning to understand how things operate and function, even in the natural realm. So when it comes to having a great marriage, you have to understand the Word of God concerning marriage, but you also have to understand the various components of marriage that make it great. A lack of understanding in this area can completely destroy a marriage relationship.

The Word of God says that people are destroyed because of a lack of knowledge (see Hosea 4:6). That verse is talking about the knowledge of God and His Word, as well as an understanding of His creation. How many times have you seen someone's life practically ruined, because he or she lacked understanding in some area, whether it was health, finances, relationships, and so forth?

As pastors, Tom and I have seen marriages destroyed, because one spouse in the marriage didn't understand the very thing I'm talking about in this chapter. The husband or wife became attracted to someone else. Instead of willfully shutting down those thoughts immediately, he or she allowed those chemicals to flow, therefore, the feelings and emotions associated with infatuation ensued. Instead of resisting, the person continued to allow those feelings to dominate his or her thoughts and actions. Soon that person was in a very bad situation, which resulted in many people getting hurt. However, this person never intended to destroy the marriage or family, but his or her lack of knowledge and understanding caused a disaster to take place, that never should have happened.

> *For wisdom will enter your heart, and knowledge will be pleasant to your soul. Discretion will protect you, and understanding will guard you. Wisdom will save you from the ways of wicked men, from men whose words are perverse, who leave the straight paths to walk in dark ways, who delight in doing wrong and rejoice in the perverseness of evil, whose paths are crooked and who are devious in their ways. It will save you also from the adulteress, from the wayward wife with her seductive words.*

> Proverbs 2:10-16

"Say to wisdom, 'You are my sister,' and call understanding your kinsman; they will keep you from the adulteress, from the wayward wife with her seductive words" (Proverbs 7:4-5). Notice the words "protect," "guard," "save," and "keep" in these verses. Walking in the fear of the Lord brings wisdom, knowledge, and understanding to your life that will protect, keep, preserve, guard, deliver, and save you and your marriage!

'Truth or Consequences?' — One King's Nightmare

When a married couple chooses to walk in the truth and in the light of God's Word, they will avoid the devastating consequences of sin.

Do not lust in your heart after her beauty or let her captivate you with her eyes, for the prostitute reduces you to a loaf of bread, and the adulteress preys upon your very life. Can a man scoop fire into his lap without his clothes being burned? Can a man walk on hot coals without his feet being scorched? So is he who sleeps with another man's wife; no one who touches her will go unpunished.

Proverbs 6:25-29

Verse 29 says, "So is he who sleeps with another man's wife; no one who touches her will go unpunished." The same is true for a man or woman who sleeps with someone other than his or her spouse. The Bible is clear that adulterers will not go unpunished. In other words, they will face consequences for their actions.

You probably know the story of David and Bathsheba. Bathsheba was the wife of Uriah, the Hittite. You can read this account in Second Samuel 11 and 12. David was anointed by God to be the king of Israel. He had sent his army off to battle while he remained at home. One night, he went up to the roof of his palace and saw a neighbor, Bathsheba, taking a bath on the roof of her home. Immediately a thought hit David's mind! David was attracted to the lovely undressed woman in the rooftop bathtub. But instead of saying no to his thoughts, he allowed the chemical, PEA, to flow. He permitted the attraction to persist, and a flood of emotions began to influence him. Still, he didn't resist. He continued to yield to those feelings and emotions, until he became consumed with them, and they began to dominate his thoughts and actions.

Perhaps David thought, *Well, I'm the king. I could just sleep with her, and then it will all be over.* What his exact thoughts were, we don't know. But we do know that he sent men to inquire about Bathsheba. In other words, David knew she was married before he ever had relations with her! So David had Bathsheba brought to his palace. Her husband, Uriah, was one of David's soldiers on the battlefield, who was laying down his life for his country. David, still refused to resist the strong temptation to commit adultery, acts beyond reason and beyond what is right. So David slept with another man's wife, and soon it was discovered that she was pregnant with his baby!

David tried to maneuver the situation by bringing Uriah off the field, so that he could have relations with his wife, so he would think that the child Bathsheba was carrying was his. But Uriah was too loyal to his fellow soldiers who were still on the field, and refused to indulge himself in the pleasure of sex with his wife. Instead, he chose instead to sleep outside the doors of David's palace until he received new marching orders.

David was in a real predicament! He concocted a plan to get rid of Uriah permanently, so he could take Bathsheba as his wife. He ordered Uriah to be sent to the frontline in battle, completely unprotected, and Uriah was eventually killed.

David was an adulterer and a murderer! Then God sent the prophet, Nathan, to David, and Nathan finally got through to him that God had seen David's selfish, arrogant actions and revealed it to His prophet. Then Nathan delivered the really bad news that David was going to suffer the consequences of his actions.

"Now therefore, the sword shall never depart from your house, because you have despised Me, and have taken the wife of Uriah the Hittite to be your wife." Thus says the Lord: "Behold, I will raise up adversity against you from your own house; and I will take your wives before your eyes and give

> *them to your neighbor, and he shall lie with your wives in the sight of this sun. For you did it secretly, but I will do this thing before all Israel, before the sun."*
>
> 2 Samuel 12:10-12 NKJV

It's just as Proverbs 25:27-28 says—when you allow yourself into a situation like that, you are playing with fire, and you will be burned. In other words, you are going to get hurt, and your family will suffer the consequences of your sinful actions, too. There is no such thing as "private" sin. The sin you engage in will eventually, directly or indirectly, affect others around you. In the case of adultery, not only is a spouse betrayed and emotionally devastated, but children, friends, and extended family members are often hurt as well. After David's affair with Bathsheba, he never had complete peace in his circumstances again. Consider the following consequences of David's actions:

1. His firstborn child with Bathsheba died (2 Samuel 12:18).

2. His daughter was raped by his son (2 Samuel 13:11-14).

3. His son mocked him by sleeping with his concubines in the presence of all Israel (2 Samuel 16:21-22).

4. His own son tried to overthrow his kingdom and kill him (2 Samuel 17:14-26).

5. His son was killed (2 Samuel 18:14-15).

These consequences were a huge price to pay for one moment of attraction, that David yielded to and gave himself over to! Influenced by thoughts and overcome by emotions induced by brain chemicals, he brought much destruction and ruin into his life. "But each one is tempted when he is drawn away by his own desires and enticed. Then, when desire has conceived, it gives birth to sin; and sin, when it is full-grown, brings forth death" (James 1:14-15 NKJV).

Death and destruction are what King David experienced in his life, because he "despised" God and His commandments (2 Samuel 12:10). In other words, David failed to walk in the light of God's Word. Before we judge David, when a person commits adultery today, he, too, is despising the commandments of God. Remember we said that God is love (1 John 4:8). So if we are walking with Him, we are walking in love—in the very love of God. That love will not intentionally violate His Word. The love of God within us will compel us not to do anything to hurt our spouse or family.

The Power of a Thought

We talked about the fact that thoughts affect the brain, which physiologically can affect the emotions, which in turn can even affect the body. So how do we keep ourselves from giving undue place to infatuation—infatuation outside the context of marriage? It begins with the fear of the Lord—with our relationship and our walk with God—and with our thoughts! "...I [Jesus] tell you that anyone who looks at a woman lustfully has already committed adultery with her in his heart" (Matthew 5:28).

It's amazing how many people entertain sexual thoughts about someone other than their spouse, and somehow think that, because they have not "acted" on those thoughts, it's okay. When thoughts come and are entertained, then lust is conceived in their heart. It's not just young people who fall prey to giving wrong thoughts, feelings, and emotions a place in their lives. Even older people are ignorant of how *phenylethylamine*, or PEA, can work against them, through the power of a thought. Although it has been discovered that it can occur in middle-aged women as well, men are especially vulnerable to what has been termed the midlife crisis. Both genders go through a sort of "change of life," in which chemical changes occur in the body, and can seriously affect behavior in the unlearned and naïve.

Have you ever seen a man who was approaching mid-life, and, suddenly, he leaves his wife, buys a sports car, and marries a significantly younger woman? He leaves "the wife of his youth" (Proverbs 5:18; Isaiah 54:6; Malachi 2:14-15). He devastates his family, including his own children, and affects the generations to follow. This misguided man is flying high with feelings of euphoria of being "in love" with someone else.

After a couple of years, when the chemical PEA begins to wash through the man's body and subside, he often realizes that the new life he created for himself is not that great, but it's too late. Lives have been hurt, and lifestyles have been altered forever. In cases like this, God can restore individual lives, but the families will likely remain broken. And to think that it all began with one thought that went unguarded and unchecked.

Take Action Now

The life we live here on earth is just a vapor, but eternity goes on and on without end. So why live foolishly and with regret? No matter what you may be experiencing in your mind at this stage of your life, there is help in God, and now is the time to take action. The Spirit of God will lead you into all truth in every situation and circumstance (John 16:13). You may need to see a good doctor who can test you for hormonal imbalances. You may need to talk to your pastor. Whatever you do, don't allow your marriage to be destroyed. In the face of temptation, invite God into your situation and pray earnestly about it. He can do more than you can ask or think—"exceedingly abundantly" above and beyond your own wisdom, power, or feelings (Ephesians 3:20)!

The life we live here on earth is just a vapor...So why live foolishly and with regret?

How Looking Ahead Can Keep Your Marriage From Being Derailed

Most marriages that fail don't just collapse overnight. In most failed marriages, there were certain conditions that the couple allowed to persist. These conditions made their relationship vulnerable to destructive forces. If they had exercised a little more diligence and foresight in their marriage, then they could have seen the dangers that loomed ahead, and their relationship could have been salvaged and healed. Some people are emotionally numb and "distant" in their attitude toward their spouse. This condition is a setup for failure. Perhaps the husband has devoted so much of his life to making money, that he has become indifferent to having an intimate relationship with his wife. Or maybe the wife has been so consumed with her children, or other interests and activities, that she no longer desires her husband.

Priorities can change and cause real damage to the relationships in our lives that God considers the most important. Next to your relationship with Him, your marriage is the most vital relationship you have. So why not invest the time, effort, and energy necessary to keep your priorities in check, and your marriage closer to the top of the list where it belongs? There are times in life when we need to reflect on what we truly value—what really matters to us. When you value something, you are more inclined to protect and preserve it. You will spend time and money to keep what you value in tip-top shape.

Tom and I have a great marriage. We are so happy, and we are very close as a couple. We are truly best friends. We enjoy being with each other and hate being apart, but it hasn't always been that way. Our marriage is blessed, but it took a lot of work—a lot of time and effort—to get to where we are today. Tom and I weren't saved when we got married, so when we got saved, we were first-generation Christians. There was a lot of divorce on my side of the family, and Tom's parents were also divorced.

We both brought a lot of "baggage" into our relationship, but we were determined to get it right! We valued the institution of marriage and our commitment to each other, and we knew we could have God's highest and best if we worked at it. We also knew that if we didn't work at it, our relationship would ultimately be derailed, and we would become just another statistic in the record books of marriage and divorce.

People can get their priorities out of order, and over time, marriage can seem to lose its value. Many couples don't value the relationship they have with each other. They value jobs and other activities more than their marriage. Or maybe only one person in the marriage values the relationship. One party works on the marriage, while the other party sort of floats along, indifferent in his or her attitude. This hurts a marriage, because it takes the effort of both the husband and the wife to nurture and grow a marriage into something beautiful and fruitful.

When marriage doesn't hold the place of honor and importance that it should, then a husband or wife can become more susceptible to outside interferences. For example, you may be a wife whose husband is negligent toward your relationship, but at work, a handsome man pays a lot of attention to you, and you sense an attraction between the two of you. If you don't shut those thoughts down, before long, you are going to begin thinking, *I've fallen out of love with my husband, anyway. He isn't doing right by me or the marriage.* Now you're "in love" with "Mr. Right" at work. But it's not even the real thing. You have feelings of love, but it's infatuation—the result of the chemical PEA—feelings that are very real, yet deceiving.

If you are a husband, your wife could be so wrapped up in your children and their activities, that she has neglected herself and has really let herself go in terms of her appearance. Maybe she is overworked and just doesn't care anymore. You go to work and there's a secretary there who is always well-dressed, and she tells you that you're the smartest man in the world. She always looks nice, smells nice, and acts nice. Before long, you're thinking, *I deserve better than what I'm getting at home. My wife is always telling me what's wrong. I want to hear something good for a change.*

Both of these arguments may sound reasonable and convincing, but they are not biblical or justifiable. However, if you allow yourself to be consumed with thoughts of being with someone other than your spouse, your senses will eventually override the voice of your conscience, and you will begin traveling down a path of deception and destruction in your marriage.

What so many people are calling true love is nothing more than infatuation, and medical science bears that out. Why, then, are so many otherwise intelligent people deceived by these feelings? Often it's because they have traded the value of their marriage for the value of having their own needs met, despite what the consequences will mean to their spouse or their marriage. Human love is selfish, but the God-kind of love puts others first, and it's that kind of love that ultimately never fails! (See First Corinthians 13:8.)

How to Restore 'Lost' Love

A person's relationship with the Lord is closely connected with his or her relationship with others. In fact, the closer you walk with the Lord, the better you will treat others, and the better you will do at marriage, successfully navigating the storms and the twists and turns of life that come against every married couple. When you walk closely with the Lord, you make a much better marriage partner than someone who doesn't walk closely with God.

But what happens if your walk with the Lord needs to be restored as badly as your marriage needs to be restored? Of course, you know you can ask the Lord to forgive you, and you can be restored in your relationship with Him. Well, it's possible to restore your relationship with your spouse, as much as it's possible to restore your relationship with God. Perhaps you have even thought that the love between you and your spouse can never be regained. But with God, it's possible to discover and renew that love again.

I think back to when I was first saved. I was so in love with Jesus that all I wanted to do was talk to Him and spend time in His presence. It wasn't physical attraction, but I was so consumed with His love for me that I gave myself totally to the Lord in my thoughts, words, and actions. And guess what? My brain released that PEA. I was on a "high," so to speak. Now, I realize that everyone doesn't react or respond this way when he or she gets saved, but that was my experience. I wanted to pray and read the Bible, day and night. Thoughts of the Lord consumed me continually.

This is the experience of many Christians. Just as the infatuation stage of a relationship between a man and woman is designed to teach them how to act, this early stage of a believer's walk with the Lord is supposed to teach him how to act in order to retain his joy over the long haul. Often a believer who began his relationship with the Lord in a euphoric state of mind, doesn't continue those "first works," after those strong feelings for the Lord subside.

A person's relationship with the Lord is closely connected with his or her relationship with others.

This is not a unique scenario. In Jesus' seven messages to the seven churches in the Book of Revelation, He said the following to the entire Church at Ephesus: "Yet I hold this against you: You have forsaken your first love. Remember the height from which you have fallen! Repent and do the things you did at first...." (Revelation 2:4-5). Jesus had commended this church for their good works in certain areas, but then He delivered to them the hard truth that they had forsaken their first love—the first love they had for Him. Then He told them to repent, or change their minds completely, and to do the things they did at first—when they first got saved and had a revelation of God's love for them (a love which hasn't changed, by the way).

He told them, "Remember the height from which you have fallen! Repent and do the things you did at first..." (v. 5). How does this apply to the "fallen" relationships in marriages that we see today? Since our walk with the Lord affects our relationship with others, especially our spouse, it is very much connected. If your relationship with your spouse has reached this "fallen" state, I'd say you have forsaken your "first love" for your spouse. I encourage you to remember the height from which you have fallen in your relationship with him or her. Then repent, turn around, and do those things that you did at first!

In other words, in the same way that we need to remember the works we did when we first got saved, we need to remember the "first works," that we did when we initially became attracted to our spouse. I encourage you to think back and recall the consuming feelings of euphoria you felt in the beginning of your relationship with your spouse. Remember the fun times you enjoyed together and the thoughtful things you did for him or her when you began dating. Were you more attentive to your spouse then than you are now? Were you more supportive? Protective? Kind, gentle, and thoughtful? These are great questions to ask yourself. You can relive these fond memories again and again, until you bring those loving feelings back into your marriage.

In Psalm 51:12, David wrote, "Restore to me the joy of Your salvation, and uphold me by Your generous Spirit" (NKJV). With God, restoration is possible no matter how far you have fallen in your relationship with Him or your spouse. So I encourage you to meditate on these truths and apply them to your heart and marriage. In so doing, you will begin to understand the difference between mere emotions born of the senses, and love which is real and lasting. This understanding will preserve you spiritually and morally. It will also help prevent a potential train wreck in your marriage, and restore joy to your relationship.

'But I Married the Wrong Person'

As I said before, when the strong feelings of infatuation subside in marriage, some people think that the person they are with is not the right person for them. That could not be further from the truth! Did you know that when you get married, your spouse becomes the will of God for you, because marriage is sacred in the eyes of God. It's not a game. When you entered the covenant of marriage, you made a vow to God and your spouse. Your marriage became the will of God. So don't ever let the enemy tell you that you married the wrong person. You need to stand down every thought that comes to your mind to that effect, and you need to say, *No, my spouse is the right person for me.*

Certainly, I'm not talking about situations in which one spouse is being physically abused by the other. Some marriages end, not because God necessarily "willed" the marriage to end, but because one person made ungodly choices that endangered his or her spouse, and that person refused to seek help to make the necessary changes. These are extenuating circumstances that sometimes make it impossible for a marriage to continue. However, these cases are few and far between. What we see happening with divorce in the world today—and even in the Church—is more or less the result of a lack of understanding about God's Word, and a lack of understanding about relationships and, in particular, our physical makeup. In other words, an alarmingly large number of people don't understand the difference between infatuation and love. But if you have Jesus in your heart and your spouse has Jesus, then no matter where you are in your marriage, God is in your marriage and He's for it, not against it. The Holy Spirit lives in both of you, and He is working the desire to do God's will and to be changed by Him from faith to faith by the power of His Word (Romans 1:17). He can do great things with even the most hopeless situations. So I encourage you—don't break up before you get your breakthrough!

A Word to Singles

Understanding the difference between love and infatuation is so crucial for someone who's single. Infatuation is fleeting, because it's based largely on the senses, and it can change with the seasons of life. But love that is grounded in God and His Word is stable and committed through every season. If you are single and in a dating relationship with the wrong person, then you can turn those feelings off, gradually or suddenly. First, you need to say "no" and keep saying "no" until your thoughts of not allowing that relationship to continue begin to affect your brain, which in turn will affect your feelings and emotions.

We know that the Bible says, "Do not be unequally yoked together with unbelievers. For what fellowship has righteousness with lawlessness? And what communion has light with darkness?" (2 Corinthians 6:14 NKJV). Now apply what you know about infatuation. You can see that even though a sinner says and does the most loving, romantic things for the one he "loves," once that infatuation phase is over and the *phenylethylamine,* or PEA, begins to wane, they are still the same person that they were before. Unless the person has gotten saved, he or she will still be in the same lost condition as he or she was, before they became physically attracted to each another. *Phenylethylamine* can be released by a person's brain, whether or not he's saved! This chemical that causes such feelings of euphoria, is physiological in nature, not spiritual.

Infatuation in Its Place

Infatuation has its specific place in a relationship. If you are single, its purpose is to bless you and the person that you are going to marry. If you are married, its purpose is to bless you and your spouse. Outside of that, infatuation has no place in your life! Although it's certainly important to be physically attracted to your spouse, physical attraction and infatuation cannot sustain a permanent marriage relationship. Those things can help lay a proper foundation for marriage, but they can't act as the foundation itself.

Infatuation isn't wrong in itself, but we must know its purpose and its place. When infatuation lays the foundation for a permanent relationship that's blessed by God, it can be a blessing. The Holy Spirit can work with infatuation if you are teachable, and He can use it to develop you further in your love walk than you ever thought possible. Even after you are married and you are long past being infatuated with your spouse, you can be anointed to be the husband or wife that God intended you to be and enjoy a marriage that's "Heaven on earth." I know it's true, because Tom and I are living our "dream marriage" today!

Of course, I know of people who have gotten married and never seemed to go through the infatuation stage in their relationship. I'm not saying that infatuation is necessary to have a good marriage. I'm simply saying that when present, those strong feelings and emotions have a purpose—to mentor and train you to be the lifelong partner that God intended.

10
WHAT TO DO
WHEN YOU'RE
'JUST NOT FEELING IT'

Drs. Tom and Maureen Anderson

Over the years, we have witnessed many marriages that seemed shattered and broken beyond repair, but were restored by God's bountiful grace. However, His grace was only effective, as these couples embraced the help that God offered them, which He offers every couple today through His Word. Because of the finished work of Christ, there is victory available to us in every circumstance of life. We must eagerly avail ourselves of that victory through our willing obedience to the Word and the will of God in every area of our lives, including our marriage.

If there's one thing we have learned in our own lives and in ministering to others, it's this: *Great marriages are made of great people, and when two people in a marriage strive to build up the other person, the marriage, as a matter of course, will always blossom and thrive.* But what happens when a couple loses all hope concerning their marriage? They are "just not feeling it," and the future looks anything but bright. There is hope in God! God extends hope to every person who is willing to believe beyond his or her feelings, and beyond the challenges of the moment.

Tom:

From 'Caterpillar' to 'Butterfly' in Your Marriage

"And do not be conformed to this world, but be transformed by the renewing of your mind, that you may prove what is that good and acceptable and perfect will of God" (Romans 12:2 NKJV). We know that our emotions stem from our thoughts, and our thoughts come largely from the words we hear, including the words we speak! By purposely changing our words, we can eventually change our thoughts. Through changing our thoughts, we will change our beliefs and our actions. Then this will transform us and our circumstances, in much the same way as the metamorphosis of a caterpillar takes place, transforming or changing it into a beautiful butterfly.

Thoughts are so powerful, and we can see this in the study of human behavior. For example, scientists have studied the brains of people who seem to bounce from relationship to relationship. In one study, it was discovered that these types of people have unusual neurological patterns associated with thinking negative thoughts over a prolonged period. These subjects developed certain "ruts" and "grooves" in their patterns of thinking. In other words, after thinking along the same negative lines over time, something happened in the brain that caused them to behave erratically, especially in their relationships.

God extends hope to every person willing to believe beyond his or her feelings and beyond the challenges of the moment.

Volunteers in this study were then given an assignment: to think and speak only positive thoughts for the span of two months. In a nutshell, after just two months of successfully completing the assignment, brain scans revealed that those "grooved" patterns had been reversed! Isn't it amazing that just the act of thinking and speaking positively can break cycles of destructive behavior in a person's life?

We Build—or Destroy—with Our Words

Proverbs 18:21 NKJV says, "Death and life are in the power of the tongue, and those who love it will eat its fruit." In the same way that our words can tear down and destroy, they can also build up and give life. When you sow life with your tongue—with the words of your mouth— you will reap the "fruit" of life. So, as a husband, when you bless your wife with words of praise, you are sowing life into her spirit, as well as your marriage.

We know that man is the provider of seed. We also know that the Word of God is referred to as "seed" (Mark 4:14; Luke 8:11). So, as a husband, when you speak the Word over your wife, you are planting seeds into her heart and mind. Then she will incubate those seeds, causing them to germinate and grow, and when they do, they will return to you—the sower—a harvest, in the form of a wonderful marriage.

You Can Create the Marriage of Your Dreams

God extends hope to every person who is willing to believe beyond his or her feelings and beyond the challenges of the moment. "By faith we understand that the worlds were framed by the word of God, so that the things which are seen were not made of things which are visible" (Hebrews 11:3 NKJV). Your vision for your marriage will come to fruition based on what you are speaking or confessing. I'm not just talking about the words you quote by faith to God and in your own heart; I'm talking about the words you speak to each other.

You can "fashion" your marriage, put it in order, and equip it for its intended purpose, by the words of your own mouth! For example, simple words—such as, *I admire you; I appreciate you; I'm so in love with you; You're the love of my life; I'm blessed to have you; You're so good-looking;* and so forth—are words that build and heal your spouse, instead of tearing him or her down and inflicting injury and pain.

Think about how loved you would feel if you heard your spouse say these things to you! Words are powerful—they are carriers of energy. Loving words carry and convey love. No matter how far from grace you think you have fallen in your marriage, positive, love-filled words spoken consistently have the power to save that relationship and cause it to flourish. Remember, love never fails (1 Corinthians 13:8).

Stop It Before It Starts — How to Stop Wrong Words in Their Tracks

We have already seen that women are great "meditators," or "incubators" of words—good words, as well as bad words. For example, when a woman broods over the Word of God in the midst of a challenge, then wisdom and blessing come forth. She meditates until wisdom is produced. However, there are potential problems that can occur when she meditates on the wrong things. When she over-thinks the wrong things, harmful emotional reactions can occur. We are all accountable to God for the thoughts that we meditate on. In other words, we can control our thoughts; we can choose what we will and will not think on.

Through the years, I haven't always been the example of a model husband for Maureen. I'm not perfect, but I'm growing. I'm further along now than I was years ago, and I will continue to learn and grow even more as long as I'm alive on this earth! During those years when I was developing to be a good husband, there were times when I said things to my wife that were not appropriate. But that's not the end of our story. Maureen had the ability to refuse to receive them—and she did! When I said things that were wrong, she decided to let those words go, instead of allowing them into her heart to incubate as seeds and produce something harmful to her emotions and, ultimately, to our marriage.

A woman who knows God and knows the Word, has the ability to refute thoughts that come to her as a result of wrong words that are spoken into her life. She can say, "No, that isn't worth building a situation out of." Of course, Maureen has the freedom to address me when I miss it and say to me, "That was inappropriate." Since I choose to walk reverently before God and tenderly toward my wife, I am man enough to respond to her, "You're right, and I'm sorry. Can we put those words to death and move on?"

When I said things that were wrong, she decided to let those words go rather than allow them into her heart.

I'm not perfect, and I don't always say everything just right. There are also times when I say one thing, but she hears another. However, instead of arguing the point, we have found ways to work through those situations through communication and trust. In other words, Maureen is not easily offended, so she is patient and calm enough to ask, "Here's what I just heard you say. Is that what you meant?" If she had misunderstood me, then I would explain what I intended to communicate to her.

This is where integrity and trust come into play. I have to be honest with Maureen. For example, if I said something in a sarcastic tone, I knew it, so I would have to own up to that. I can't lie to her and say, "I did not say it like that. What's your problem, anyway?" Since Maureen knows my character, she trusts that I would never lie to her or purposely hurt her. So through honest communication, we have been able to work through situations in which one or both of us had mis-communicated something or misunderstood something the other one was saying.

It's very difficult for a wife to trust her husband, if he has earned a reputation over the years of being very volatile and unsteady in his treatment of her. When he continually hurts her week after week, month after month, and year after year, she has a problem trusting that he won't do it again.

You have probably seen people who are what you might call "moody" or up one day and down the next. It's not easy to trust a person like that.

In fact, he or she hasn't earned any trust, because trust is earned over time. When you display certain godly characteristics over a period of time, then you build trust with those around you. Then when something happens to cause someone to momentarily doubt you, you can easily work through it. Because of your overall good character, one misunderstanding or even a lapse in judgment won't be enough to destroy the trust that you have built over time.

Although a woman is a "meditator" and "incubator" of words, she has the ability to stop wrong words from being sown as seeds into her heart. She can uproot them and keep them from growing. In fact, she must uproot them, because the principle of seedtime and harvest works, no matter what it is that we are "seeding" or sowing. Whether grains of corn or hateful words, every seed that is planted has the potential to produce after its own kind! We don't have to allow the sowing or planting process to take place. We don't have to nurture and grow everything that has been planted into our lives. In fact, we need to destroy those things that we don't want to reap a harvest from!

"Let no corrupt word proceed out of your mouth, but what is good for necessary edification, that it may impart grace to the hearers" (Ephesians 4:29 NKJV). I don't understand why husbands who know this principle of sowing and reaping, continue to sow grief and pain into their marriage. A man who does this will never enjoy the great marriage that God intended for him, because he refuses to sow the right kinds of seeds. He shoots himself in the foot, so to speak. The power to have a great marriage is in his grasp, but whether through ignorance or stubbornness, he refuses to do the right thing. Because of the wrong words he speaks, his wife constantly struggles to keep herself spiritually healthy and emotionally stable—while her trust in him has fallen by the wayside.

As a husband, you can't expect your wife to bless and minister life to you, if you are filling her with death and destruction. To expect blessing when you are sowing cursing defies the law of sowing and reaping, and it will not work. Woman is truly the "wombed" man. So why not sow romance and tenderness into her life? Then instead of reaping corruption because you are mistreating her, you can choose to enjoy a harvest of blessing.

The Word of God in Your Marriage

All Scripture is given by inspiration of God, and is profitable for doctrine, for reproof, for correction, for instruction in righteousness, that the man of God may be complete, thoroughly equipped for every good work.

2 Timothy 3:16-17

God desires that our marriages be strong, complete and thoroughly equipped, but we are going to have to follow the instruction and correction of the Word of God, in order to have the blessing of God in our marriage. Romans 1:16 NKJV says, "For I am not ashamed of the gospel of Christ, for it is the power of God to salvation for everyone who believes, for the Jew first and also for the Greek." God's Word is His power to do whatever needs to be done in your life. In other words, there is enough power in God's Word to change you and your circumstances, including your marriage.

You need to be open to God's Word. You have to eagerly accept and embrace the truth when you hear it. If you will do that, then the Word of God will change your life for the better. Romans 12:2 NKJV says, "And do not be conformed to this world, but be transformed by the renewing of your mind, that you may prove what is that good and acceptable and perfect will of God." This verse was written to believers, not to unbelievers, or to those who are unsaved. As believers, we are a new creation in Christ. Second Corinthians 5:17 says concerning the New Birth experience, "Therefore, if anyone is in Christ, he is a new creation; old things have passed away; behold, all things have become new" (NKJV). This verse is talking about your spirit, or your heart. Your spirit was re-born—made completely new—in the New Birth. What about your soul, though? Just as you still had the same body after you got born again, you still had the same soul.

Your body and soul did not become "new" in the New Birth. So you still had many of the same attitudes and beliefs that had been formed over the course of your life, largely due to your circumstances and environment. Many of those beliefs were wrong; they did not line up with the Bible. That's why Romans 12:2 says that you must renew your mind with the Word of God. You must allow your mind to be transformed—changed—by the power that's in God's Word.

We are responsible for what we incubate and grow.

"Submit to God and be at peace with him; in this way prosperity will come to you" (Job 22:21). "Agree with God, and be at peace; in this way good will come to you" (Job 22:21 NRSV). When we are truly sub-mitted to God, we will agree with and yield to His Word and His will for our lives—including our marriages. As a result, His blessing will be upon us, and our household. We have His Word for it!

Maureen:

A Focused Mind and a Guarded Heart

"Keep your heart with all diligence, for out of it spring the issues of life" (Proverbs 4:23). Although a husband is responsible to guard his words and "let no corrupt word proceed from his mouth" (Ephesians 4:29), a wife has some responsibility in building and strengthening her marriage, too. She must "keep her heart with all diligence" (Proverbs 4:23). In other words, she must guard her heart concerning her marriage, because from her heart will flow an attitude of life or death, regarding her relationship with her spouse. I'm talking about focus. As a wife, you can choose to focus on your husband's faults, or you can focus on his strengths. If you focus on his faults, those faults will become magnified, and they will eventually cause a wedge of separation or division between you.

The Birth of an Emotion

Every emotion is born from a thought. Women must understand that they are incubators; therefore, we need to think on and nurture the right kind of thoughts. If we fail to think correctly, we will develop the wrong kind of emotions—strong negative emotions that will affect our marriage. The right thoughts equal the right emotions. When a woman comes to me and says, *I just don't love my husband anymore,* by talking with her, I can usually take her back to the place where she began to incubate negative thoughts about her husband. In some cases, the wrong thoughts a woman nurtures over time produce such strong emotions that she's ready to act on those feelings in divorce court. A woman in this position usually doesn't need to change her marital status—she needs to change her thoughts and emotions.

Some women become so ingrained with wrong emotions that they are completely captive to their feelings. Their emotions are more real to them than the truth of God's Word. However, thoughts and feelings can change. You can change your feelings the same way you got those feelings in the first place—by changing what you have been thinking about. It's sad when marriages fail because a wife doesn't grasp this important truth. She buys into the lie that her husband will never change, and that "the grass is greener on the other side."

The Wisdom of Guarding Your Thoughts

'The wise woman builds her house, but with her own hands the foolish one tears hers down" (Proverbs 14:1). This verse in Proverbs can apply to men, too. By our thoughts, words, and deeds, we are creating the marriage that we will either be privileged to enjoy, or be forced to endure. If we want the right kind of marriage—marriage as God intends it—we will think on His Word, speak His Word, and act on His Word concerning marriage.

When you feel unhappy with your spouse, the first step in overcoming that is to recognize it as just a feeling. Then you need to resist that feeling, so you can work constructively, not destructively, on the problem. If you act on what you believe according to God's Word, instead of on your negative feelings, then positive feelings will eventually follow. But so many people don't want to take that first step, because it involves "casting down" the wrong thoughts and replacing them with the right thoughts, and that takes work! "Casting down imaginations, and every high thing that exalteth itself against the knowledge of God, and bringing into captivity every thought to the obedience of Christ" (2 Corinthians 10:5 KJV).

We know that thoughts produce feelings, whether good or bad. Good thoughts produce good feelings; bad thoughts produce bad feelings. In order to cast down bad thoughts, we must replace them with good thoughts. We can do that by speaking good words, especially God's words. That sounds simple enough, but it seems that women especially struggle with this. Many don't understand that feelings are just that— feelings— and that these feelings and emotions can be controlled by controlling their thoughts.

Change Your Thoughts and Change Your Life!

How do you turn negative thoughts about your marriage into positive ones, and feelings of frustration and unhappiness into feelings of joy, peace, and contentment? One way is by remembering the good times, by remembering what caused you to fall in love with your husband in the first place. You know you can do this, because how many times have you done it in reverse? In other words, how many times have you relived an argument with your husband or some painful moment in your marriage? Just as you can relive a bad moment, you can relive a season in your life when you had intense feelings of love for your husband. You can think about the things that made you laugh together. If you can't remember those times, ask the Holy Spirit to help you remember. Then as He brings those things back to your remembrance, write them down. Rehearse them in your thinking over and over again.

What are you doing when you actively replace negative thoughts with positive ones? You are doing battle in your mind! It won't always be easy, but if you will fight for your marriage, you can win these battles of the mind and enjoy the reward and the victory that will ultimately come. Doing spiritual battle means you are not always going to go with your feelings. When your feelings contradict the Word of God, you need to go with what the Word says instead. You are going to be a doer of the Word (James 1:23), instead of just responding to your feelings and fleshly impulses.

"Casting down arguments and every high thing that exalts itself against the knowledge of God, bringing every thought into captivity to the obedience of Christ" (2 Corinthians 10:5 NKJV). You can stop the cycle of negative thought patterns, by guarding your heart and by taking every negative thought captive to God's Word. When your thoughts are "talking loud" and clamoring for your attention, you can talk even louder! You can boldly and confidently say, "I don't feel it right now, but I appreciate my husband. I admire and esteem him. I choose to respect him."

...you can relive a season in your life when you had intense feelings of love for your husband.

...and let the wife see that she respects and reverences her husband [that she notices him, regards him, honors him, prefers him, venerates, and esteems him; and that she defers to him, praises him, and loves and admires him exceedingly.]

Ephesians 5:33 AMP

I have heard many women use the excuse that because their husband had done so much that was wrong, they could no longer respect him. Instead of using their thoughts to think on their husband's positive traits, they were using their thoughts to meditate on his faults, failures, and shortcomings.

Wrong thoughts produce wrong emotions. When you think on your husband's strengths and take notice of his accomplishments, you will feel better about him and your marriage. He may not be where you want him to be, but one thing is certain: *He's never going to get there while you're being negative!*

If you look for your husband's weaknesses, you will find them, but if you look for his strengths, you will find those too. Most people are very trained and adept at looking for weaknesses, so it may take some time to train yourself to meditate on your husband's strengths. But once you begin thinking more and more about your husband's good points, you will also start talking more about them.

I realize that many women struggle with this verse in Ephesians; they struggle to respect their husband. However, it is possible to obey this verse, and it starts with a willing heart. You must practice thinking the right thoughts. You may have to pray about it and ask the Lord, "Show me his strengths." Then God will answer you, and He will bless your acts of obedience every step of the way.

Dreams Don't Just 'Come True' — Sometimes You Have to Call for Them

...(as it is written, "I have made you a father of many nations") in the presence of Him whom he believed—God, who gives life to the dead and calls those things which do not exist as though they did.

Romans 4:17 NKJV

(As it is written, I have made thee a father of many nations,) before him whom he believed, even God, who quickeneth the dead, and calleth those things which be not as though they were.

Romans 4:17 KJV

Abraham "called those things which be not as though they were." He walked by faith in what God had said, despite what he could see with his natural sight. We can learn a lesson from Abraham. We can talk about what we want our husband to become, instead of what he appears to be right now. We can call "those things which be not as though they were." When we do that, our thoughts will produce the right emotions. We will be building a positive environment of faith in which God can work in us, in our husband, and ultimately in our marriage.

"By faith we understand that the worlds were framed by the word of God, so that the things which are seen were not made of things which are visible" (Hebrews 11:3 NKJV). With our words we create our own world and with God's words in our mouth, we create the kind of life that He desires for us. He wants us to prosper in our health, finances, and relationships—especially in our marriage.

Marriages don't come pre-built. We have to put forth the effort to build a life together with our spouse. Often people will look at a couple that has a great marriage and say, "I wish I had a marriage like theirs." Those people don't realize the work that went into building that great marriage.

Romans 1:16 says, "For I am not ashamed of the gospel of Christ, for it is the power of God to salvation for everyone who believes..." (NKJV). God's Word is His power! In other words, His Word is self-fulfilling. The opposite is true, too. You can speak negative things over and over, and they will come to pass, too! They will produce negative emotions and negative consequences in your life. So why not speak the Word of God's power over your marriage?

Years ago, I ministered to a woman who overcame her negative feelings toward her husband. Her marriage was restored by doing what I'm sharing with you. In fact, this woman's feelings went beyond having feelings of disrespect: *She literally despised her husband.* This woman needed help. She didn't want to feel that way about her husband, but she felt trapped by her thoughts, emotions, and beliefs concerning the man she had married. She opened her heart to the Lord and to His Word, and she began "arresting" every negative thought that came to her mind about her husband. Instead of thinking on a negative thought, she began quoting scriptures that dealt with marriage, especially those that talked about a godly husband, or a man who fears the Lord.

When she first began doing this, she would get angry, because emotions flooded her mind and thoughts assailed her: *You're lying! Your husband is NONE of these things!* In fact, every time she tried to speak out the Word of God over her husband and her situation, she was attacked by negative thoughts and emotions that had become strongholds in her mind. She had allowed these thoughts to work in her, so she had to recognize that and deal with it, before she could move on.

She kept doing this, and over the course of time, it became easier and easier to 'nip wrong thoughts in the bud' about her husband and her marriage. The Word of God in her heart, spoken out by faith, began to change her, and, gradually, her husband began to change, too. Instead of allowing her emotions to control her, she took control of her emotions. As a result, today this woman and her husband have a beautiful, loving marriage!

A Wife's Responsibility

A woman can build her home and her marriage, instead of tearing it down by thinking and speaking negatively (see Proverbs 14:1). It's true that women are incubators of words, but we are also responsible for what we incubate and grow. We must focus on thinking positive thoughts and speaking words that are based on the Word of God. "When they observe the pure and modest way in which you conduct yourselves, together with your reverence [for your husband; you are to feel for him all that reverence includes: to respect, defer to, revere him—to honor, esteem, appreciate, prize, and, in the human sense, to adore him, that is, to admire, praise, be devoted to, deeply love, and enjoy your husband]" (1 Peter 3:2 AMP).

As a wife, you might be thinking, *Help me—I just don't feel that way about my husband anymore!* But you can develop these feelings and emotions once again. God wants you to have feelings for your husband, and He's showing you how to get those feelings back. You don't have to get them all back by midnight tonight. However, you need to begin to restore your emotions by the power of God's Word. It's not only possible—God is calling you to do it!

You are going to have to pay the price to lay down your old thoughts and to pick up new ones. Your emotions will change when your thoughts change. You may flip-flop in your emotions when you first start out, but in time—as you consistently think on the right things—your emotions will change. The atmosphere in your home will change, as well as your marriage. Then your husband will be also be free to be everything God has called him to be.

Many women don't want to take that kind of responsibility. They don't want to hear that they are the ones who could be making or breaking their marriage. The saying, *Behind every great man is a great woman* is true. What is a great woman? One who has faith in her man—not someone else's man—but her man! She looks at him as a man of greatness, no matter where he is in his walk right now. Why?—Because God says he's great!

Every man is born with a purpose; God has a plan for every person. A man has to realize this fact, understand God's plan, and have the support of his wife and family, if he is ever going to carry out his God-ordained purpose. I have known wives who were married to their husbands for years, and those men just seemed to be going nowhere in life and taking their families with them! These wives had just about had it and were ready to throw in the towel concerning their marriage. I counseled some of these women to do the things I'm sharing with you, and within months, their marriages and their lives began to turn around!

Many women wonder where their marriage went wrong. Somewhere along the way, there were disappointments and hurts in the marriage, and, although the wife made the decision to forgive and be at peace with her husband, her emotions didn't recover and "catch up" with her decision to forgive. Now she must aggressively change her thinking process and retrain herself to think positively, so she can produce positive emotions.

Emotion-Driven or Spirit-Led?

Emotions are a powerful, driving force in our relationships. They can be used for good, but they can also be very destructive to the wife, her husband, and their relationship as well. Although we, as women, are emotional by nature, we must guard against being led by our emotions. We must be Spirit-led, not emotionally driven. If we "incubate" the Word of God, and let the Word develop in us, that Word will take us where our heart wants to go. No woman wants to feel cold toward her husband. No woman wants to disrespect the man in her life. Most women desire a passionate relationship with their husbands.

Years ago, the Lord spoke to me and said, "Every day, I want you to look for something good in the man I've given you. Then I want you to tell him the good that you see." So I would look for something in Tom every single day. And every day, God would show me something. I would find a way to tell Tom, "I'm so proud that you're a great leader," "You're so wise," "You take such good care of me and the kids," "You're so handsome," and so forth. These words blessed Tom and made him happy. Who wouldn't be happy to hear words of affirmation every day from someone you love?

The Male Ego: Handle With Care

God created man with an ego, and that ego can be easily crushed. A man should be able to trust his wife not to bruise his ego, yet a wife can bruise or even crush her husband's ego like nobody else. A man is at his best and functions at his highest potential, when his wife believes in him. He does not function well when his wife is upset with him. So as a wife, you have a tremendous amount of influence in your husband's life. It's a great responsibility, and you must fulfill it with love and great care.

Psalm 100:4 says, "Enter into His gates with thanksgiving, and into His courts with praise. Be thankful to Him, and bless His name" (NKJV). Your thanksgiving and praise to God gives you entrance and access into His gates and courts. Similarly, when you praise your husband's good qualities, you open his heart so that emotional connection is possible. Your words of praise and affirmation build trust in your marriage relationship. Remember, great marriages are made of great people. In the process of building up your spouse, you are building your marriage, too, and causing it to become a relationship that honors God, and brings blessing to your own life. In thought, word, and deed, your marriage will be happy and blessed!

11
TRUE LOVE:
THE 'CONSTANT'
THROUGH LIFE'S
CHANGING SEASONS

Dr. Maureen Anderson

Years ago, a secular song hit the top of the charts that asked the question: *What's love got to do with it?*[1] First, we need to understand infatuation. Although feelings of infatuation can motivate and compel us to do things that are loving and kind, these feelings are not the same as love, as we will see.

Since there seems to be so many different kinds of love, a better question might be: *What is true love?* People often talk about love in various contexts, such as their love for a certain kind of car, food, clothing, jewelry—or even a favorite song. Of course, people also talk about love as it relates to those they hold dear—such as spouses, children, parents, siblings, and friends. What about the deep fondness some feel for their pets? Love can have various meanings and applications to each one of us, but what does God say about the subject of love?

We know that God is love (1 John 4:8). We also know that He gave us—mankind—His very best in the gift of His Son Jesus Christ (John 3:16). So right away, we know that true love originates from God and that giving is a characteristic of someone who loves. Since marriage is the picture of Christ and the Church (Ephesians 5:25), we know that love is unconditional. Christ loved the Church and gave Himself for it—not

189

because we did anything to deserve or merit His sacrifice, but because He loved us unconditionally, with an everlasting love.

Simply put, true love in marriage is about your spouse, not about yourself. Loving your spouse effectively—in the way that he or she best receives love—is not a lofty goal that we can never attain. Romans 5:5 NKJV says, "...the love of God has been poured out in our hearts by the Holy Spirit who was given to us." So if we are saved, we can love! We know that love is not a feeling. It becomes a feeling when we choose to love as an act of our will. In other words, love is about giving; it's about a choice to give, serve, and bless our spouse. We must will, or choose, to give the love that's already in our heart as a believer.

Since marriage is a picture of Christ and the Church, one purpose, for the love of God in our hearts, is marriage. A Christian marriage is designed to show how much Christ loves the Church—His Bride—and how much the Church loves Christ. How we give place to God's love in us helps determine the level of fulfillment we will experience in marriage. If we allow love to flow out of us freely, we will reap the benefits that go along with sowing love into the life of our spouse.

Seasons in Marriage

There are two seasons in every marriage—high seasons and low seasons. Low seasons come when a need is not being met over a period of time. It's during those low seasons that many couples begin to focus on the negative qualities in the relationship and in their spouse. They begin to focus and meditate on their faults and failures. In other words, they forget about love! This is very dangerous to the marriage, because negative thoughts often have a way of coming to fruition and bearing very bad fruit.

So we must will, or choose, to give the love that's already in our heart as a believer.

We must guard against thinking on negative thoughts that come to our mind, especially during low seasons. When our needs go unmet over a period of time, certain chemicals are released in the body that can cause us to begin to think negatively. As our emotions become affected, our thoughts and feelings can spiral further downward and lead to discouragement, depression, and, eventually, complete hopelessness. We must fight against negative thoughts that are induced by those brain chemicals or neurotransmitters, by thinking positive thoughts.

When we choose to love our spouse, we become more rooted and grounded in the Word of God and the love of God, which helps us grow to the next level in our marriage.

Finally, brethren, whatever things are true, whatever things are noble, whatever things are just, whatever things are pure, whatever things are lovely, whatever things are of good report, if there is any virtue and if there is anything praiseworthy—meditate on these things.

Philippians 4:8 NKJV

What you think about will eventually produce strong feelings, because emotions are always borne out of thoughts.

Once negative emotions start flowing from the negative thoughts that you have allowed to persist, these thoughts will become even more powerful, because emotions are even more difficult to control. Many married couples find themselves in this very situation. They have meditated so long on the negative things in their marriage, that they have become discouraged and confused. They simply don't know what to do. They don't have a vision of victory on the inside of them, and unfortunately, that's when many opt to end their marriage instead of fighting for it.

Recognize Your Season and Formulate Your Plan

It's important to recognize the low seasons when they come, so that you can grow through them and come out on the other side, stronger and more deeply rooted in love. This begins with a determination that you are going to have a Kingdom marriage no matter what. You need to invest your time studying the Word of God and materials on enjoying a successful marriage. You will also need to fellowship with your spouse. You also need to know how to fast and pray. You must be willing to walk by faith concerning your marriage, and to pay the price to succeed, remembering that faith works by love (see Galatians 5:6).

When you recognize that your marriage is in a low season, that's the time to guard against every negative thought that comes to your mind about your marriage and your spouse. Did you know that you can plan your thoughts? You can plan to think only on positive things, where your marriage and your spouse are concerned. You can also plan to think only on things that are loving, kind, and praiseworthy. You might need a pen and paper to formulate your "thought plan," by writing down your spouse's strengths and the things that you love about him or her. Then you can record memories of when you first met and of your dating experience. You can recall and relive the days when you sort of "glowed," when he or she walked into a room.

Here is a simple exercise that will help you keep the right attitude during a low season, so you can grow and go to the next level of love in your marriage. Concerning your spouse, simply ask yourself, *What are the positives about this person?* So often, we focus on the negatives, but what are your spouse's positive traits? I encourage you to write down five good things about your spouse at the beginning of each day—five things that you are grateful for. Do it first thing in the morning. Don't wait until you become frustrated again. Tell your spouse that you appreciate those things about him (or her). Rehearse these characteristics to yourself. Talk about them constantly so that you can form new, positive thoughts to replace the old, negative ones.

Do this every day. Begin with a new list each day. Think about traits you admire in your spouse. Think about and relive fun times you have enjoyed together. Think about things that remind you of your love and dedication to each other. For example, if you are a wife, does your husband have a job? Does he go to that job every day to earn a living? Write these things down and focus and meditate on these things, instead of the negative thoughts that come to your mind. It may help if you talk about what you have written, to rehearse out loud the positive things that you have written about your spouse. Also, if you have recorded a fun activity that you remember, perhaps you can make plans to do that activity again.

People do this simple exercise in reverse all the time. They may not keep a real, written list of things they don't like about their spouse, but in the low seasons, they will focus and meditate on those things until those thoughts form negative emotions and strongholds, or belief patterns, that become difficult to change. Then they start talking negatively about their spouse because emotions demand expression. Out of the abundance of the heart, the mouth speaks! (See Luke 6:45).

After they have meditated on and spoken those negative things continually over a period of time, they begin to act on them. As a result, many divorces occur out of the low seasons in a marriage.

The following is provided as a guideline to record the thoughts, you plan to think about and meditate on, when negative, accusing thoughts assail your mind.

My spouse's greatest characteristics:

1.

2.

3.

4.

5.

My favorite memories together:

I met my spouse at _____

He [or she] looked _____

I knew I was in love when _____

We went _____ on our first date.

My favorite memory is the time when _____

Someone might argue, "I remember all the good times, but things just aren't that way anymore." Although that may be true, continuing to think that way will not change anything for the better. If you want to re-create those feelings from your days of dating and courtship, you will have to begin with your thoughts and emotions —reliving those moments when your thoughts were positive and your emotions were high. If you truly want to see a change for the better in your marriage, you must get rid of your old way of thinking and begin to think positive, faith-filled thoughts.

Remember, love is not a feeling, but your thoughts of love can produce "feelings" of love. When you sow thoughts and words of love, that are in line with God's Word, the feelings you re-create won't be fleeting, like the thoughts that come and go. Instead, your thoughts and feelings will become a habit. In time, they will also begin to develop within you, feelings of love that will last a lifetime. Think about it!

How to Turn a Mountain Back Into a Molehill

You have no doubt heard the saying, *You're making a mountain out of a molehill.* That's actually what happens when you continually think and meditate on your spouse's faults and shortcomings. Negative emotions will always follow, and you will create a destructive mountain on the inside. The more you think on those negative things, the larger that person's faults loom - high above any possibility of marital happiness! However you can reverse that process. The same way in which you created your mountain, you can also diminish it—and you can turn your mountain back into a molehill!

Usually, traits we don't like in someone else exist in us.

Here is another simple exercise you can do during a low season in your marriage, when you are feeling frustrated with your spouse. Write down three characteristics of your spouse that you would like him or her to change. In other words, list the things that seem to come up over and over again when you are in a low season. Then ask the Holy Spirit, *How do these characteristics show up in me?* Usually, what we don't like in someone else, are traits that exist in us. We might become bothered from time to time, about these things in our own life, yet they seem to be magnified or intensified in the lives of those closest to us.

> *And why do you look at the speck in your brother's eye, but do not consider the plank in your own eye? Or how can you say to your brother, "Let me remove the speck from your eye"; and look, a plank is in your own eye? Hypocrite! First remove the plank from your own eye, and then you will see clearly to remove the speck from your brother's eye.*
>
> Matthew 7:3-5 NKJV

The thing that really bugs you about your spouse might be a "speck" in him or her, but it could be a "plank" in you! So before you try to change your spouse, you need to ask the Holy Spirit, *Is this a problem in my own life? If so, how can I get free from this myself? How can I get victory in this area?* If you criticize and become hyper-sensitive about what the other person is doing, the Bible says that while you are judging that person, you are condemning yourself (see Romans 2:1).

Low Seasons Do Not Have to Be Long Seasons

During the low seasons of marriage, you need to remember and meditate on the good times. This will have a positive affect on your emotions and help you usher in the high seasons again. Your low seasons don't have to be long seasons! By thinking right, speaking right, and purposely reminiscing and reliving the high, positive seasons, you can quickly reverse the low seasons of your marriage. Let's look at a Spirit-inspired prayer that the Apostle Paul prayed for the Church concerning the love of Christ—a prayer that we must continue to pray today.

> *...that Christ may dwell in your hearts through faith. And I pray that you, being rooted and established in love, may have power, together with all the saints, to grasp how wide and long and high and deep is the love of Christ, and to know this love that surpasses knowledge—that you may be filled to the measure of all the fulness of God.*

> Ephesians 3:17-19

What does love have to do with the seasons of life? Thoughts, words, and acts of love can act as a "constant," in the changing seasons that we all experience. They will produce positive emotions within us, even when dark clouds of negativity loom over us. Expressions of love can sustain a relationship, strengthen it, and help propel it to a higher level of love in the next season. Another facet of love in the changing seasons, is properly dealing with conflict and differences. In the low seasons, conflicts often escalate and can bring destruction to a marriage if they are not resolved.

When Hope Seems Lost —
What To Do When You Don't Know What To Do

As we have seen, when a person's needs go unmet for a period of time, their body releases a chemical that begins to influence emotions. Of course, that doesn't mean that you have to follow your emotions. You can resist that process by guarding your thoughts and going to God in prayer. However, instead of praying and resisting negative thoughts, many people just allow their emotions to bring them down. They forget that Jesus is their High Priest, who ever lives to meet their needs (Hebrews 7:26). We can always go to the Lord with whatever is bothering us, and He will be a present help in time of trouble. "God is our refuge and strength, a very present help in trouble" (Psalm 46:1 NKJV).

"Let us therefore come boldly to the throne of grace, that we may obtain mercy and find grace to help in time of need" (Hebrews 4:16 NKJV). In our own experience, prayer and fasting has made all the difference in how Tom and I relate to each other today. Although we both came from broken, dysfunctional homes, our families were opposites—and so were we. In fact, our dysfunction was just about the only thing we had in common! Not only did Tom and I have adjustments to make and hurdles to overcome, but we also faced obstacles in our marriage that seemed impossible to overcome!

In the early days of our marriage, we had small struggles, as well as huge ones. Of course, God gets all the glory for enabling us to make it through those early years with a love story greater than we ever thought possible. Today, we have a marriage that's "Heaven on earth"—a Kingdom marriage. We are so much in love, because we learned the secret of true love in marriage. However, God could not have taught us if we weren't determined to overcome the obstacles in our marriage and make it a success, no matter what the cost.

Remember, the goal of marriage is to create intimacy between the husband and wife. Emotional baggage often interferes with the intimacy that should be experienced in marriage. To say that Tom and I entered marriage with a lot of baggage is an understatement. We had freight trucks and moving vans full of baggage that we each brought to the table in our relationship! My father was abusive, and my parents divorced when I was only eight years old, so I never really had a dad in my life. Tom's mother left him and his family when he was four years old.

So the only thing that we had in common were issues concerning abandonment, rejection, worthlessness and low self-esteem. These are the kinds of things that had been planted into our minds and subconscious from a very early age. Consequently, every response and reaction that we had as adults was based on these negative thoughts and emotions. Naturally speaking, we were a "divorce waiting to happen"— but to God, we were a challenge!

How to Share Your Relationship Baggage

Before God could help us, He had to do a work in both of us, so we would have a willingness to desire His best for our marriage. So every time an issue would arise, we had a prearranged way of settling it. Instead of screaming and yelling for days, or giving each other the silent treatment, we would pray together and ask God to show us what to do. When Tom and I had a problem, we would sometimes go on a three-day fast together and spend as much time as possible over those three days, earnestly praying and seeking the Lord. Then the gifts of the Holy Spirit would manifest on our behalf (1 Corinthians 12:8-10) and we would hear from the Lord. He came through with the wisdom and the answer we needed every time! He would reveal the root of the problem, so we always knew exactly whose issue was causing the problem—mine or Tom's. But it really didn't matter whose issue it was, because we were in this together—we were a team. Tom's victories were my victories, and my victories were Tom's victories.

When you are going through a low time in marriage, it's not time to drift apart. Instead, you should draw closer to each other, even if only one of you are going through a difficult time. You need to pray and seek God together. As a Christian, you are indwelt by the Holy Spirit, who leads you into all truth (John 16:13). Often when one spouse is dealing with intense emotional issues, the other spouse sort of abandons him or her to deal with it alone. You are not supposed to abandon each other in marriage. You are supposed to stand and fight together, united as one in purpose, shouldering each other's issues. That's love in action, and doing that brings the favor, power, and provision of God into whatever it is you are dealing with.

Now, when I say that Tom and I stood together in our marriage, I'm not saying that we never got angry with each other, or spoke a harsh word to each other. However, we got over our offenses quickly and learned to walk in love and forgiveness. Otherwise, we would have become isolated from one another—and it's in those times of isolation, that people tend to become vulnerable and fall prey to discouragement and hopelessness.

Communication Do's and Don'ts in Marriage

Fasting and prayer is a big key to resolving conflict and getting rid of the emotional baggage that can destroy a marriage. Communication is another big key used in resolving conflict. Even if you have to talk about the same issue over a period of time, if you are communicating truthfully and peaceably in a godly manner you can eventually work the issue out with God's help. But when you stop talking, it's almost guaranteed that your problem will not be solved.

I know of husbands and wives who sleep in separate rooms at night, because they remain constantly offended by each other. Early in our marriage, there have been times that I was tempted to close myself off from Tom when we were dealing with something, but he would not allow it. He would follow me into the other room! He also prayed in the Holy Ghost all night at times. Tom has never been passive about our relationship, but how many men just let things drag on for weeks and months at a time—and sometimes let the relationship deteriorate until it is completely destroyed?

You can walk into some people's homes and just sense strife and offense in the atmosphere. Why? Because conflict was left unresolved and unchecked, and it continued building and gaining momentum until everyone became affected—the husband, the wife, and the children. You don't have to allow those attitudes to dwell in your home. You have the power—especially if you are the husband, the head of the home—to "take the bull by the horns," and determine that you are not going to give up on God or your marriage, until you have reached the other side—and you are both experiencing "Heaven on earth" in your marriage.

Wrong Ways to Handle Conflict that Yield Very Wrong Results

People react differently to difficulty and hardship—to the low seasons of life—so don't expect your spouse to react the same way as you would in every situation and circumstance. Instead, accept each other's differences and stay positive and supportive. Give one another the benefit of the doubt. In other words, walk in love! Often during hard times, we become impatient and intolerant of others, especially our spouse, and that only makes matters worse. In many cases, if couples simply knew what not to do during the storms of life, they would be a lot further along in their marriages than they are now. That's why I want to discuss four negative responses to difficulties: criticism, withdrawal, defensiveness, and contempt. We must recognize and overcome these, in order to endure the low seasons and enjoy the high seasons of marriage and life.

Negative Response Number One: Criticism

The first negative habit that some people fall into when they feel disappointed, is criticism. When they become dissatisfied—especially with their marriage—they often use words that tear their spouse down, instead of building him or her up. Obviously, that's not the wisdom of God, because the Bible says that a wise woman builds her house, but a foolish one tears hers down (Proverbs 14:1).

Thankfulness and praise open our hearts and allow connection to happen.

Of course, this can apply to men, too. When a husband is frustrated over some behavior of his wife, he can begin to point out all her faults and failures. His needs are not being met, so he uses criticism as a mechanism to deal with it.

Using criticism to try to get your needs met does not work. When a husband and wife pick each other apart with their words, they tear down their marriage. Marriage is an institution that involves two people—and when those people are torn down, the marriage goes down with them. I urge you to avoid being critical at all cost. Criticism does not produce anything godly in a marriage; it only destroys or tears it down. In fact, nothing constructive at all comes from criticizing your spouse in a critical, mean-spirited, or demeaning manner.

The root of criticism is impatience. In other words, if you are critical, you want to see a change now, even if it's a forced change. You want to have your say now, even if feelings get hurt in the process. A critical person is emotionally driven, and when you are emotionally driven and not Spirit-led, then your conversation can be very destructive. Criticism does not build intimacy in a relationship, instead it tears down any intimacy that was present to begin with. People who struggle in this area also deal with feelings of pessimism and extreme negativity. They are the ones who see the glass half empty, and they are blinded to what they have in life, because all they can see is what they don't have.

If this negative habit describes you, then make a commitment before God today that you are going to search for, acknowledge, and be thankful for what you have and praise Him for it. Even if you have to get a journal and write down the good things you have—including the good qualities in your spouse—I encourage you to do it. Write down the things that you are thankful for, and meditate on those things. Begin each day by reviewing what you have written.

"In everything give thanks; for this is the will of God in Christ Jesus for you" (1 Thessalonians 5:18 NKJV). "Give thanks in all circumstances, for this is God's will for you in Christ Jesus" (1 Thessalonians 5:18). This verse doesn't mean that God brings every circumstance into our lives, whether negative or positive, nor does it mean that we are supposed to be thankful for everything. It simply means that we should be thankful "in everything."

Here are a few more verses about being thankful. "And let the peace of God rule in your hearts, to which also you were called in one body; and be thankful" (Colossians 3:15 NKJV). "Enter into His gates with thanksgiving, And into His courts with praise. Be thankful to Him, and bless His name" (Psalm 100:4 NKJV). Thankfulness and praise can open our hearts and allow connections to happen. When you and your spouse show gratitude toward each other, you are building trust. Even emotional gates that have been closed in the past can be opened again, when love and appreciation are being shown.

The opposite is true in an atmosphere of un-thankfulness, negativity, and pessimism. Darkness prevails in this kind of environment. Romans 1:21 says, "…although they knew God, they did not glorify Him as God, nor were thankful, but became futile in their thoughts, and their foolish hearts were darkened" (NKJV).

An unthankful heart becomes darkened, and a darkened heart can bring a marriage down lower and lower, unless the person makes a decision to change. Showing gratitude is a choice just like showing love is a choice. Since God has told us to be thankful, then that means we can do it!

A critical person must be willing to change. Instead of criticizing, he or she must learn to pray. Then that person must be willing to have an honest, healthy conversation with his or her spouse—one that builds intimacy instead of destroying it. (In the next chapter, we will look at how to peacefully and effectively communicate with your spouse.)

Negative Response Number Two: Withdrawal

The second negative response to frustration and discontentment is withdrawal. The person who employs this mechanism does not use words at all. He or she simply withdraws. That person is there, but not really. Instead, he or she becomes emotionally distant. When the other person asks, *Is everything okay?* the withdrawn party will usually respond, *Yes, everything is fine.* When in reality, everything is not fine. That person is dissatisfied, and instead of dealing with the issue biblically, he or she pulls away from the other person.

This behavior is so destructive. You can't bury needs, pretending that they don't exist, and expect to be happy. That's emotional dishonesty, and it breeds confusion in the marriage, because of the unwillingness or inability to be open and upfront. When you bury your emotions instead of dealing with them, these emotions don't just die. Although they are buried, they still remain alive. Whether you are consciously dwelling on them or not, they will continue to grow and produce destructive fruit in your heart and in your marriage—hatred, bitterness, wrath, resentment, and so forth. Withdrawing as a means of dealing with negative emotions doesn't work!

People who use withdrawal are usually very sensitive to criticism. They don't like to be told what to do, and criticism makes them feel inadequate. So when you criticize this kind of person, he or she will quickly withdraw. They seem isolated, but they inwardly long for connection, instead of isolation. Yet what they long for, they will never do. So, if you have a spouse that withdraws, you need to hug that person! That's what he or she really wants. You need to tell your spouse, "You're not going to withdraw. We're going to talk about this and work it out."

As I said, the person who withdraws usually does so, because he or she has some deep need that's not being met. For example, the person may have a passion about something and wants his or her spouse to share that passion. Perhaps that person loves the outdoors and desires to spend quality time with his or her spouse, while enjoying an outdoor hobby or activity. However, if the spouse does not share that passion— and has no desire to learn to like it—withdrawal can result.

We have all been guilty at times of neglecting the dreams and passions of those we love. We don't hear the excitement in our loved one's voice when something greatly interests him or her. We are not as interested as we should be, in that person's heart and in what God is doing in his or her life. Often, that person senses the lack of interest and, over time, begins to "check out" emotionally.

Since people who withdraw have difficulty expressing themselves, communication can also present a special challenge. Often they don't know how to express these issues, whether it's some kind of emotional injury or a fear that mentally tortures them. If you are a "withdrawer," for the sake of your own emotional health and the health of your marriage, you must simply make the decision that you will communicate! And you must do it in a healthy manner, not when adrenaline is flowing at a high.

You can begin with an email, voicemail message, or a letter. Just purpose in your heart to start somewhere, until you can sit down with your spouse and engage in a healthy conversation. This will be especially challenging, because a person who withdraws is not the kind of person who usually seeks out connection—yet that's the thing he or she needs the most. I'm not making excuses for the one who withdraws, because it's a trait that needs to be overcome. I'm simply saying that being sensitive to people like this—and loving them in spite of the walls of isolation that they put up—is a big key to drawing them out, and helping them make the change to communicate more effectively, and take personal responsibility in their relationships. Those who withdraw need to determine why they are withdrawing, and what their real needs are. Then they need to practice communicating those needs in a loving manner. Only then, can "withdrawers" begin to break this destructive habit in marriage.

Negative Response Number Three: Defensiveness

The third negative behavior that many resort to in low seasons is defensiveness. Defensiveness is born out of hopelessness and then turns into defiance. Someone who's hopeless might say things, such as, "I can never please her [or him]." Being defensive is the attitude that causes anger to erupt, so strife and fighting usually ensue when a person gives place to defensiveness. When one person in a marriage becomes consistently defensive, there's usually an underlying problem that's being manifested through that negative behavior.

Defensiveness includes denying personal problems and failing to be responsible. The root of defensiveness is usually a feeling of hopelessness, that you will never be able to please your spouse. You have nurtured the belief that you will never be able to make that person happy. A voice inside you declares, *You're not good enough.* Nothing you do seems to change that belief. You respond to every word and action defensively, because you find it difficult to separate your behavior from you. You identify so closely with your behavior, that it provokes more of the same defensive behavior (see Romans 7:19).

You need to realize that your behaviors and attitudes are not you; they simply live in you, in your soul. Understanding that you are a new creature in Christ (2 Corinthians 5:17) will help you drive those attitudes far from you. It may not happen overnight, but as you meditate on the truth of God's Word—that you are a beautiful new creation in Christ, made in His likeness and image—those attitudes from the past will fall by the wayside.

If defensiveness describes you, then you need to realize that you are responding from a place of hopelessness, and that's not of God. God is the God of hope! You are going to have to pray and perhaps do some fasting. Ask the Lord to show you how to deal with the doubt and judgmental attitude—toward yourself and your spouse—that has taken hold in your life.

Defensiveness leads to arguments and strife. It causes the person who's being defensive to go into "attack-mode" and become angry at his or her spouse at the slightest provocation. If this is a habit you are accustomed to giving place to, I encourage you to quickly admit when you have misunderstood something that your spouse has communicated. Instead of arguing, be peaceable. You could say, "I'm so sorry. Let's pray about this."

Defensiveness can also cause a person to spiral downward into feelings of worthlessness. The enemy wants the husband or wife to believe that there's no hope, and that he or she is a complete failure. If he succeeds, in time the spouse will begin to act out what he or she believes. The enemy is after your marriage, but, really, he's after your mind! He knows that if he can get to your mind and begin to influence your thoughts and emotions, he can destroy your marriage in just a matter of time. So instead of allowing negative voices to play in your head, you need to begin to say some things out loud from the Word of God. You need to stand down those thoughts until they become weaker and weaker. Eventually, they will have no more power over you or your marriage. When your spouse speaks, you will hear him or her correctly instead of through a filter of hopelessness, failure, and defeat.

Usually defensiveness occurs in a relationship in which one spouse is overly critical. In fact, one definition of defensiveness is an attitude that challenges criticism. But if you're the defensive type, don't connect to the criticism. Instead, the next time your spouse criticizes you, recognize it as a trigger point and say, "What is your need, Honey? I want to help you. Let's pray and seek God."

Negative Response Number Four: Contempt

The fourth negative behavior that manifests in conflict is contempt. Contempt motivates a person to ridicule his or her spouse, especially in public or in front of others. Someone who's contemptuous of someone shows great disrespect toward him or her. The person who's in contempt keeps a running list of the other person's transgressions and can't wait to let everyone else know what's wrong with him or her.

Contempt is a manifestation of the most intense lack of respect. Someone's need is not being met, so the offended party creates a sort of rap sheet on the offender and uses the person's "crimes" to insult him or her to others. He or she uses every opportunity to air the faults and failures of the other person to anyone who will listen. In the Old Testament, we see an example of contempt in Michal's attitude toward her husband, King David, as he danced before the Lord. "Now as the ark of the Lord came into the City of David, Michal, Saul's daughter, looked through a window and saw King David leaping and whirling before the Lord; and she despised him in her heart" (2 Samuel 6:16).

David was praising God and celebrating the arrival of the ark of God's Presence in the city. Afterward, Michal said, "...'How glorious was the king of Israel today, uncovering himself today in the eyes of the maids of his servants, as one of the base fellows shamelessly uncovers himself!'" (v. 20 NKJV) Her biting remark showed her disgust and contempt for her husband. Usually people who show contempt for their spouse, picked up this attitude early in life. Their contempt is actually disrespect for authority. Perhaps some authority figure let them down in some way. Maybe their parents weren't there for them, or didn't connect with them emotionally. So in marriage, they transfer this image to their spouse. They expect that this other person will also let them down.

We already talked about the power of thoughts. A person who manifests this negative behavior of contempt must arrest his or her thoughts the moment they begin to surface. This person must invoke the Holy Spirit's help to recognize those negative images from the past when they come. Then he or she must instantly replace those thoughts and images with good ones. But the person must do this aggressively. Those feelings of contempt didn't become ingrained in the person's emotional makeup overnight. This person is going to have to fast, pray, and start asking the hard question as to why he or she has given place to this destructive behavior.

If this behavior describes you, a good place to start after you have prayed, is to simply begin imagining your spouse meeting your needs! Be adamant with yourself in refusing to continue your old way of thinking. It hasn't profited you thus far, and that kind of destructive behavior will never profit you and yield you the kind of marriage God desires for you. It's important to realize that when strong feelings of frustration are present, we will each be tempted to yield to one or more of these negative behaviors. We need to determine which of these behaviors most often describes us, and when we locate ourselves, we need to ask the Holy Spirit, *Why do I do that?* Then we need to repent, give that behavior to the Lord, and press beyond yielding to it every time we get frustrated.

During the low times in our marriage, we must recognize that the reason for most of our frustrations is that an important need is not being met. That frustration is also the product of inner conflict due to a lack of communication. We lack the ability to communicate our feelings properly, so we feel frustrated and we manifest one or more of these negative behaviors. We will criticize our spouse, withdraw from him or her, or become defensive or contemptuous in our interactions.

Some people are clueless about how to resolve conflict and communicate peaceably, so they would rather have things remain the way they are than to step out and confront an issue. This type of behavior is unhealthy for the marriage. When conflict isn't resolved, nobody wins, especially the children. Everyone in the family feels it when there's unresolved conflict between the husband and wife.

It's not good for children to hear their parents criticize one another privately or publicly. It's equally unhealthy for them to experience one or both parents giving the other parent "the cold shoulder." It's also very stressful for children to witness one parent picking a fight with the other parent, because he or she has become defensive. That's another reason why all of these behaviors need to be identified and removed from our lives.

No matter how many times you have failed in the past, I encourage you to communicate your needs to your spouse without accusing or criticizing. Then invite your spouse to communicate his or her needs and be willing to meet those needs without getting into strife. Guard your words as you speak. For example, instead of saying, "You never take me anywhere anymore," you could say something like, "Honey, I really need a date night or just some alone-time with just you and me."

The Level of Your Desire Will Determine the Level of Your Success

I heard a minister once say that "wanting to" is half the battle. In other words, your ongoing desire to walk in love and improve your relationship with your spouse, is a driving force that will eventually bring forth a successful marriage. In the low seasons, you will not sputter and quit. Instead, you will rev up your engine, set your face like flint to seek the face of God, and put into practice everything that you learned about building a marriage that's "Heaven on earth." You will understand that marriage is about building a life with another person, not stopping during the construction phase, short of finishing what you began together. In other words, you are going to be a doer of God's Word (James 1:22), even in the hard times. You will hunger and thirst for righteousness (Matthew 5:6)—for the truth of God's Word, His will, and His divine order in every area of your life. And you will receive! Your life will be filled and you will be satisfied, because of your earnest desire to make things better for you, your spouse, your marriage and family, and generations of family to come.

A marriage can overcome great obstacles when two people work together as a team. That's why it's so important to build each other up—not tear each other down—in the low seasons. We must be mindful to afford our spouse the same grace, forgiveness, and mercy that we would show to anyone else. In fact, the people in our home—our immediate family members—should receive the best treatment from us, instead of the worst.

The Role of Personal Responsibility

This chapter is not intended to condemn you, but to help you face the issues that have the potential to harm you or your marriage. If you obey the Lord and His Word in getting rid of these things—in throwing out your baggage—you will be "...a vessel unto honour, sanctified, and meet [profitable] for the master's use, and prepared unto every good work" (2 Timothy 2:21 KJV). You can't just "wish" it and automatically receive it. Personal responsibility is involved and making right choices is a part of that. You have to choose to do the right thing even when "right," is not always easy.

So what do we do in the low seasons of marriage? Do we "tuck and run"—or fight our way through on our own until the relationship is in ruins? No, we need to go to God! This is the time we need to become more rooted and grounded in His love. We also need to allow those roots to go down deeper in our walk with Him. Then we need to educate ourselves, so we will be able to recognize those seasons and know how to handle them. We need to be people of prayer, depending upon the Holy Spirit to bring us the wisdom we need to please the Lord and to build our marriage, instead of destroying it. We must walk in love and control our thoughts, understanding that where our thoughts continually go, our feelings will follow.

If we want a Kingdom marriage that's "Heaven on earth," you can't be asleep at the wheel, especially in the low seasons. If you learn to rely on God's love as the one constant in every season, you can survive and even thrive in the low times. You will be able to go to the next level of love in your marriage. No matter how far your relationship with your spouse has strayed from the right path, that love will provide light and lead you to a highway of blessing and success in your marriage. Love will take you to the next level.

[1] Tina Turner, "What's Love Got To Do With It?" Capitol Records, Hollywood, CA, 1984.

12

BARRIERS TO INTIMACY— OBSTACLES THAT CAN AND MUST BE OVERCOME

Dr. Maureen Anderson

A happy and successful marriage is centered around intimacy—both physical and emotional—between a husband and wife. So you can be certain that the enemy doesn't want you to experience intimacy in your marriage on a regular basis. In fact, he would love it if you never touched or talked to each other at all! Most couples are very affectionate and intimate when they are dating, but after they get married, for many of them, there is very little touching or talking anymore. For some reason, that part of the relationship grows cold.

What happens when a couple grows cold toward each other in marriage? For one, they distance themselves from one another. A separation occurs even if the couple remains married. This isn't the will of God for two people who have become "one flesh" in marriage. Tom and I have ministered to couples that had been married for years, yet were so disconnected that they slept in separate bedrooms. For years they lived in quiet contempt or indifference toward one another, instead of resolving their issues. All those years, they weren't even trying to change their situation—and some of them even had children still living at home! The enemy had free reign in those marriages, because they were full of inner conflict and strife.

This behavior of "disconnecting" in marriage is so abnormal that it sends a message of alarm to our brain, which triggers a flow of adrenaline in our body that can put us in a state of anxiety, uneasiness, and even fear. A husband and wife who lack intimacy in their marriage, must identify the reason for their disconnection. The need to connect is a basic human need—and in marriage, it's an absolute necessity in order for the marriage to thrive.

Getting to the Heart of the Problem
Before the Problem Gets to Your Heart

The following are the primary contributors to a lack of intimacy in marriage—barriers to intimacy that we are responsible to overcome if we desire to have God's best.

- Negative experiences and emotions from the past
- Conflict with your spouse
- Unforgiveness, bitterness, and resentment
- Lack of communication with your spouse
- Sexual sin or dysfunction

Imagine a marriage that is void of intimacy, but has somehow continued year after year. It is an unhappy marriage that is lacking in fulfillment. Marriages like this don't usually last very long. So much time has passed and so much damage has occurred in the relationship, that the couple loses hope. They eventually fall apart, because they lack the knowledge and understanding that is neccesary to get them off the path they are traveling on and back on the right track.

All things are possible with God! (Matthew 19:26; Mark 10:27.) Nothing is too hard for God. He designed marriage, and He has a plan to make it what He wants it to be, so you, your spouse and your children will be blessed, as well as others around you, as they observe His blessing in your lives. In this chapter, we will look at intimacy-killers in marriage, and we will also touch on some intimacy-builders that you can begin to incorporate in your marriage today.

Dealing with Negative Emotions and Conflict

Many marriages lack intimacy because of negative emotions from the past or marital conflicts. Many people bury their feelings instead of dealing with them head-on, because they don't know what to do. If you have a tendency to hide your pain, disappointment, frustration, and anger—look out! "Out of sight" might mean "out of mind" for a season, but if you are constantly internalizing your negative emotions, then these issues will not go away; they will simply remain hidden deep within your heart and soul. These issues will resurface at some point in your marriage. They are going to come up, and they are going to disconnect you from your spouse, if you don't resolve them. Once they are resolved, you will be able to enjoy an emotionally healthy relationship with your spouse.

Wrongdoings of the past and the negative emotions that accompany them, must be faced and dealt with, not buried. The first step—even if it's something that happened long ago—is to go to God. Sometimes we need to talk to God about a situation simply to get His perspective. Perhaps the person who wounded us didn't even mean to do it. At other times, we need to go to God in prayer to receive supernatural help and healing—the kind that only He can give. And He will give it! But we must take the first step. We must ask Him for help and seek Him through His Word for the answers we need. (In the following chapter, we will talk more about dealing with emotional issues from the past.)

What Not to Do in the Heat of Battle

When we are going through a negative situation, the worst thing that we can do in the heat of battle is to jump into that conflict with both feet! If we confront conflict in the heat of the moment, we will probably see destructive results. In fact, when conflict is just based on emotions, then deeper conflict will always result. We might even say or do something that could destroy a relationship. That is completely counter-productive, because the goal in marriage is to build, not destroy. As I said, everything in marriage is centered around intimacy between a husband and wife, so resolving conflict and dealing with issues are important. If a couple doesn't know how to resolve their issues or they fail to resolve conflict properly, intimacy will be hindered in their relationship.

Confront Your Conflict—Value Your Spouse

No marriage is completely free from conflict, because marriage involves the union of two people and the blending—not dissolving—of two distinct personalities. So the goal is not to avoid conflict at all cost, but to resolve it when it arises. This way it doesn't produce a wedge of isolation in the marriage. The first step in resolving conflict—after a "cooling period," if necessary—is to face the conflict instead of avoiding it. Recognize it for what it is and deal with it.

Something good can come out of conflict when it's handled properly, or dealt with according to the principles of God's Word.

> *Finally, all of you be of one mind, having compassion for one another; love as brothers, be tenderhearted, be courteous; not returning evil for evil or reviling for reviling, but on the contrary blessing, knowing that you were called to this, that you may inherit a blessing. For "He who would love life and see good days, Let him refrain his tongue from evil, and his lips from speaking deceit. Let him turn away from evil and do good; Let him seek peace and pursue it.*
>
> 1 Peter 3:8-11 NKJV

Once you decide to deal with conflict in your marriage, the next step is to pray. Then after you have talked to God about the problem, you must also talk to your spouse. Begin your discussion by telling them how much you value them and your marriage. In doing this, you are building up your spouse, while demonstrating the value you have for the relationship. This creates instant feelings of security and an environment where there can be a peaceful discussion without anyone becoming fearful, agitated, or defensive.

Check Your Attitude at the Door

When confronting a conflict, after you have stated your positive feelings for your spouse, begin by stating the problem in gentle, non-accusing tones. The Bible says, "A soft answer turns away wrath, but a harsh word stirs up anger" (Proverbs 15:1 NKJV). Speaking in soft tones is another way to build intimacy. In other words, instead of stating the issue in a heated manner and firing off accusations at your spouse, you should be calm and gentle in your approach. For example, never use "you" statements that are accusatory, such as, "You always do this" or, "You're always that." Instead, you could re-phrase the problem with these words: "When this happens, it's probably just me, but it makes me feel…," then you can talk about your feelings without condemning or criticizing your spouse.

In other words, have a humble attitude that takes responsibility for your own feelings. For example, you could say something such as, "Maybe it's just me, but this is how I felt when…." Don't automatically put the blame on your spouse. You might feel as if your spouse is truly to blame for the problem, nevertheless you must still be gentle

…have a humble attitude that takes responsibility for its own feelings.

in the way you confront the issue. You need to check your attitude at the door! Also—and this almost goes without saying—never resort to name-calling when you have a disagreement with your spouse! In fact, if you and your spouse are calling each other names, your marriage isn't headed for trouble—trouble has already "arrived at the station," and you need supernatural help. You must have a determined desire to change, if you want to turn that situation around and send it packing!

What's Your Point?

When you are addressing an issue with your spouse, be careful to stay on the point at all times. Don't use that time to air a whole string of complaints, or to enumerate all of your spouse's faults and failures. Also, remember not to interrupt your spouse when he or she "has the floor." However, if you need to, ask politely, so you will not be interrupted when it's your turn to speak.

When you approach conflict with an attitude of gentleness and compassion, you will get further than you ever would by yelling and speaking hateful, destructive words. Ideally, when you confront a problem, you will hear the words, *"I'm sorry. I didn't mean to do that."* Or, *"What you're saying is valid. I know there are some things I need to get free of, and I'm committing myself to it, beginning now."* If you are confronted, you should respond with equal wisdom and a spirit of cooperation. However, it's important that even if you don't get the response you desire, you must always be willing to do the right thing, anyway. In other words, unfairness on the part of your spouse does not give you the right to "return evil for evil" (Romans 12:17; 1 Thessalonians 5:15; 1 Peter 3:9). In review, the following are basic guidelines to successfully confront and resolve conflict when it arises:

- Take time to cool off if necessary. Ask for a time-out so you are not emotionally driven, but Spirit-led. If necessary, walk off the "adrenaline rush" you may be experiencing. Then be certain to name a specific time when you would like to address the problem and then keep that appointment to the best of your ability.

- Pray before you begin and ask God for wisdom, and He will give it to you (James 1:5). James 3:17 NKJV says, "…the wisdom that is from above is first pure, then peaceable, gentle, willing to yield, full of mercy and good fruits, without partiality and without hypocrisy."

- Begin your conversation on a positive note by talking about some of your spouse's positive qualities.

- Always use "I" statements; never use "you" statements. Be careful not to accuse, condemn, or criticize.

- Use gentle tones. The tone of your voice is an important aspect of conflict resolution. A soft tone and a gentle spirit or attitude is a must.

- Don't yell or call your spouse names!

- Don't interrupt the other person.

- Stay on point and talk about one subject at a time.

Forgiveness Bridges the Distance Between You and Your Mate

Of course, there are situations in which conflict remains in a marriage over a period of time, because the couple refuses to deal with it. In a case like that—or even when one spouse desires the forgiveness of the other—it's so important that we learn to forgive, and refuse to keep score of each other's wrongdoings.

It [love] is not conceited (arrogant and inflated with pride); it is not rude (unmannerly) and does not act unbecomingly. Love (God's love in us) does not insist on its own rights or its own way, for it is not self-seeking; it is not touchy or fretful or resentful; it takes no account of the evil done to it [it pays no attention to a suffered wrong].

1 Corinthians 13:5 AMP

If we are going to "take no account" of wrongdoings, then we will have to make the decision not to be a victim in life. When we hold on to wrongs committed against us, we can fall into that mindset of feeling sorry for ourselves. In fact, we can pay so much attention to the suffered wrongs that we become obsessed with them. When God says that His mercies are new every morning (Lamentations 3:23), why do we want to keep reminding people of things they have done that they have already repented for? When we keep bringing up past problems and mistakes, intimacy is impossible. If we refuse to let go of things from the past, that may have hurt our feelings or even our relationship, then seeds of bitterness will begin to grow in our heart. If this bitterness is not stopped (see Hebrews 12:15), it will eventually defile our marriage.

His mercies are new every morning.

The Bible says that God is love (1 John 4:8). Since He's in us, our new nature is to love others, instead of being bitter or resentful. We need to be true to this new nature in us, instead of yielding to wrong thoughts that try to keep us focused and obsessed with a wrong that's been committed. Often we want to wait until we feel like forgiving others before we actually forgive them. But forgiveness is not a feeling—it's a commitment! Forgiveness is a commitment to refuse to pay back evil for a wrong that's been committed against us. Paying back "evil for evil" can destroy a marriage.

Another reason we should desire to forgive others freely is because God said that He would not forgive us if we fail to forgive others (Mark 11:25). Even if someone who has done something wrong to us, fails to repent or ask for our forgiveness, we are not supposed to be overcome by evil—we are supposed to overcome evil with good (Romans 12:21).

Talk to Your Mate!

Many couples often miss it in marriage because they grow dissatisfied over unresolved issues. Instead of drawing near to God and communicating with each other, they disconnect or grow distant in their relationship. Perhaps they don't even know or believe that God can help them. Maybe they don't believe in their spouse or their marriage, as they should. But if that's the case, then that's when they need to purposely draw near to God and connect with their spouse!

There is no substitute for spending quality time communicating with your spouse. In other words, talk to each other! Many couples have no problem talking about superficial topics, such as the weather or the news. They can even engage in conversation about the kids' school or something that happened at work, with relative ease. However, there is a deeper level of communication that needs to take place between a husband and wife. They must talk openly and often about their love for one another, their value for their relationship (this includes resolving conflict when it arises), and their future goals and dreams. This kind of communication is valuable, because it involves sharing life together, and this kind of sharing helps build intimacy.

There is no substitute in marriage for spending quality time communicating with your spouse.

At times, they need to talk about the past by engaging in occasional walks down memory lane. Reflecting on the past—on the things that brought them together and on the fun moments they have shared—can be a tremendous bonding tool in marriage. Often when two people have been married for a while, they forget those early days in the relationship when they were first attracted to each other and fell so deeply in love. The only way to keep those memories alive is to talk about them.

Although it's important for a couple to reflect on pleasant memories from the past, a couple must also talk regularly about their future. One thing that keeps many couples from growing together emotionally and spiritually, is a lack of communication concerning their future plans and goals. Every couple needs to have a vision for tomorrow—for the seasons of life ahead. They need to know where they are going in life and then have a well laid-out plan for getting there. They need to depend on God and His Word to guide, direct, and bless them—and to even tweak those plans from time to time if necessary! Vision is created with words, so I encourage couples to talk to their spouse about the future. They can keep their vision for a beautiful future alive, by communicating on a daily basis with each other.

...the first part of communication is listening; the second part is speaking.

The Power of Communication

Never underestimate the value and power of communication. When communication is lacking in a marriage, then misunderstandings and speculations can give rise to suspicion, distrust, and attitudes of cold indifference. The devil is a liar and a thief, who thrives in the dark places where there's no communication. In fact, he often uses a lack of communication and information to supply misinformation—to "fill in the blanks" with his lies, so a couple will drift further and further apart, until the marriage is eventually destroyed.

When a husband and wife are talking regularly to each other, then the enemy's accusations and schemes can be exposed in the light of their open and honest communication. So it's important to talk to your spouse—and then listen to him or her talk back! We know that communication is a major issue in marriage, and listening is a vital part of communication. So, we must seek to understand our spouse, and then seek to be understood by him or her. The first part of communication is listening and the second part is speaking.

Four Techniques to Improve Your Hearing

"A wise man will hear and increase in learning..." (Proverbs 1:5 NKJV). Did you know that one of our deepest needs in a relationship is to be heard? We want our heart to be heard and understood. So when we are really listening to our spouse when he or she speaks, we are meeting a deep spiritual and emotional need. The following are four simple things you can do to improve your listening skills, so that you can truly hear what your spouse is saying.

First, respond to what your spouse has said. Attempt to assimilate or understand the message, and then paraphrase what you heard or think you heard, to clarify the intended message.

Second, ask follow-up questions to obtain a clear picture of the speaker's intended meaning. In other words, if you are not sure you understand, it's okay to ask questions. In fact, unless you are putting the speaker on the defensive by taking a wrong attitude or tone, asking questions shows that you are interested in what's being said.

Third, you need to communicate your desire to understand your spouse's feelings. A big key to effective communication and a great marriage, is understanding the other person's feelings. Doing this can be as simple as saying, "I want to understand your feelings." When you are attempting to understand your spouse's feelings, it's important to listen with your heart, as well as your ears. In other words, you may feel lost in terms of what the other person is really feeling, but you can ask the Holy Spirit to help you, because He knows exactly what's going on in that person's heart.

Actually, the speaker may not even understand his or her own feelings. But as you communicate your desire to understand, and you ask guiding questions, the heart can begin to open up, because that person will perceive that the environment is safe for communicating. When a person feels safe and loved, he or she will be more willing to open up and share from the heart. Intimacy happens when the heart opens.

Fourth, when listening to a speaker, maintain good eye contact and body language. It's amazing the level of comfort and care that eye contact can provide in a conversation. When you are looking the speaker directly in the eyes, it communicates that you care about the person and that you are interested in what he or she has to say. It says that you are stopping everything, and putting all of your focus on that person.

Intimacy happens when the heart opens.

On the other hand, if your eyes are darting around the room, or you are looking in another direction while the person is talking, it communicates that you don't really care about the speaker's feelings or what he or she has to say. Body language says a lot about how well you are listening to someone, who's sharing his or her thoughts and feelings with you. When your spouse is speaking to you, if you lean slightly forward in his or her direction, then you will be communicating interest, as well as a certain level of respect.

It's also a good idea to nod occasionally as the other person speaks, because nodding communicates affirmation —not only are you affirming what's being said, but also the person who's doing the speaking! Without words, you are communicating that they are valuable and important, and that what they have to say is important, too.

The last big key to effective listening is to ask how you can best help the speaker. In other words, don't just automatically volunteer counsel or advice. Perhaps your spouse just wants you to listen, not try to solve a problem. So if you immediately start telling them what they should do, it could push that person further away. It's okay to politely ask, "Would you like me to try to provide some solutions to this problem?" Most of the time, the speaker just wants someone to listen and understand his or her feelings.

Steps to Greater Intimacy

Whether or not you and your spouse have experienced problems with intimacy, or "staying connected" in your marriage, there are things you must do consistently as a couple if you desire to maintain intimacy in your marriage. First, you and your spouse must commit to praying together on a regular basis. We have heard the saying, *The family that prays together stays together.* Many have thought that was just a cute saying, but there's more truth to it than they have realized.

I'm not saying that all of your praying must be done with your spouse. Certainly, every believer must have his or her own time of prayer and fellowship with the Father. Actually, the Bible commands us to pray always—with all kinds, or types, of prayer (see Ephesians 6:18). We should never be out of fellowship with God, instead we should be in constant communion with Him, and ready to connect in prayer at a moment's notice for ourselves or for others.

In addition to our own prayer time, we need to create a special time to pray together just with our spouse. We can pray together about matters that concern our family, for wisdom and direction for our future, for each other, or for others.

Every morning, Tom and I pray, make confessions from the Word, and then pray awhile in the Spirit (see Acts 2:4; First Corinthians 14:14-15; Jude 20). In doing this, not only are we building ourselves up and setting the tone for our day and our future, but we are also bonding in our marriage. Tom doesn't just pray with me—he also prays for me.

In His relationship with the Church, Jesus sets the example for husbands and wives. Jesus is our Intercessor. Hebrews 7:25 says that He ever lives to make intercession for His Bride, the Church. Similarly, a husband must cover his wife in prayer. He is in a tremendous position of authority to pray protection and blessing over her, and to pray for the fulfillment of her destiny. It doesn't have to be a long prayer; he simply needs to make sure the devil knows whose wife she is and that she's covered with the blood of Jesus!

I'm not saying that a wife has no responsibility to pray for herself, or for her husband and family—because she is responsible to do her own praying. But just as Christ loves the Church, the husband must also love his wife and lay down his life, or give of himself, for her (see Ephesians 5:25). That includes laying down his life for her in prayer.

Ways to Draw Closer to Your Spouse

Besides spending time praying with your spouse, it's important that you bond with your mate by making time alone together a priority. Remember, we have seen that love gives. So, you sow and minister love to your spouse when you give to him or her, and that includes giving your time. Whether the two of you are enjoying an activity together or talking about future dreams and goals, spending quality time together creates an emotional bond and contributes to greater intimacy in your marriage.

Another way to bond and create intimacy with your spouse, is to show him or her affection. In other words, hold hands with your spouse every chance you get. Hug your spouse often. Touch is very crucial in a marriage. Your spouse needs to be touched by you every day! (We'll talk more about affection in a later chapter, which deals with sex in marriage.)

Other ways to develop intimacy in your marriage include:

- Flirt with each other often.

- Show appreciation, even for the little things.

- Express your love for each other several times per day. This can include verbal and non-verbal communication. For example, you can tell your spouse you love him or her—you can also write your spouse a note expressing your feelings of love and admiration.

- Laugh together. A cheerful heart is like medicine (Proverbs 17:22).

- Play together. Plan activities that you can enjoy together.

- Encourage one another regularly and support each other's goals.

A happy marriage in which both parties are enriched and fulfilled doesn't happen by chance. Intimacy is fostered and nurtured in a happy marriage—both physical and emotional intimacy. And it is up to each couple to keep the fires of intimacy burning brightly and to deal with those issues that threaten closeness in the marriage.

As I said, the need to connect is a basic human need. In marriage, it is a necessity. As a husband and wife, you owe it to yourselves and to God to root out every obstacle that would distance you and your spouse, and prevent intimacy in your marriage.

13

IS YOUR MARRIAGE OVERWEIGHT? HOW TO RID YOUR RELATIONSHIP OF EMOTIONAL BAGGAGE

Drs. Tom and Maureen Anderson

Almost everyone enters marriage with some kind of "baggage"—issues that are a result of negative experiences or associations from the past. When you are married, your issues become your spouse's issues and vice versa. So it's the responsibility of you both to help each other get rid of the baggage, so that it doesn't harm the marriage. In other words, it's not important who has the baggage, you both must decide that whatever it takes—fasting, praying, and seeking the Lord together—you're not going to let emotional baggage remain in your marriage. In a marriage, each spouse is responsible to help the other work through behaviors that don't line up with the Word of God. It's your responsibility to pray for each other, instead of criticizing each other.

Facing the Facts

Many people are in denial about certain characteristics in their life that cause great stress in their relationships. For some reason, they are not willing to face the facts and own up to their failures and mistakes. They have not realized the great benefits that await them, once they get rid of the baggage and the behavior that accompanies it. It won't profit us if we resist God's dealings, and refuse to acknowledge that we have issues or problems that we need to work on in our marriage. The Bible says that God resists the proud but gives grace to the humble (see James 4:6; First Peter 5:5). If we refuse to deal with issues in our life that keep coming up, we are simply going to have to keep going "around that same mountain," so to speak, until we finally get to the root of the problem. The "out of sight, out of mind" solution doesn't work! In fact, we could say concerning these issues: *Deal now or pay later.*

We have observed that people who choose divorce over dealing with emotional baggage from the past, often find themselves going around the same mountain again and again in their new marriages. They never deal with certain issues, so those issues just keep coming up. The names change, but the problems basically remain the same. So it's important to deal with the issues that prevent you and your spouse from enjoying the physical and emotional intimacy that God intends for your lives.

Maureen:

'Naked and Not Ashamed'

One reason that people don't face their issues from the past, is they don't feel unconditionally loved and accepted. Therefore, they are unwilling to open up and make themselves vulnerable to another person. The concept of working through things together—as "one flesh" and as a team—is foreign to their thinking.

"And they were both naked, the man and his wife, and were not ashamed" (Genesis 2:25 NKJV). When God created Adam and Eve, it says they were "naked and not ashamed." This verse is talking about their physical nakedness, but in marriage, we must also be able to reveal, or "make bare," our feelings to one another without feeling afraid or embarrassed.

Tom and I always have felt comfortable and safe while making ourselves vulnerable to each other. Early in our marriage, I would ask Tom from time to time, "Do you think I have a problem in such-and-such area?" And he would often say, "Yes, Honey, you do"! However, he didn't abandon me in the midst of my problems, leaving me to figure out how to fix them on my own. He never took the attitude, *Good luck with that.* Instead, he would say, "Let's fast and pray and get to the root of this so we can deal with it. I will help you get through this." With Tom standing with me, I would always get free from whatever had me troubled or bound. With every freedom that I obtained—our marriage got better. So, as Tom and I committed to stand together and work through each other's problems, our marriage kept improving, because we both kept getting free from the baggage of the past. "Freer" people make better marriages!

When two people enter marriage, they bring issues from their up-bringing—past associations and experiences, whether good or bad. We were no exception. There were times early in our marriage, when we experienced some real low points. We were frustrated and had no idea what to do. But we didn't abandon the marriage. Since we were both committed to the marriage, Tom would say, "Let's get to the bottom of this. Let's fast and pray for a couple of days and find out what God is saying." That sounds simple, but that's truthfully how we dealt with our issues. We never buried issues; we faced them and dealt with them head-on. We did it together, and we worked them out with the help of the Holy Spirit.

A Real Identity Crisis

Some Christians won't admit that they have issues, because they are too embarrassed or ashamed to face them. They identify more closely with the issue than with their identity as a new creation in Christ. In other words, they have allowed their baggage to define who they are—and the way they deal with that is to bury it and refuse to acknowledge it. "Therefore, if anyone is in Christ, he is a new creation; old things have passed away; behold, all things have become new" (2 Corinthians 5:17 NKJV).

If you are a Christian, you are a new creature in Christ. Your spirit has been reborn; it is completely new. In your mind and emotions, however, all things aren't new. That's why Romans 12:2 tells us to renew our mind with the Word of God. The power of the Gospel can change and shape our thinking until we produce the right kind of emotions.

It's also important to understand that your baggage is not you! It's the stuff that is in you—in your soul. For example, you might have some garbage in your house, but the garbage isn't the house—the garbage is simply inside the house.

How can you remove garbage from your home or from your life if you are not aware that it is there? To be successful in life, especially if you are married, you need to have some self-awareness. You need to be able to step outside of yourself, so to speak, and say, "Okay, this behavior is not godly. I've seen it in my mother, my brother, and my grandfather—and now I'm acting the same way. It's time to stop this. It's time to get the garbage out."

You can face your issues and identify them without identifying 'with' them. You have to acknowledge the baggage before you can get rid of it. If you fail to acknowledge and deal with issues from the past, those things are going to start stinking—just as garbage will begin to stink if you leave it inside long enough!

> *It's time to get the garbage out.*

When garbage is allowed to remain in a couple's life long enough—when the stench of their issues becomes almost unbearable—one or both parties is usually ready to throw in the towel and quit.

Your 'Baggage' Can Weaken Your Gifts and Hinder Your Success

We saw that whatever "baggage" your spouse may be carrying from past experiences, is actually your baggage, too. In a marriage, the two become one. That means that your victories are your spouse's victories and your spouse's victories are your victories. So we should want our spouse to be successful and happy in life. We should work to build up our spouse, instead of tearing him or her down!

What happens when a couple lacks this understanding and fails to work together as a team to rid the marriage of issues that cling to the relationship and weigh it down? One or both parties in that marriage has gifts and strengths that will never get developed. To illustrate this point, let's suppose that a man and woman enter their marriage with the following issues:

The Husband

His mother was bossy and controlling. She manipulated the entire family and never allowed him to step up and become the man that he should be. He feels betrayed and rejected by his mother, and as a young man he makes an inward vow never to let a woman boss him around again.

The Wife

She came from a home that was filled with physical and emotional abuse. She became very unsure of herself and her place in the world. She reverts to emotional passivity in order to keep the peace and minimize her pain.

These two people, who have two very different backgrounds, get married. Now they are supposed to join forces and combine their strengths. He doesn't know how to initiate vision for his new family or provide the driving force that will propel them forward in life. The wife doesn't even know that she has any strengths! They are married and in the same boat, all right, but this couple isn't going anywhere on the sea of life. They are just sitting in their boat, in a state of inertia—paralyzed by their issues from the past.

Now suppose the wife begins to deal with her issues and starts renewing her strengths. Instead of being passive, she attempts to utilize these gifts in their marriage. Suppose that the husband has not overcome his sensitivity to his overbearing mother. The minute his wife tries to contribute something to their marriage, he tries to throw her overboard! He wants her out of his boat! Why? She's only making suggestions that she feels will benefit them both, but he sees her actions through the clouded lenses of his past. He feels his wife is being controlling and manipulative and that it's his "Mom" all over again. He doesn't exactly want to take the helm in the marriage, and when he feels pressured in the least way, he's ready to cry, "Mutiny!" or abandon ship himself.

When two people can't seem to combine their strengths, they need to ask themselves why, and then deal with that situation at its root. If they don't understand the behavior, they should ask the Lord. He understands it perfectly, and the Holy Spirit will reveal the answer to them. Some married couples live their whole lives without experiencing the best life possible, because they are not fully utilizing their strengths. Things are standing in their way, and they have allowed those things to continue for years. This is a sad situation.

On the other hand, there's nothing more promising or exciting than to see a husband and wife cheering each other on. Together in the same boat, they are working together to navigate the sea of life successfully. Yet they want each other, individually, to be the best that he or she can be.

Tom:

Relationship Dynamics and Dysfunctions

Just as there are dysfunctional relationships in marriage, there are also dysfunctional relationships in churches between a pastor and his congregation. Dysfunctional churches generally stop growing when they reach about eighty to a hundred people, or so. That's about as big as they can grow. There is a connection between the dysfunctional attitudes that exist in marriage and those that can be found in some churches. Just as a dysfunctional church won't grow, dysfunctional attitudes—emotional baggage—that are allowed to remain in a marriage will stifle the growth of that relationship.

There are generally three reasons for dysfunction in the church. I will share these three scenarios:

Church scenario number one: The pastor is a victim. He or she has an entire congregation of enablers or "rescuers," that attend that church to take care of the pastor. The pastor always seems to need help, so they are always ministering to the pastor, bailing him out of one situation after the other. In return, these enablers are deriving their sense of value and worth from helping him. It's a very unhealthy relationship that produces a stagnant, sickly church.

Church scenario number two: The pastor is an enabler. In constantly helping his congregation, he has all kinds of victims—and he is "saving" them all! He has become almost like Jesus to his congregation. They are trained to look to the pastor instead of to the Lord. Instead of cultivating a living relationship with Jesus, the people look to the pastor to solve their problems. He is usually available for counseling at all hours of the day, every day of the week—24/7. His church never grows any larger than what he and his wife can take care of.

Oh, pastor, you're the only one who can help me! This is the mantra of the enabling pastor's sheep. They eat up all of his time, so he never prays, runs his race, or accomplishes anything in terms of his calling. Consequently, the members of the congregation are hindered in their own race.

Now let's relate this to a marriage situation in which one spouse is constantly needy and "under-acts" in the relationship, while the other party continually "over-acts," or over-compensates, to make up for the lack of participation from the needy spouse. The enabling party is not completely altruistic or self-sacrificing. By continually meeting their needy spouse's requirements and demands, the enabling spouse derives feelings of worth from his or her repeated "rescuing," of the other person.

Unless this cycle is broken, these "over-actions" will become exhausting and—in the end—unfruitful. Besides encouraging unhealthy dependence on another and crippling the needy person emotionally and spiritually, the enabler is hindered in his or her own personal growth. This kind of marriage might continue to exist, but it will never thrive, unless changes are made by both people in the marriage.

Church scenario number three: The pastor is a persecutor or abuser. He has a church full of victims and he "beats them up" every time they go to church. Every Sunday, he's calling them (in so many words), "You low-life, mud-crawling worms. Get your lives straight, you bunch of sinners!" People respond to that by repenting, getting saved, and crying, bawling, and squalling. They get "saved" every week, and then he beats them up again. Yet they keep coming back for more. It's a very abusive, dysfunctional relationship that halts church growth.

Here's how this relates in marriage: One spouse continually abuses the other spouse, attempting to control them by beating them up physically and/or emotionally. Since the abuser isn't dealing with his or her insecurities and fears, the abuser can only be assuaged by inflicting damage on their spouse in order to "break" that person's spirit. Once the victim is broken, the person doubts his or her self-worth and becomes the compliant party who yields to the persecutor's manipulative demands. A marriage in which one or both spouses are de-valued, dishonors God and will not flourish. Until both parties learn to value what God values—people—the marriage will remain sick and weak.

> *A marriage in which one or both spouses are de-valued, dishonors God and will not flourish.*

Responsibility and Accountability in Marriage — 'And the Two Grownups Shall Become One Flesh'!

"And the two shall become one flesh'; so then they are no longer two, but one flesh" (Mark 10:8 NKJV). I showed you examples of dysfunctional relationships in the church and in marriage. Now let me show you a "functional" relationship. In a healthy relationship, there are times when one party will under-perform, while the other party over-performs, such as in the case of a sickness, injury, stringent work deadlines or requirements, and so forth. A helper mentality can be prominent for a season, as it should be, because marriage requires teamwork. Also, a helper mentality can be prominent, simply due to the personalities in the marriage. One spouse simply enjoys serving more than the other spouse. However, in a healthy marriage, there is a scope and limit to the help that each party provides. A healthy helper correctly believes, *I am accountable for me. You are accountable for you. You make me accountable; I make you accountable. We speak truth in love. I am responsible TO you; I am not responsible FOR you.*

> *Be willing to let go of the things that hinder you.*

Healthy people enjoy that kind of relationship. Unhealthy people usually seek out dysfunctional, unhealthy relationships. For example, people sometimes leave our church—a very large, thriving church—for no other reason, except they want to attend a small church that remains small. Many of them are saying, "I need to be beat up regularly," or "I need to have a close relationship with my pastor, so I can help him."

Have you ever wondered why some people are so "on again-off again," concerning their church membership or their personal relationships? Emotionally and spiritually, unhealthy people cannot maintain healthy relationships—whether at church, on the job, or at home. They try for a while, but soon they either bail out of, or bring some kind of destruction to the relationship. They often sabotage their own opportunities for change and happiness—as well as the happiness and well being of others.

A Surefire Solution for an Overweight Marriage — Let the Baggage Go!

Just as there is a dynamic that exists between every pastor and his or her congregation, there is a dynamic that exists between every husband and wife. It needs to be a healthy dynamic or the marriage itself will not be healthy. With all the extra weight that emotional baggage brings to a marriage, who wouldn't want to get free of the things that are a burden to the marriage? I encourage you, no matter how shocked, dismayed, or discouraged you are at the baggage that's in your life, don't deny it, but be willing to let go of those things that hinder you or your marriage.

What are your issues? It may be painful to acknowledge, but it's important to know specifically what you are dealing with. Do you have abandonment or rejection issues? You may have a deep-seated fear of loss that has paralyzed you and kept you "stuck" in one place for years. Perhaps that fear has kept you, as a husband, from affirming or complimenting your wife, because you are afraid that she is going to leave you.

Did you know that cases of physical and emotional abuse can stem from this kind of fear? The person isn't trusting God, so he or she is yielding to that fear and trying to control and beat the other party into submission—all of this just so the abuser can have a temporary moment of "peace," without having to permanently deal with the very painful issue at hand. Hurting people hurt others, and hurting people are not joyful, peaceful, or fulfilled individuals. So why would they avoid being delivered and healed from what's causing them so much continual pain and fear? We need to know and understand the driving force behind the things we do to tear down our marriages. Then we can stop those forces dead in their tracks, and begin to build the kind of life and marriage that will bring us true happiness and be pleasing to God.

14

WHEN SEX HAS BEEN ABUSED – RIGHTING THE WRONGS FROM THE PAST

Drs. Tom and Maureen Anderson

We have been looking at some of the barriers between husbands and wives that make physical and emotional intimacy impossible: negative emotions, "baggage" from the past, conflict, unforgiveness, and lack of communication. However, we couldn't do justice to this subject without looking at a huge barrier to marital intimacy, and that is sexual dysfunction. Sexual dysfunction in a marriage can range from sexual sin and abuse, to issues with sexual health and even sheer ignorance about sex and what it means to your partner. In this chapter and the following chapter, we will discuss these topics in more detail. We encourage you to continually educate yourself in regards to the important subject of sex. This is a subject that has been overlooked by the Church at large, for too long.

God created the institution of marriage, and that means that God created sex! Ignorance concerning sex is not bliss and it won't bless your marriage—but we don't have to be ignorant. God has given us the means to grow in every area of marriage, including the area of physical intimacy with our spouse.

Your Body Is the Lord's

God intended for sex to be enjoyed in the context of marriage. However, outside of the marriage union, sex is considered to be immoral. This isn't just our opinion. This is what the Lord says, too. "'Food for the stomach and the stomach for food'—but God will destroy them both. The body is not meant for sexual immorality, but for the Lord, and the Lord for the body" (1 Corinthians 6:13).

Please read carefully the rest of this passage in First Corinthians 6.

Do you not know that your bodies are members of Christ himself? Shall I then take the members of Christ and unite them with a prostitute? Never! Do you not know that he who unites himself with a prostitute is one with her in body? For it is said, "The two will become one flesh." But he who unites himself with the Lord is one with him in spirit. Flee from sexual immorality. All other sins a man commits are outside his body, but he who sins sexually sins against his own body. Do you not know that your body is a temple of the Holy Spirit, who is in you, whom you have received from God? You are not your own; you were bought at a price. Therefore honour God with your body.

1 Corinthians 6:15-20

According to the Word of God, sexual immorality is the only sin committed in the body. All other sins are committed outside of the body. The one who participates in sexual immorality is sinning against his own body, which is God's (vv. 19-20). We are the temple of the Holy Ghost. We are not our own, but we have been bought, spirit, soul, and body, with the precious blood of Jesus. When we are born again, we become His—yet we must yield ourselves to Him instead of doing what our body desires or dictates.

It is possible to avoid sexual immorality. God wouldn't command us concerning this very thing, if it were not possible for us to obey Him. He plainly tells us, "Flee sexual immorality" (v. 18). In other words, if that's what it takes, we must flee or run from it! That denotes a very serious, purposeful, determined action on our part. We are not supposed to hang around the wrong people or get ourselves into precarious situations with those of the opposite sex just to see how close to the creek we can get without falling in! We are not saying this to criticize or condemn anyone who has been involved in a sexual relationship outside of marriage. Through faith in the precious blood of Christ that saved you, you can be free from the sin and guilt of your past. You don't have to let the things of the past come between you and your spouse today.

Maureen:

Forgetting and Forsaking Your Past

There are intimacy issues in so many marriages today because of sexual sin and baggage from the past that have never been dealt with. Some people were sexually abused as children and young people. As a result, they struggle with intimacy in their marriage. There are also various kinds of sexual sins that have seemingly been "passed down" from generation to generation. For example, in some families adultery is a widespread problem. In other families, pornography is rampant.

Too many hold on to the things of the past instead of "closing the book" on what happened yesterday.

God wants you to be free from the sins and addictions of your forefathers. He not only wants you to be forgiven, but He also wants you to forget and to forsake your past. Too many people hold on to the things of the past instead of "closing the book" on what happened yesterday. You may be tempted in certain areas, but it's time to start a new book based on your new life in Christ! You have the power to withstand every single temptation through the blood of Jesus, the Word of God, and prayer.

Pray and Don't Give Up!

"Then Jesus told his disciples a parable to show them that they should always pray and not give up" (Luke 18:1). I encourage you to read this passage in Luke 18, about the widow's petition to the unjust judge. Many people use this parable as an analogy, comparing God to the unjust judge. But God is not unjust, and that's not the lesson that Jesus is teaching here. He's talking about the "importunity" of faith—the persistence of faith—or, in other words, faith that won't give up!

God has called you to be one with your spouse and to enjoy physical and emotional intimacy with them. So if you are struggling in this area, you can go to God and expect answers. If it's a sin from the past that you are dealing with, He forgives and washes away the past, so no matter what has happened or what you have been through, today can be a new day for you! God, by His grace, can restore you to a condition that's even better than before, or better than you could ever imagine. There's power in the blood of Jesus—more than enough power to wash every sin and every memory associated with sin, away from your life!

In talking about physical intimacy, or sex, in marriage, we're not talking about something that's dirty or perverted. God created sex, but the enemy, Satan, attempts to pervert everything that God has created, including sex. Sex has been perverted in the world, where many people—sadly, even many from the Church—have exchanged the beauty of sex and intimacy in marriage for something that is twisted, filthy, and destructive.

Keep Pornography in Its Place — Out of Your Life and Your Marriage!

Pornography is a perversion of the sexual relationship that God gave to a man and woman in marriage. Pornography in marriage is an "intimacy-killer;" it's a thief of the physical and emotional intimacy that God desires between a husband and wife. If you have a problem with pornography, you must get free from that. When you engage in pornography, you are tainting the gift of sex that God has given to you in marriage. You must face this bondage squarely and get free of it through prayer and fasting and, if necessary, through professional counseling. Any kind of sexual act outside of engaging in sex with your spouse, is wrong behavior. Being interested in someone other than your spouse is wrong and needs to be dealt with. I'm not saying this to condemn you, if this is a problem in your life. I'm saying it because with God, there is an answer—if you truly desire God's highest and best.

Whether it's abuse, pornography, or some other kind of dysfunction, if you feel there are situations in your marriage that prevent intimacy and the sense that the two of you are truly one, you need to face those things and refuse to allow them to continue. Encourage your spouse that you are a team and that you would like to fast and pray together about the situation. Tell him or her, "Let's get to the bottom of this. Let's get free from whatever hinders us from being what God has called us to be in marriage."

Sometimes sexual sin such as pornography is a result of a generational issue that has come down the family line from generation to generation. In other words, it's a stronghold that a person struggles with—seemingly more than anything else that he or she has to deal with in life. As a Christian, you belong to God. Your spirit and your body are His (1 Corinthians 6:20). A Christian has the power of choice to say no to these spirits that come to tempt, harass, and try to lay claim to God's property. But many don't fully realize or understand that fact, and they struggle needlessly for years when, instead, they should be "cutting off the giant's head" (see First Samuel 17:51). In other words, they can get free from that curse through the yoke-destroying, delivering power of God!

Please understand me. God does not curse people. In fact, He has redeemed us from the curse of the Law (Galatians 3:13). You can't curse what God has blessed! But the enemy will try to tempt people to give place to things that will stop the blessings of God and hinder or completely cut off what God wants to do in their life. So, you see, if a person yields to the temptation, then he or she can open the door to a curse.

Generational sins cannot force themselves on you! They keep getting passed down from one generation to the next because of people's wrong choices. The enemy wants to perpetuate sin and iniquity, but he can be stopped when someone simply says, "Enough!" In other words, someone must take a strong stand on the Word of God and on the redemption that is his or hers in Christ. That person can give place to the Holy Spirit and the blood of Jesus Christ and break the power of that stronghold, preventing it from traveling to future generations.

If you have been plagued with sins and things in your life that you recognize as being a pattern in your family's history, you can break free of that. Whether it's pornography, adultery, divorce, or even poverty or disease, Jesus has paid the price for your freedom, and He says that you are free! (See John 8:36: Romans 6:14; Galatians 3:13: Galatians 5:1; Hebrews 2:14; 1 John 3:8.) So what will you say about it? I encourage you to pray the following prayer from your heart.

Father God, there have been generational curses in my family in the area of sexual sin—of temptations that were yielded to from generation to generation. I call it sin, Lord, and I renounce it where my life and my children's lives are concerned. I love my forefathers, but I hate their sin. I love what You love, and I hate what You hate. I want the fear of the Lord in my life—that attitude of reverence toward you that guards us from evil and gives us life [Proverbs 14:27; 19:23; 22:4].

So right now, Lord, where there's been pornography, adultery, fornication, or anything that's sexually impure, I want that out of my life. Forgive me for yielding to those temptations. I haven't taken my place of authority, as I should have. I haven't hated that sin, as I should have. But I hate it, Lord, and I see it nailed to the Cross, because Jesus paid the price for my complete freedom.

I let go of that baggage by faith. I cut off all ungodly ties and relationships. I've been washed in the blood of Jesus, and You said that if I confess my sin, then You are faithful and just to forgive me and cleanse me from all unrighteousness [1 John 1:9]. I receive my forgiveness and cleansing. I belong to Christ; my body is Yours, so I consecrate my body to You now as an act of my will. I am not an instrument of sin or a slave to sin, but I am an instrument of righteousness [Romans 6]. I am one with You, and I am one with my spouse. Thank You, Lord, for setting me free. In Jesus' name, Amen.

Tom:

There's a connection that takes place in our spirit, soul, and body during the act of sex. That's why sex outside of marriage is so dangerous—it damages people's lives. This needs to be taken very seriously. There are many reasons why people fall into the sin of adultery; however, it finds its roots in issues pertaining to the heart. Of course, Satan is the tempter, but the best defense against his tactics is a firm decision of the heart to obey the wisdom of God's Word and commit oneself wholeheartedly to pleasing Him in marriage and life.

You Are Not Your Own—You Really Do Belong to God and to Each Other

1 Corinthians 7:3-5 says:

The husband should fulfill his marital duty to his wife, and likewise the wife to her husband. The wife's body does not belong to her alone but also to her husband. In the same way, the husband's body does not belong to him alone but also to his wife. Do not deprive each other except by mutual consent and for a time, so that you may devote yourselves to prayer. Then come together again so that Satan will not tempt you because of your lack of self-control.

First Corinthians 7:5 says, "Do not deprive each other except by mutual consent and for a time, so that you may devote yourselves to prayer. Then come together again so that Satan will not tempt you because of your lack of self-control." As I said, Satan is the tempter, but we can avert his plans and schemes simply by knowing what the Word says, walking in its wisdom, and obeying God at every turn in the road. So when we read First Corinthians 7:5, we need to obey that. If we are not obeying that verse, then we are putting our marriage in harm's way. Simply put, if you are married, you belong to your partner in marriage.

You have a duty, then, to understand sexuality in marriage and to do your part to protect your sex life from outside influences that will try to undermine your marriage relationship.

Sexuality and Health

In this chapter, we are talking about dysfunction in the marriage as it pertains to sex and intimacy. Maureen has covered several spiritual aspects of overcoming dysfunction that resulted from abuse and mistakes from the past. I'm going to cover some natural aspects of dysfunction that have been overlooked, largely because people have not known where to look! In other words, they know there's a problem, but they don't have a clue where to begin to look for answers.

The Lord gives wisdom. Sometimes His wisdom dictates that we fast and pray and root out the "curses" and sins that have plagued generation after generation in our family line. At other times, His wisdom reveals other hidden causes for our problems, and some of these causes are very practical in nature.

What is dysfunction? Briefly and simply, it's the failure to function normally. For the believer, "normal" is merely the standard of God's

Word and His will. So when a husband and wife aren't physically and emotionally intimate, we know that some dysfunction is occurring in their marriage, and they need to find out why.

Sex and Hormones

I believe that so many problems in marriage, including emotional problems, are directly associated with hormone levels in the individual—and I'm talking about both women and men. The good news is that this is a problem that can be easily corrected. With the use of natural hormones, you can bring every hormone level into balance and see drastic changes in your physical health, your outlook on life, and your family relationships. I can't even begin to count how many people we have counseled who had tried everything and couldn't seem to resolve longstanding emotional issues, both personally and in their marriage. Once they were tested and realized how imbalanced their hormones were, they were able to immediately correct the problem. Their lives completely turned around for the better!

Help for Those Who Struggle

The body is absolutely amazingly put together by God. Who better than our Creator to give us the wisdom we need to function at our very highest and best? I've said it before, but it bears repeating: *If you're having problems you can't seem to resolve, check your hormone levels before you do anything else (after you've read this book, of course).* You could save yourself months and even years of frustration and agony, if you will follow this simple nugget of wisdom and counsel.

Remember we read First Corinthians 7:5, which says, "Do not deprive each other except by mutual consent and for a time, so that you may devote yourselves to prayer. Then come together again so that Satan will not tempt you because of your lack of self-control." Let's suppose, for example, that a husband is experiencing a rise in his testosterone levels, but his wife is experiencing a deficiency in her levels of progesterone and other hormones that affect her libido. She rejects her husband's sexual advances. That husband is then placed in a vulnerable position that could potentially undermine and destroy his marriage. His hormones are at unusually high levels, and he's now dealing with issues of self-control.

> *...sexual intimacy is crucial to the vitality and success of a marriage.*

If a seductress—a wayward woman (Proverbs 6:20-35; 7:1-5)—crosses his path to tempt him, he could give in to the temptation to have sex with another woman.

Now, I am by no means suggesting that a husband should have an affair—nor would I ever justify or condone that kind of behavior. *Two wrongs don't make a right,* as the saying goes. We each must answer to God for our own obedience or disobedience to His Word. Even if you find yourself in a position of agonizing temptation, you have the responsibility to say, "No, I don't mess around; I'm not going to do that." But you also have the responsibility to talk to your spouse about your sexual needs.

Marriage, including the physical or sexual aspect, requires communication in order to work. In other words, sexual problems are not issues that one party in the marriage should simply resolve on his or her own. When you are in the throes of temptation, that's not the time to withdraw and be silent. That's where the enemy thrives—when one partner in a marriage isolates himself or herself from the other person. You need to set a standard of openness in your marriage and refuse to allow the enemy to come between you and your spouse on any level.

However, the Word of God warns you that if you deny your spouse sexual intimacy, you are giving the devil a foothold in your marriage. We have counseled couples that had not been sexually intimate in years. It was by God's grace that these marriages survived to the point that we were able to help them. In these situations, we always endeavor to get to the root of the problem first. For example, *Is it just that sex is not a very high priority in the marriage? Are hormone levels low or off-balance? Is some other sickness present? Are there negative emotions, such as unforgiveness, that one or both people in the marriage have failed to deal with? Is there a problem with pornography? Are both parties faithful to their partner in the marriage?* There are any number of reasons why couples struggle in this area, but the issue must be dealt with, because sexual intimacy is crucial to the vitality and success of a marriage.

The Road to Restoration and Recovery

Maureen and I have seen so many turnarounds in marriages by exposing the hidden problem of hormone deficiencies and imbalances in people's lives. I am convinced that hormones are at the root of many of the problems that couples face in marriage. In one of our recent marriage seminars, we provided a means for those in attendance to have their hormone levels checked, and many of them tested low on certain hormones that affect their sex-drive. Once the problem was discovered, the couples could work on repairing the problem.

The study of hormones has been somewhat of a mystery for years, but now researchers are discovering that hormones are life-givers to the body. They have the capability to keep disease at bay when they are properly balanced. Usually, hormone levels drop significantly when a person reaches his or her mid-forties. I don't think it's a coincidence *...have a humble attitude that takes responsibility for its own feelings.* that people usually begin dealing with greater occurrences of disease at that stage of life. Many Christians are sick due to a lack of knowledge and education about how to take care of their bodies. However, I don't believe any amount of education or treatment should take the place of a genuine heart faith in God's Word. Yet some have gotten out of balance in the area of healing. They have chosen to ignore the care of their body or they have violated certain natural laws under the guise of "just walking by faith."

Two Schools of Thought

There are two schools of thought concerning the problem of hormonal imbalances. One is the belief that these imbalances should be controlled by pharmaceuticals. The other is the belief espoused by naturalists, who believe that the natural forms of these depleted hormones, can remedy the problem by helping the body regain its own ability to correct these imbalances. Medical doctors are trained to prescribe pharmaceuticals, and very few of these doctors embrace the "natural" view of balancing hormones. I'm not doling out medical advice, but I do know that there are published warnings regarding most hormone replacement medications. Even labels warn that these drugs can cause certain cancers, such as breast or cervical cancer, as well as heart attacks and strokes.

I personally take a more natural view and believe that the bio-identical hormones are very powerful and effective, with little or no side effects. I also believe that maintaining the proper balance of hormones can prevent virtually all serious illnesses. God put these hormones in our body and balanced them perfectly. If we keep them balanced through diet, exercise, and, if necessary, bio-identical hormone replacement therapy, our body has everything it needs to fight disease, maintain the proper weight, and slow down the aging process.

A good doctor can test you and discover if you are suffering from a hormone imbalance that is severe enough to affect your health and lifestyle. We know of people in their twenties and thirties who were tested and found that they were seriously imbalanced and in need of bio-identical HRT. If they did not receive this type of intervention, I have no doubt that many of these people would have been destined for disease early in life.

In many of the cases involving these young people, they had lost all sexual desire prior to being diagnosed and treated. They were simply co-existing with their spouse, hoping that maybe what they were experiencing was normal. But it isn't normal to lose interest in sex with your spouse! A diminished libido causes so many problems in marriage, including emotional hurts and problems with self-worth because the sexually healthy spouse usually has to battle thoughts, such as, *Is it me?*

Couples in this predicament need to talk to each other and be very open and honest in their communication. They also need to seek medical advice. The first step that I would recommend is hormone testing. I received hormone testing years ago, and it was discovered that I needed to undergo bio-identical HRT. Within four or five months of the therapy, I felt like a thirty-year-old man again! I still feel that way today, and I don't plan to change! Addressing a physiological problem can be as simple as taking replacement hormones—and it can make all the difference in your relationship with your spouse.

Exposing the Lies and the Shame of the 'Mid-Life Crisis'

Women go through menopause and often lose interest in sex during this time. Men also go through a similar stage in life, known as "mid-life crisis." Both are symptoms of an underlying hormone imbalance. Problems occur when a man doesn't understand why he is losing interest in sex with his wife. Often, instead of seeking help, he may turn to something else to fill this void in his life, such as pornography, another woman, or some other radical behavior—spending unreasonable amounts of money, buying a sports car, changing his wardrobe, and so forth.

When a man resorts to sinful behavior, he often alienates those who are the closest to him. They are hurt and confused by his actions. He may try to blame his wife or other people in his life for his feelings of frustration, insecurity, and inadequacy. Instead, he should be talking to his pastor, doctor, or even his wife! These are critical times that must be worked through, but that becomes difficult, if not impossible, when the lines of communication are closed.

Where Do We Go From Here?

Since men are generally more emotionally guarded than women, it's easier to identify a hormone related problem in a woman. For example, if she is an emotional yo-yo—crying one minute and laughing the next, two or three times a day—or if she seems depressed for long periods, that's usually a sign of a problem with hormones. *DHEA, melatonin,* and *pregnenolone* are three over-the-counter hormone supplements that can help a woman who is experiencing the negative effects of menopause, or even perimenopause. However, there are other considerations, such as the need for thyroid, estrogen, progesterone, or growth hormones. That's why I recommend that women—especially those who are menopausal or perimenopausal—see a good doctor or qualified practitioner in naturopathy, who can prescribe certain therapies that are natural, but might require a prescription.

For men, I recommend *DHEA, melatonin,* and *pregnenolone,* which can be purchased over-the-counter—and thyroid, testosterone, and growth hormones, which must be prescribed by a health-care practitioner. However, even OTC treatments should be taken under the guidance of a professional. Only a qualified professional can test you and accurately prescribe the more potent supplements that you may need to help restore proper balance to your endocrine system.

Many people suffer with symptoms of menopause or "mid-life," yet they won't discuss it and receive the help they need. They suffer silently and alone, floundering in their personal lives and their marriages through ignorance and feelings of guilt and shame. If they would simply open up and seek the help they needed, then they could obtain victory and get on with their lives. God is ready and He delights in healing, delivering, and restoring relationships and lives. He is able and willing to right the wrongs that have occurred in the past and in our marriages, and He will meet us where we are when we seek Him.

15

MADE FOR EACH OTHER: SEX AND THE COVENANT OF MARRIAGE

Dr. Tom Anderson

G od created sex for marriage. Sex is a gift from God that was meant to be enjoyed in the context of marriage, beginning on your wedding day. He intended sex for pleasure and pro-creation, but it is also a symbol of the covenant between you and your spouse—a covenant to remain together through life as "one flesh" (Genesis 2:24; Ephesians 5:31). The world does not identify sex as being symbolic of a covenant. This can be seen in the promiscuity that's so commonplace today, especially in our country. Young people, in general, don't place the same value on virginity or abstinence before marriage as they once did. For example, fifty years ago, seeing a pregnant girl in high school was almost unheard of; however, in today's society, it is fairly commonplace.

Focusing on the Future—Forgetting the Past

Over the years, we have lost sight of the covenant that God designed to be consummated through marriage. Biblically, a first-time marriage was intended for a man and a woman who would reserve themselves for marriage, so they could give themselves to each other on their wedding night. This act of giving oneself was supposed to be a powerful symbol of purity, fidelity, and emotional security. In other words, when a man and woman were joined in marriage, and they consummated that union through the act of sex, there should not be any images from their past relationships that have to be "erased"—no memories or imaginations to bring into the marriage from old relationships. "...I do not count my-

> *That act of giving oneself was to be a powerful symbol of purity, fidelity, and emotional security.*

self to have apprehended; but one thing I do, FORGETTING those things which are behind and reaching forward to those things which are ahead" (Philippians 3:13 NKJV, emphasis mine).

There is grace and power to "forget" and to forge a new life and a new marriage beyond your past relationships. The Apostle Paul, who had to learn to forget some things himself, wrote these inspiring words: "...forgetting...and reaching forward..." (Philippians 3:13). However, just think how blessed a relationship is that doesn't have any ungodly images and memories from the past. This was God's original plan for marriage. Certainly, He's the God who causes us to overcome, despite our mistakes and sins of the past, but when we follow His will from our youth, there's very little to overcome!

Taking the time to communicate with young people about this subject is a big key to helping them avert the dangers and heartache of sexual promiscuity. If you have children or grandchildren, sharing the truth about sex and marriage from God's Word can encourage them to "save themselves" for marriage.

At our church, one of our sons teaches a class on sexual purity for young high school students. It's a great program in which the students make a heartfelt commitment to remain pure until they get married. These young people are not just parroting words that they heard someone else say. By the time they finish the program, they truly understand God's plan for sex and the incredible importance of the institution of marriage. We certainly don't condemn you if you have missed it by having sex outside of marriage—and neither does God (see Romans 8:1). We are simply trying to paint a picture of the value of marriage and of sex in the context and confines of marriage.

Playing for Keeps

Isn't it wonderful how God designed sex and marriage? Think about what the world has done to that design. The world has perverted it, so that the idea of "waiting" until marriage is scorned. Sadly, that mentality has even crept into the Church, but it's not biblical. Marriage does not consist of two people setting up house together for a while to see if everything will work out. Marriage is a covenant commitment to build a life together for the rest of your lives. That commitment should be taken very seriously; it should not be entered into lightly or without a lot of consideration and prayer.

What is a covenant? A covenant is a solemn, binding agreement or compact. God takes covenants very seriously. In the Old Testament, if someone entered into a covenant and then broke that covenant or vow, he could be hunted down and killed. Often, the curse for breaking a covenant not only came upon the guilty person, but also upon their entire family. A covenant was designed to last forever, and was considered to be the strongest contract known to God and man.

A covenant was designed to last forever.

God considers marriage so important that He set it up as a covenant relationship, comparable to the one established between Christ and His Church. Just as God and His children share covenant rights, husbands and wives also share covenant rights in marriage. One of these covenant rights is the right to share physical intimacy with their marriage partner. Sex is not only a covenant symbol in marriage, but it's also an act of physical intimacy that God created for husbands and wives for their enjoyment and pleasure. It is God's desire that every Christian couple find sexual fulfillment in marriage.

Don't Be 'in the Dark' About Sex

A couple's attitude toward communication is so critical to the health and vitality of their marriage. This is especially true in regards to communicating about sex. Open communication is critical to sexual fulfillment. Traditionally, couples have assented to this truth, but they have only gone so far in communicating about sex. It seems that one or both spouses have been unwilling to fully expose their feelings about what they consider to be sexually fulfilling. How often do you and your spouse talk about sex? Do you know what your spouse likes or dislikes when it comes to sex? If you can't truthfully answer this question, "Yes!"—beyond all shadow of a doubt, then I encourage you to take the first step in breaking down those communication barriers in your marriage.

I have a saying that anything "left in the dark" between you and your spouse, can hurt you and your marriage. If it should have been said but it hasn't, then it needs to be communicated! God intended sex to be enjoyable, healthy, and satisfying for both the husband and wife. Yet there are many couples that are languishing in this area because of a lack of knowledge and because of a lack of willingness to communicate concerning that lack of knowledge.

For example, some wives endure pain during intercourse because they don't want to communicate that with their husband. Some think that if they tell the truth, it's going to offend their spouse and cause bigger problems. However, they are depriving themselves of sexual fulfillment because of their unwillingness to communicate.

There are many great books about sex that are available. They are educational and not pornographic, and were written to help married couples find the sexual fulfillment in marriage that God intended. However, if people won't avail themselves to these kinds of books, or if all they have ever been taught came from a dirty movie or magazine, then they are destined to stay on the wrong track in their sex life unless they make a change. Married couples should not be afraid to read a book about sex and sexual intimacy. Sex in marriage is a covenant act. Our sex life is important to God, and it should be important to us as well.

Feast or Famine?
It Depends on Who You Ask

"He brought me to the banqueting house, and his banner over me was love" (Song of Solomon 2:4 NKJV). This verse is talking about a feast of food, a "banqueting house." But just as good food nourishes a person, a good sex life will nourish you as well—your life personally and also your marriage. A person can be full or famished in this area of sex!

What a husband and wife consider as "famine" in the area of sex can mean two different things altogether. If a woman describes her sex life as a famine, she may not be talking about the number of times she's having sex, but rather the quality of her sexual experience. Quality is more important to women, whereas quantity tends to be more important to men. What actually constitutes quality sex to a woman? We have heard it said that for a woman, sex begins long before the physical act. That's absolutely true.

A sense of security is essential for a woman in order for her to enjoy a satisfying sex life. She must feel loved, cherished, secure, and protected in order to freely give herself sexually to her husband. These things are absolutely critical in making a woman's sexual experience a feast instead of a famine. On the other hand, a man gains greater connection with his own emotions, after having physical intimacy with his wife. When he makes himself more vulnerable and more open to her physically, he reconnects with her emotionally. A man's ego is greatly influenced by how well he performs.

About That Male Ego

We have already seen that men are very strong by nature. They are tough, protector types, and that's a good thing. A man is a macho, "can-do," knight in shining armor. But if you criticize him sexually, then he's a mess. It is absolutely necessary for a husband to have the assurance from his wife—the one person who he trusts—that he is a great lover.

A man's ego is a very fragile thing. Studies show that most impotence is not caused by physical or physiological conditions, but by too much criticism! A man's ego is greatly influenced by how well he performs and how well he's encouraged.

Men have been graced and equipped to take on a great responsibility in marriage. A man may be looked at as a pillar of strength, but his ego is fragile; it's his greatest weakness. Famine, for a man where sex is concerned, can occur because of a wounded ego. When a man's ego has been wounded, it affects him sexually. For example, if he has been made to feel incompetent on his job, those feelings of insecurity could affect his desire for sex.

Wrong Words, Right Words — The Cause and the Cure

A man can be rendered sexually impotent by speaking the wrong words to him. Words are the cause, and words can be the cure! With all the television advertisements we see for cures for Erectile Dysfunction, or ED, I promise you that a majority of cases can be cured simply with words—the right words. If you are a wife, then tell your husband often that he's a good man—a good lover and provider. Find things that you can compliment him for.

You also need to look your best for him, because taking care of yourself, communicates love and respect to him without words. If you don't take care of yourself, it communicates just the opposite, and he will feel that you don't respect him. We live in an image-based society, but I'm not saying that we, as Christians, should allow ourselves to be conformed to that mindset. However, we must not throw the baby out with the bath water, either! In other words, we need to look our best. Since men are predominantly visually oriented, a wife especially needs to boost her husband's ego by being the best she can be. (We'll talk more about "desirability" in marriage later in the chapter.)

Whether he's been incessantly criticized, or his wife has simply lost interest in him, if a husband feels unloved, unworthy, disrespected, or ill esteemed by her, it will affect him sexually. If he feels that way over a prolonged period of time, he may grow cold and indifferent toward his wife if he doesn't communicate his feelings. One of the reasons many marriages suffer from this "famine syndrome," is the lack of understanding that exists within the Christian community regarding sex. There simply aren't a lot of people talking about it.

...the wise person will arm himself with the truth of God's Word

The first time I taught on the subject of sex at our church, I announced it in advance and forbade anyone under the age of twenty-one to come in the sanctuary that Sunday. Once we made sure we had an "adult-only" audience, we closed the doors and had a closed meeting. I was very candid as I taught on this subject that day, and the congregation gasped! But that's okay; I didn't apologize. God created sex, and church leadership needs to talk about it.

Satan, sin, and the world have perverted the gift of sex. Lives have been messed up because of wrong teaching on this subject. Sex has been portrayed as a 'meaningless' experience that was designed purely for one's own gratification. Believers must stand up and tell the truth about God's gift of sex in marriage.

Just Sex—Or Sexual Fulfillment?

Without sexual fulfillment in your marriage, you are not receiving God's best for your marriage. It's God's will for you to prosper and be abundantly blessed and fulfilled in every area of your life. Satan is the author of mediocre and dull, and he doesn't want you to have God's best in any area, including your marriage and sex life! It's not often that you will hear someone tell you that Satan's will for your life is a mediocre, unsatisfying sex life—but that's exactly what I'm telling you. He deceives people, and that's how he's able to steal, kill, and destroy (see John 10:10). Whether it's your health, finances, relationships, and so forth, the enemy is a thief and a destroyer. The wise person will arm himself with the truth of God's Word, because it's the truth that a person knows and embraces that will set him or her completely free (John 8:32).

It's also important to be wise concerning the differences between the genders. The Bible says, "Husbands, likewise, dwell with them [their wife] with understanding…" (1 Peter 3:7 NKJV). By the same token, it will profit a wife to have an understanding of the male gender. Ignorance is not bliss in marriage! Knowledge is power. The more you know and the more you put into practice what you know, the happier and healthier your marriage will be.

Getting Sex in Perspective

We have already covered the fact that men are primarily planters and women are primarily "receivers" or "incubators" of that which is planted. So in the context of sex, we could say that men tend to be ready to "plant" at a moment's notice! On the other hand, women are not always ready to receive; they are more seasonal when it comes to sex. In other words, like the soil in a garden, the wife must be properly prepared and cared for—cultivated—prior to enjoying physical intimacy. Whether it's "feast" or "famine" in a couple's sex life is often dependent upon perspective: the husband's or the wife's. Gaining a more clear understanding of what each party needs and wants in the relationship, will ensure physical and emotional security and a marriage that's "Heaven on earth."

The Real Truth About Sexual Incompatibility

We know that in marriage, a man's and woman's needs are different. Because our emotional needs are so different, our sexual needs are different, also. If we don't understand that, then problems will result. In a previous chapter, we looked at how to overcome certain barriers to emotional intimacy and a satisfying sex life. In this chapter, we are going to look at some problems and issues with sex that aren't nearly as complex. We will start with desirability in marriage.

Dress for your man, not every man.

Problems with sex in marriage can be related to a spouse being physically undesirable to his or her spouse. I'm not talking about any physical traits that may be perceived as negative, including being overweight. I'm talking about the way in which you care of yourself. You can be your best and be attractive for your spouse. You don't have to be wealthy enough to afford cosmetic surgeries or be as thin or well-built as an actor, model, or athlete. But you can endeavor to be the best you possibly can be at every season of your life and marriage.

Your Spouse Is Looking at You

I'm talking about taking care of yourself and looking your best for your own sake and for the sake of your spouse. For example, what type of clothing does your spouse like? There's a saying for wives that goes something like this: *Dress for your man, not for every man.* The same could be said for husbands: *Dress for your woman, not for every woman.*

You don't have to own designer clothing or have a "hair allowance" worked into your monthly budget, but you can make sure your clothes are clean and neat, and that your hair is brushed or combed and styled. It isn't fair to woo your mate in courtship looking nice, but then after you get married, you look disheveled and unkempt most of the time!

One of the things about Maureen that has always impressed me, is that there are no days that she doesn't dress nice, put on makeup, and fix her hair. She dresses well every day. Over the years, that has inspired me to shape up in this area, too! I have been known to hang around the house on my days off wearing cutoffs, a raggedy T-shirt, and flip-flops. But Maureen has truly motivated me to look my best at all times. We often hear that looks aren't everything or that looks aren't important, but they are very important. I'm not saying we need to look as if we have just stepped out of a Hollywood clothier or salon; I'm simply saying that we each need to try to be the very best we can be for ourselves and for our spouse.

What Women Want

Notoriously, we have said that "looks" or appearances matter more to men than to women. But in the following passage from Song of Solomon, I think it's interesting that the woman is looking at the man's physical features here, beginning with the top, his head, and working her way down!

My lover is radiant and ruddy, outstanding among ten thousand. His head is purest gold; his hair is wavy and black as a raven. His eyes are like doves by the water streams, washed in milk, mounted like jewels. His cheeks are like beds of spice yielding perfume. His lips are like lilies dripping with myrrh. His arms are rods of gold set with chrysolite. His body is like polished ivory decorated with sapphires. His legs are pillars of marble set on bases of pure gold. His appearance is like Lebanon, choice as its cedars. His mouth is sweetness itself; he is altogether lovely. This is my lover, this my friend, O daughters of Jerusalem.

Song of Solomon 5:10-16

In this passage, the woman notices the tenderness of her husband's eyes, but she doesn't neglect the strength of his hands and legs. This passage is so reflective of the female gender! She's looking for tenderness and strength, romance and friendship. She finds all of these things in her ideal mate.

What Men Want

As I said, men are well-known for being "visual" people. In other words, they are very moved by what they see. Let's look at the following passage at the way Solomon notices his wife.

How beautiful your sandalled feet, O prince's daughter! Your graceful legs are like jewels, the work of a craftsman's hands. Your navel is a rounded goblet that never lacks blended wine. Your waist is a mound of wheat encircled by lilies. Your breasts are like two fawns, twins of a gazelle. Your neck is like an ivory tower. Your eyes are the pools of Heshbon by the gate of Bath Rabbim. Your nose is like the tower of Lebanon looking towards Damascus. Your head crowns you like Mount Carmel. Your hair is like royal tapestry; the king is held captive by its tresses. How beautiful you are and how pleasing, O love, with your delights! Your stature is like that of the palm, and your breasts like clusters of fruit. I said, "I will climb the palm tree; I will take hold of its fruit." May your breasts be like the clusters of the vine, the fragrance of your breath like apples, and your mouth like the best wine. May the wine go straight to my lover, flowing gently over lips and teeth.

Song of Solomon 7:1-9

Solomon was obviously very attracted to his woman! He compared her body to a beautiful tree and then communicated his plans to get very close to that tree! There has been so much foolish controversy in the Church about how a woman should look. I'm saying there's nothing wrong with a wife taking care of herself—with decorating the "tree"!

Beyond looking your best, smelling good is important too. If you are a husband, you especially need to know that your wife is not into sweat! I say this in fun, but if you're in doubt, take a shower. Being clean and fresh is always better. Do you think smelling good is that important? Even if my nose didn't know, the following verses cause me to believe it is.

> *Pleasing is the fragrance of your perfumes; your name is like perfume poured out. No wonder the maidens love you.... While the king was at his table, my perfume spread its fragrance. My lover is to me a sachet of myrrh resting between my breasts. My lover is to me a cluster of henna blossoms from the vineyards of En Gedi.... Who is this coming up from the desert like a column of smoke, perfumed with myrrh and incense made from all the spices of the merchant?*

Song of Solomon 1:3,12-14; 3:6

That sounds to me like a little aftershave or cologne might be beneficial in your relationship with your wife! A pleasant scent or aroma makes a great impression on a woman—just as it makes an impression on a man. It seems that women are better than men at smelling nice. The pleasant scent of a woman's cologne or perfume is very attractive to her husband. We will also see from the following verses that pleasant-smelling breath is an important trait to have when it comes to sexual compatibility with your spouse.

> *Your lips drop sweetness as the honeycomb, my bride; milk and honey are under your tongue. The fragrance of your garments is like that of Lebanon. You are a garden locked up, my sister, my bride; you are a spring enclosed, a sealed fountain. Your plants are an orchard of pomegranates with choice*

*fruits, with henna and nard, nard and saffron, calamus and cinnamon, with
every kind of incense tree, with myrrh and aloes and all the finest spices.*

Song of Solomon 4:11-14

A Touching Response

We have talked about the importance of looking good and smelling good in regard to sexual compatibility. Appealing to the senses of sight and smell is an attractive quality in a spouse. Now we are going to look at appealing to your spouse's sense of touch—in other words, responding to the sexual advances of your spouse.

When we talk about giving your spouse the appropriate attention during foreplay and sex, it's important to talk about what not to do. For instance, watching television over your mate's shoulder is not conducive to sexual compatibility! Answering the phone while your spouse is flirting with you is another "mood-killer," that can hurt the relationship, because it communicates disinterest or disrespect.

In Song of Solomon 7, where Solomon notices his wife's physical features, it's interesting that he didn't start at her head as she did when she noticed his features. He started somewhere else in beholding the beauty of his ideal girl! He started with her feet for some reason and then worked his way upward toward her curves. Then he spoke of physically being near. He says, "'...I will go up to the palm tree, I will take hold of its branches.' Let now your breasts be like clusters of the vine..." (vv. 8-9).

Some have said, "This is too explicit to be in the Bible." But, remember, God created sex; it's a gift from Him for marriage. It seems that some Christians have a very skewed view of sex. They see it as dirty, instead of a gift from God to be enjoyed. They must renew their mind to the truth of God's Word (Romans 12:2) and get rid of those wrong ideas about sex. Sex is not dirty in marriage; it's holy. And what Solomon is saying to his wife, here in verses 8 and 9, is not dirty or crude. He's simply talking about his anticipation of foreplay and sexual intercourse as acts of love, to be enjoyed between the two of them as husband and wife.

In writings from the Early Church and Old Testament history, we can find that it was common for married couples to read from the Song of Solomon on the Sabbath and then participate in sexual intercourse. As you know, the Sabbath was a holy day set apart for God's people under the Old Testament, just for rest and relaxation. Certain activities were forbidden, yet intercourse was considered as an act to be partaken of on that holy day! What did the patriarchs know back then that perhaps we don't know today?

More Than 'Icing on the Cake'

Sex is not just some benefit of marriage or "the icing on the cake"; it's an integral aspect of the bond of marriage. In fact, sex and the covenant of marriage cannot be separated, anymore than the ingredients in a cake can be separated once they are mixed! So we must never be guilty of downplaying this important function in a marriage relationship. Sex in marriage plays a big part in how bonded we feel to our spouse. It's a scientific fact that the act of sex creates chemical changes in the brain that bring feelings of euphoria, and then great peace and calm. It's at that moment that two people in a marriage feel the most bonded.

Sex also promotes and deepens the bond of love between a husband and wife. In fact, the chemical *peptide oxytocin* that's released during sex actually encourages more affectionate behavior between the couple. Ironically, the more affectionate you are with your spouse, the more *peptide oxytocin* is released!

When *peptide oxytocin* is released in the body, it helps block negative memories. Hollywood has made jokes about "makeup sex," but there's a real truth to utilizing sexual intimacy with your spouse to eradicate negative feelings that challenge the relationship.

During sexual intercourse, the brain actually releases "memory blockers" that help you focus on the present and on each other again, instead of on a fight you may have just had. These brain chemicals promote feelings of well-being, happiness, and "forgetfulness" where an offense is concerned. "...Do not let the sun go down while you are still angry, and do not give the devil a foothold" (Ephesians 4:26-27).

God has provided us with everything that we need, so that there wouldn't be any footholds of the enemy in our lives. So when you become angry with your spouse, don't stay mad—get close to him or her and allow your positive feelings for each other to wash over any emotions of anger or frustration. Engaging in sex as a married couple even has health benefits. A certain study revealed that one sexual encounter burns the same number of calories as running five miles!

Endorphins that are released during sex also have anti-aging effects on the body. Endorphins help produce energy, burn fat, and strengthen the immune system. They can also produce an analgesic effect that lessens the sensation of pain. God made no mistake in creating sex to be enjoyed between a husband and wife in the covenant of marriage. In fact, the two—sex and marriage—were made for each other as gifts and the blessing of God.

16

RESPONSIBLE WITH MONEY, READY FOR A BRIDE

Dr. Tom Anderson

We have seen that one of a husband's biggest responsibilities in marriage is to protect and provide. In fulfilling this responsibility, he creates an atmosphere of security and trust for his wife and children. I cannot talk about this subject adequately without specifically addressing the topic of money in marriage—or, more specifically, men and money in marriage. Some men don't have a clue about how to create or stay on a budget. Often a husband is buying "toys," or the things that he wants, while he can't even pay the rent or mortgage. That is irresponsible, and that lack of taking responsibility creates stress and feelings of insecurity in a man's family.

I know that it's not popular to lay the responsibility for the finances strictly on the husband. I've heard countless times the excuse, "Well, my wife is better at that kind of thing than I am." That might be true. Many women are more detail-oriented than men. But if you, as a husband, don't balance the checkbook and pay the bills, then you don't know exactly what you're bringing in as income, what you owe, or what you have on hand. You need to know all of those things, otherwise how will you know whether you have enough money or whether you need more money?

Often husbands leave it to their wife to make ends meet and to figure out how to stretch their income in order to meet the family's needs. This is not God's intent. The husband is the head of the home, and it is his responsibility to manage the financial affairs of that home. If you, as a husband, have not taken your place as the leader in your financial affairs, I strongly urge you to take a bookkeeping class or basic class on business math, so you can build security and trust in your marriage by properly managing your money.

> *The husband is the head of the home, and it is his responsibility to manage the financial affairs of that home.*

One thing you need to do is set up a budget, cutting expenses if necessary to ensure that money is not always "tight" at your house. For example, it's important that a husband pray about making large purchases, such as buying a home. I encourage you not to make a large purchase until you know it's God's will. Don't get ahead of yourself and jump into a large commitment, such as a home purchase, that puts your family in a bind financially.

This happens more often than you might think. A family becomes overcommitted financially, and the wife feels pressured to go out and work. The wife begins taking on responsibility that belongs to her husband. I'm not suggesting that it's wrong for a wife to work outside the home if she desires to do so and if she and her husband are in agreement about it. But if she has to forfeit doing the things that fulfill her as a wife and mother because she's forced to take on outside work, chaos and disorder will eventually set in because the home is operating outside of God's design and order. Simply put, it is the husband's responsibility to create and manage the household budget so that the family doesn't become overcommitted financially.

Our son, Jason recently bought his wife a nice car. She said to him, "You need a nice car too." He told her, "Not now. I can't buy two cars right now. I will drive the 'junk' car so that you can have a nice one." In buying his wife a nice car while he drove the older one, Jason showed his wife that he valued her and that she could trust him with their financial future. It's not that Jason doesn't like new cars; he likes them very much! However, he understands his responsibility in the home, and that he must protect and provide for his family first above all else, including above his own desires.

I have seen husbands spend money frivolously on themselves, and then tell their wife that there was no money to buy her a new outfit or take her out on a date. If he spends $200 playing golf, but she can't have something nice, something is wrong with that! As a husband, protecting and providing for your family entails taking leadership where the finances are concerned. If your wife is the one who's responsible for knowing what you have and what you owe, you have just added to her a responsibility that belongs squarely with you, not her. Consequently, you have added unnecessary stress to her life.

A Job First, Then a Wife

"Then the Lord God took the man and put him in the garden of Eden to tend and keep it." (Genesis 2:15 NKJV). Clearly, God gave the man the responsibility to tend and keep the garden. Notice that God gave Adam a job before He gave him a wife! Adam had to do the work; it was his assignment from God. And it is no less the husband's assignment and responsibility today. As I said, I'm not condemning a wife for working outside the home if she desires to do so, or if the husband and wife are in agreement with that arrangement for a season. But ultimately, the husband is responsible for managing the finances and making sure that enough money is coming in to support his family.

It's very important that the husband accept responsibility as the provider for his family. If his wife wants to have a profession, that's great.

However, if you, as a husband, have a wife whose heartfelt desire is to stay at home with her children, it's your responsibility to make certain that she is able to do this. When our children were young, there was a season during which I held two and three jobs to make it possible for Maureen to stay home with our children. That's what was in her heart to do. She had a college degree, and she could have had a career. But she desired to stay at home and raise our children. I'm so thankful and glad that she was able to invest that time in our sons at that stage of their lives.

I realize that some women are doctors, lawyers, and business owners. Maybe you are a husband who earns less money than your wife and your wife enjoys her career. The responsibility to make sure that the bills are being paid and that the future is being provided for is still yours. Your wife's income isn't what brings her security. It's the way you manage the family's finances that bring her comfort and security in life.

It Boils Down to Trust

Women need two important things from a man: unconditional love and security. In fact, the entire home needs that. This comes down to an issue of trust. In other words, can your wife trust you to look ahead and foresee the future needs of the family? Or is she anxious because she thinks you can't see past the here and now? Sometimes people go to the local church looking for help when they are about to be evicted from their house or lose their car tomorrow. They should have known they were in trouble long before then. If a husband foresees that his home is in jeopardy, he can get a second job and avert a crisis. Even working at a fast-food restaurant can help him earn enough to make his late car payments.

In my way of thinking, a forty-hour workweek is a lie from the pit of hell! Ask any business owner you know who's successful and doing well and he or she will tell you that a forty-hour workweek is a myth! I worked seventy to eighty hours a week most of my life. I don't understand the mentality of someone who comes home after eight hours and just sits there while his financial future is in jeopardy.

Most people waste forty hours a week watching TV, anyway. They could make wiser use of their time working to get their family caught up and even ahead. But instead of bringing their budget back in line, they often complain, "My job just doesn't pay enough."

What about Christmas season? If you, as a husband, are meeting your budget but don't have extra money for gifts at Christmas, you can get a seasonal job that will pay for your family's Christmas. The same is true concerning vacations. Your family needs at least one vacation together every year. It's your responsibility to make sure the extra money is budgeted or comes into the family somehow for you to be able to do that. Extra money for Christmas gifts and vacations may not seem like absolute necessities in life, but as a leader in the home, when you provide these things for your family, beyond blessing them, you also build trust and security into those relationships—trust that will last a lifetime. You can't put a dollar amount on that in terms of the value it holds.

Your Kids Are Watching You

As a father, you largely influence the relationship your kids will have with God, as well as their own children someday. My son, Scot vividly remembers the time I got laid off when he and Jason were children. I sat the family down and said, "I got laid off from work, and eve-rything is going to be fine. I will do everything I can do, and God will provide for us. So let's go out and eat!"

Your children need to feel like you're an immovable, unshakable rock!

Scot recalls the emotion of that moment even more than the details of the layoff. He said he learned that day that no matter what happened, Dad would always take care of it. He also learned to trust God as his

Heavenly Father. Now, as a dad himself, Scot instills this same sense of confidence and security in his own wife and children. Your children need to feel like you are an immovable, unshakable rock! You may need to go to the Rock, Christ Jesus, to receive the strength you need, but your family needs to see that no matter what the circumstance, Dad won't be crushed by it; he's an overcomer.

Early Lessons and Challenges

In my younger days, finances were a bit of a challenge for me. However, I overcame this challenge, and I want to share with you my simple system for getting started on the road to financial responsibility and stability in your life and marriage. I developed this system when I was in college, and it has served me well for many years. In fact, I have taught this system to businesses, organizations, and families all over the world.

These principles are practical and useable today. They are simple, yet profound, and you can incorporate them into whatever system of management that you choose to use. You simply need to find what works for you, and then stick with it as a discipline, until it becomes a habit. In other words, the longer you stick with it, the easier it becomes to do.

Find out what works for you, and then stick with it as a discipline, until it becomes a habit.

This system of organizing and managing your finances will give you the means to know where you stand financially twenty-four hours a day, seven days a week, all year long. You will know in a given situation, whether you should spend money or not. That's the problem with most people—at any given time, they don't know where they are with their budget. So they tend to overspend. They make costly mistakes with their money, and if they keep making too many of those mistakes, it will eventually ruin them financially.

A Simple Assignment

The first part of this system involves an assignment. Get a notebook or loose paper that can be placed in a binder and write down all of your expenses. It's important not to leave anything out, but you don't have to know every bill to the exact cent, because there will be variables each month, especially with utilities.

Begin with your tithes, offerings, mortgage and automobile payments. Then list your home and/or automobile insurance payment and your utilities (electric, water, phone, and so forth). After that, list any other personal insurance you might carry, as well as any medical or retail payments that you might make besides your car payment. For now, leave off groceries, fuel, and other expenses such as clothing, eating out, and miscellaneous items.

This is a great program whether you get paid weekly, bi-weekly, monthly, or even semi-monthly, such as on the first and the fifteenth each month. It will even work on commissioned sales, but you will have to improvise when you don't receive income on a regular, consistent basis.

You Must Know What You Owe and Earn

Now, add up the expenses you listed on your worksheet. These are your standard, finite expenses, because they can readily be defined. Your other expenses such as groceries, fuel, and so forth can be classified as relative expenses, because they can change from month to month. For instance, you could cut your grocery bill by eating different kinds of foods or buying the store labels at the store instead of the name brands. You could carpool or take the bus or public transportation, instead of driving to work every day. You could forego buying clothes for a period of time, or you could change where you shop for clothes (consignment stores versus the department stores and so forth).

You could also sacrifice eating out for a season—or eating out as often. You could rent a movie instead of going to the cinema. All of these expenses can fluctuate from month to month. After you have listed your standard expenses, total what you earn, or take home, during that same period. For the sake of this teaching, let's just say you figured your monthly standard expenses at $2,750.00 per month. Now let's say that you take home $750.00 per week. With those figures in mind, if you were to multiply your weekly net earning by four (because there are four weeks in an average month), you would have $3,000.00; therefore, you would have very little surplus for groceries, fuel, and so forth—only $250.00.

$750.00	weekly net pay
x 4	number of weeks in an average month
$3,000.00	monthly net pay
- 2,750.00	monthly standard expenses
$ 250.00	disposable income for groceries, fuel, etc.

However, there is an average of four weeks and three days in a month, not just four weeks. So if you get paid every week, you would need to figure your budget a little differently, because you would get paid fifty-two times a year, not forty-eight.

$750.00	weekly net pay
x 52	number of weeks in the year
$39,000.00	annual net pay
÷ 12	number of months in the year
$ 3,250.00	monthly net pay
-2,750.00	monthly standard expenses
$500.00	disposable income for groceries, fuel, etc.

Of course, certain months contain five weeks, but with this system, you will know in advance what you can and cannot spend each month. In other words, you will know on June 1, for example, not on June 30, if you are going to be short on money. The important thing is that you always know where you are with your finances.

Using the preceding scenario, just because there are 5 weeks in a month doesn't mean you can make a larger purchase during that fifth week—unless you have based your expenditures on a four-week budget, instead of a 4.3-week budget. In the former case, you could then use your "surplus" in that fifth week to buy extra groceries and so forth.

This is not a complicated program, and you can use it at the beginning of each month to plan for the month ahead. People who work for commission often have problems when they receive a large payout. Sometimes they "blow it" quickly, instead of spreading it out over several less profitable months so they can pay their bills on time and meet their monthly budget. That is why knowing exactly what you owe and planning ahead are so vital to a healthy financial picture.

Some people have a separate checking account where they deposit a predetermined amount of money each pay period to meet their monthly set or standard expenses. They don't write any checks on that account except to pay those expenses. Then at the end of the month when it's time to pay the following month's bills, all the money is there. They simply write out the checks and pay each bill. They pay all of their bills on time and even pay most of them early. Besides taking the stress out of bill-paying, it helps their credit score, too.

The way some people operate their budget is, as a bill comes in, they write a check for it. Even if it's the bill for their mortgage, they will write the check, and then they have to borrow from the next pay period to make ends meet. Then they usually have to borrow from the week after that, and so the cycle continues. In time, they are months in arrears. Occasionally, they get caught up because of an extra week in a month. But then the cycle begins again. That's a very stressful way to pay bills. It's not healthy emotionally, and it's not good for a marriage.

When There's 'Month' Left at the End of Your Money — A Short-Term Cure for Shortfalls!

You might say, "That's all well and good, Reverend Anderson, but what happens if I figure my budget, and I see that I just can't make ends meet?" Many people avoid creating a budget because they don't want to see on paper what they already know—that they are spending more than they are earning. However, avoiding the issue will not repair the situation or make it go away. That's why I said that knowing what you owe and earn as the leader in the home are the basic, vital steps for bringing health and vitality into your finances and your marriage. Marriage and finances are so intricately linked. So it's important to have your financial affairs in order, for your own sake and for the sake of your marriage and your posterity—your children and your children's children.

When you figure your budget—your standard expenses and your standard earnings—what if there's not enough for food, fuel for your car, and so forth? I have been in that situation before. I went out and got a second job to ensure we had the money for those things. If you find that your bills are greater than your income, you may need to increase your income until you can decrease your bills. You might need to take a second job. If your wife is not already working, perhaps the two of you will come into agreement about her finding temporary work.

Of course, taking such measures is not a long-term solution but a temporary fix. Yet it's your responsibility as the leader in the home, to ensure that you have enough funds to meet your family's needs. Really, it's simple economics: You must either decrease your outflow—what you owe and spend—or increase your income—what you earn. If you owe more than you earn each month, there's an imbalance, and some kind of action must be taken to return that situation to a condition of stability.

Taking the Next Step:
Ensuring Cash Flow for Your Family

What happens when you figure your budget and you have enough to pay your standard bills and to cover the cost of food, fuel, and reasonable clothing and entertainment? At this point, you need to invest and save. You need to ensure cash flow for the well-being of your family, both now and for the future. Cash flow is an especially critical issue in America right now. Even banks are discovering how vital cash flow is—it will determine whether they stand or fall.

Besides doing long-term investing for your retirement years, you need a short-term savings account to ensure cash flow in the event that you lose your job or are unable to work for some reason. This account should contain funds to cover three to six months of living expenses. In other words, if your budget is $5,000.00 a month, you should have a minimum of three months' worth of expenses—or $15,000.00—in the bank to sustain your family, while you find other means of earning an income.

When the Mundane Becomes Dramatic

If you will set yourself up on this program or one like it and stick with it, then it will change your life for the better. It hasn't always been easy, but I have utilized this system for forty years. I set our church up using this system, and I have helped many businesses set up their accounting systems with this program. They know what their expenses are, so a predetermined amount gets deposited regularly into a separate account that is set aside for meeting those expenses. No one touches those accounts until it's time to disburse payments to meet the obligations of those businesses.

These things might not seem fun or exciting, but they will be dramatic and life-changing, if you will put them into practice! When the opportunity comes for you to buy something on credit, you will know immediately whether you will be able to pay for it, or whether you will have to give up eating steak and go back to soup in order to do it! By the end of each day, no matter where you are with your finances, you can use this system to discover whether you are in trouble financially or whether you simply need more cash flow for your family's needs, in case of an emergency. Whether you need to remedy a bad situation or simply take additional steps to ensure a prosperous future for your family, I encourage you as the leader in your home, to implement this plan or devise a similar one of your own.

As you pay down your debt, don't take on new debt. Use that extra money to save and invest in your future. Debt is a very dangerous thing and it can ruin an individual, a family and also threaten entire nations. It's a well-known fact that Americans, as a whole, do not live within their means. Our system of credit has made it easy to spend more than we earn (it's called "living above our means"). Even the Bible says that it's not good to live above our means—in other words, to be poor, yet try to appear to be rich. "Better to be a nobody and yet have a servant than pretend to be somebody and have no food" (Proverbs 12:9).

Most of the people I know who are genuinely rich, are not showy and don't appear as rich. They don't necessarily earn piles of money, either. They simply know how to utilize what they earn and how to live within their means. I promise you, they utilize their money wisely, they are not "willy-nilly" with money, but they operate according to some kind of budget and financial plan.

Proving the Plan In My Own Circumstances

Years ago, I was laid off from work for seven months. I used my own system during that time, and it worked fantastically. I signed up for unemployment and because I knew all my standard expenses, I knew exactly what it would take to supplement my unemployment pay so I could meet those expenses. I took part-time jobs to supplement the unemployment. I did whatever work I could find to make sure I deposited $400 per week into an account for meeting our standard expenses.

During this time that I was laid off from my job, God gave me a word: *Take no thought* (see Matthew 6:25). Yet I understood that I needed to utilize this system, which I believe was the wisdom of God for my life. As a result, I never missed paying my tithe and I never missed paying a bill. I could go to bed each night and get up each morning without a care—"taking no thought"—because I had a system in place.

During the time I was laid off, I hung wallpaper and bought and sold cars. I had never hung wallpaper before, but I learned. I did so well at it, that one time I was offered a job hanging sixty double rolls in a brand-new house. I ended up earning more money during that time period than I would have earned at my old job! Although the hours were long, during that time I actually had more days off than I would have where I previously worked. Just to show you how much God blessed my efforts, I actually had enough money, after paying all of our bills, to buy a couple of three-wheelers and I was able to spend a lot of quality time with my children that summer. I'm not saying this to brag. I'm

God expects excellence of us, and He certainly gifts and graces us to be the best.

endeavoring to show you what God can do in your life and your family's lives, if you will step up to the plate and accept your financial responsibility in the home.

Certainly, I'm not saying that the seven months I was laid off was like a vacation! But because I had a system in place, my finances were in order instead of in chaos and disarray. I had a plan. I worked the plan— and the plan worked for me! It will work for you, too, if you will put it in place in your own life.

When the economy is suffering, there is always work to do. It may not be what you want, and it certainly isn't something that you will likely have to do forever. But there's work to do; you simply have to find it. During those months of unemployment, I also did cleanup at construction sites. That was a dirty job and a lot of hard work! But, because I always found work to do, at the end of those seven months, I earned more than if I would have continued my old union job, making $25 an hour. Back then, that was big money!

While I was unemployed, since I had a financial system in place and knew I needed to deposit $400 a week into an account for paying bills, I could plan special family outings without worry. We were also able to spend quite a bit of time together as a family and even took a trip to Disneyland during that hiatus! But I knew my bottom line. I knew what I had to accomplish each week.

Be the Best

In tough economic times, corporations are forced to become "lean." When jobs must be cut, generally only the best employees will be kept on board. That's why it's important as Christians, to always be the best workers possible. God expects excellence of us, and He gifts and graces us to be the best. As we walk in that, He can protect our situation when others are vulnerable during tough times.

These are some very practical, yet rich truths that you can learn and apply to secure your family's financial future. Remember, God gave Adam a job first before He ever gave him a bride. If you haven't already done so, as the leader in your home, I encourage you to take your place of responsibility in managing the money in your marriage. As you do, new doors of opportunity will open up to you, because you will be ready to step through those doors with confidence and skill. Your wife will be exceedingly blessed, your children will be happy, and life will be different for you.

17
WHAT'S WORKING IN YOU? THE SECRET TO SUCCESS IN MARRIAGE AND IN LIFE

Dr. Tom Anderson

To illustrate a point, I have taken the following excerpt from my son, Scot's book entitled, *More Than a Dad* (Winword Publishing, Phoenix, Arizona, 2005):

A man was being tailgated by a stressed-out woman on a busy boulevard when, suddenly, the traffic light turned yellow just in front of him. Although he probably could have accelerated and "beat" the light, the man did the right thing by stopping his vehicle at this busy crossroad. The woman tailing him became furious, honking her horn and screaming in frustration. In a frightening rant, she didn't hear at first the tap on her car window by a very concerned policeman. The officer ordered the woman out of car and escorted her to the police station, where she was fingerprinted, photographed, and placed in a holding cell. After a couple of hours, she was led back to the booking desk, where the arresting officer was waiting with her personal effects. "I'm very sorry for the mistake," the officer told her. "I pulled up behind you and saw you 'flipping off' the driver in front of you and cursing and yelling. Noticing the 'What Would Jesus Do' and 'Follow Me to Sunday School' bumper stickers on the bumper and the chrome-plated fish emblem on the trunk, I just assumed you had stolen the car."

This is a humorous commentary on the lack of character that many Christians exhibit today. I used this particular anecdote because it involves a woman—and it seems that men love to blame the women in their lives for their problems! In this chapter, I'm going to share five secrets for avoiding many of the problems of life that we face as men. Blaming the woman in our life is not one of them! It's unfortunate that it took me so many years to discover these secrets and put them into practice, but if I can share them with you, as a husband and leader in your home, life can better for you than you could ever imagine—and sooner than you think!

How to Measure Success

What is success? We know that success cannot be measured by money alone. All we have to do is look at some of the major corporate failings in recent history and the enormous bonuses paid to chief officers at taxpayers' expense to see that this is true. You can't prosper materially at the expense of your soul, and still be truly happy and prosperous.

Success is ultimately measured by a man's character—by what's working inside him, in his heart. A man's character often produces outward manifestations of success, as we tend to measure success. However, we must never confuse outward, material blessings with true success. Character is the pathway of true success in life, and there are no shortcuts. The following are five "characteristic" secrets to lasting success in life—for yourself and for your family.

Success is ulimately measured by a man's character.

Secret Number One: Commitment

What is commitment? I will share another humorous story to illustrate the characteristic of commitment—this one is about a chicken and a pig that ran away from a farm. Traveling all night, the chicken and the pig became very hungry. Up ahead, they saw a diner with a sign out front that read, "Bacon and Eggs—99 Cents." Excitedly, the chicken says to the pig, "Eggs and bacon! Let's get something to eat!" Reluctant, the pig says to the chicken, "That's easy for you to say: From you, they just want a donation; from me, they want complete commitment!"

In short, commitment means you put your life on the line. Commitment in marriage means you commit to your spouse for life—not just while emotions are high, or when things are going smoothly. Marriage is a lifetime commitment, from which there is no turning back. Commitment is the first key to success as a man, husband, father, leader, and provider. Commitment to whom or to what?

- commitment to God
- commitment to your wife
- commitment to your children
- commitment to your job
- commitment to your church

As a man, you have many responsibilities in life. However, to be truly successful, those responsibilities must all be kept in order. For example, some pastors and ministers get ministry out of order and begin placing more preeminence—more time and energy—on ministry than on their own family, or even on their relationship with God. However, if a minister really wants to minister and serve (because ministers are servants), he should minister first to the Lord and then to his wife and family, before he ever thinks about ministering to others.

Handling responsibility successfully is about prioritizing your time and commitments. As we have seen, our first commitment is to the Lord; our second commitment is to our wife; our third commitment is to our children; our fourth commitment is to our job or our employer; and our fifth commitment is to our church. If we keep our commitments in this order in terms of our priorities, we will find ourselves on the road to success.

Commitment to God

What does commitment to God—our number-one priority—look like? Commitment implies relationship. That means we don't just "flop" our Bible open and read it. We read God's Word purposefully and fellowship with Him around His Word. If we don't take this attitude toward the Word and have the sense of purpose that we are committed to the Lord for the rest of our lives, we will never do this consistently.

I encourage you in your reading, to pick a subject or topic and look up word meanings. Even if you only begin doing this five minutes a day, you can do a little bit more the following day. If bodybuilder Joe Weider could build a "muscle man" in just a few minutes a day, God can do a whole lot more for you in the same amount of time. However, you must have a vital relationship with Him, because apart from Him, you can do nothing (John 15:5).

Handling responsibility successfully is about prioritzing your time and commitments.

It's important to realize that without a commitment to God and to self, your commitments to your wife, children, job, and church will not likely stand the test of time. When I talk about commitment to self, I'm not talking about a commitment to selfishness. I'm talking about a commitment to self-growth and self-improvement. You must constantly commit to being better tomorrow, than you were today.

Commitment to Your Wife

In order for a marriage to thrive and for a man to be truly successful in his professional and family life, he must make a one hundred-percent commitment to his wife. Many marriages hang on and last, because of the woman's commitment. But that's not God's highest and best. He doesn't just want your marriage to "hang on" year after empty year. God wants your marriage to thrive and be a source of great happiness and contentment.

Dedication on the wife's part is wonderful and great, but without the husband eventually engaging in the growth of the relationship, the woman will finally "give out" and give up. That's why we are seeing three out of four marriages end in divorce today. These statistics show that most marriages end in divorce! This was never God's intention, concerning His institution of marriage.

A woman's emotions can eventually run dry. However, a man's commitment can go on and on without stopping because he doesn't operate on feelings; rather, he operates on the power of his will and his mental fortitude. Don't ever allow your wife to carry something in the marriage that you should be carrying. She was not anointed to carry it, and if you don't take your place and fulfill your responsibilities in the marriage, chaos and catastrophe will be the ultimate result.

Commitment to Your Children

Commitment to your children, like commitment to your wife, entails so many areas of responsibility. It's a commitment of your love, time, energies, and strength—the very best of you. As husbands and fathers, we simply must be committed to giving our family our very best. Where children are concerned, that commitment also includes the commitment to discipline, teach, and train, and to do it consistently, throughout their young lives.

I've had parents come to me in tears because their children were skipping school, and the mom and dad felt completely helpless about the situation. Some were worried sick that their child wouldn't graduate from high school. If necessary, I would have told my sons as they were growing up, "You will attend school. If you skip a class, I will take time off from work, and I will follow you to every class. I will sit with you in class and in the cafeteria. I will hang out with you at recess, and I will follow you to the bathroom. I will sit with you while you do your homework. You will graduate from high school."

In fact, there was a brief season in which one of our sons began hanging around a young man who was a bad influence on him and others. This young man drank alcohol and had already been in trouble with the law. He would come to church and then skip out on church and influence other kids to follow him outside, behind one of the church buildings during the service. I made this same "proposition" to my son. I offered to follow him around church and school. He knew I wasn't joking (and I wasn't). Needless to say, I never had a problem with that renegade friend again.

There was another season in which my boys thought they were really tough and began to take a certain attitude with me. I remember one night as they stood in front of me, side by side, I placed one hand on each boy's shoulder and "sat" them both down simultaneously. Don't misunderstand me; I love my sons. It is a well-understood fact that discipline and rules without relationship breed outright rebellion. But that was never an issue in our house. My children knew that I loved them. They still know it. We were always a very close, tight-knit family. But I wasn't about to give up my position as head of my home and let anarchy reign just because two teenagers wanted to see if they could challenge me!

As fathers, we simply need to ask ourselves, *How committed am I to my family?* We must determine our level of commitment to our God, our family, and the things we value most. We must ask ourselves, *Am I going to do whatever it takes to do the right thing, to usher God's blessing into my life and my family's lives? Or am I going to falter and wilt at the first sign of trouble?*

You—Dad—must take your position in the house and fulfill your role. Don't allow your wife to carry the weight of matters pertaining to the family. That's your job, so commit yourself to God first and then to your family—that you will be the very best you can be and do the very best you can do for them. Although your children will "leave and cleave" when they get married (see Genesis 2:24), you will be a parent for the rest of your life. You can still train your grown and married children by your lifestyle and example, and provide for them lessons without words that will serve as a support for them as they attempt to navigate their way through life.

If you are walking with the Lord and have a teachable heart, you will always have twice the wisdom and experience as your children. You still have something to offer them, even as they grow older, but it takes commitment on your part to walk in truth and be ready to impart truth when the time is right.

Commitment to Your Job

Being committed to your job or vocation means sticking with it whether you like it or not. You may not like the particular job or season you are in right now, but the attitude you take toward the work that is set before you can make or break your future and your family's future. Jesus said that He came not to be served, but to serve. He was the consummate "Servant-Leader" and *...submitting your will to the Lord's will to serve, you'll find great freedom as a servant of Christ.* our example that we should follow as believers, especially as men. Jesus served because He loved the Father and because He chose to live pleasing to Him. We have that same power of choice today.

There is a great difference between being a servant and being a slave. If you are doing something and you feel as if have to do it, you are a slave to whatever it is you are doing. But if you are doing something because you desire to serve and you have a heart of service—even if it's only for a season—you are truly free. "Bondservants, obey in all things your masters according to the flesh, not with eyeservice, as men-pleasers, but in sincerity of heart, fearing God. And whatever you do, do it heartily, as to the Lord and not to men" (Colossians 3:22-23 NKJV).

There is true freedom in serving. Even if you are not where you want to be in life right now, you can change your attitude toward your work and, before long, you will love serving God and others in whatever capacity you are in. Yes, it will take a little bit of death to "self," but in submitting your will to the Lord's will to serve, you will find great freedom as a servant of Christ.

Commitment to Your Church

Commitment to your church can be closely related to your commitment to your children, in the sense that your commitment to attend church will serve as the model or example that your children will follow as they grow older. Volunteer service aside, let's just talk about church attendance for a minute. Studies have shown that almost eighty percent of children whose fathers took them to church will stay in church even as adults. That figure is astounding! Fathers have largely let the mothers provide the spiritual nurturing for the family, yet the same studies reveal that only about half that amount—about forty percent of children—will continue attending church into adulthood when just Mom took them to church. So a dad has the responsibility to build into his children the importance of church attendance.

I have actually heard fathers say, "Well, my teenager just doesn't want to go to church." My question is, *Since when do teenagers make those kinds of decisions for themselves!* I always took the attitude that any teenager living under my roof must attend church. If I had to pick him up, throw him over my shoulders, belt him in the car, and carry him into the sanctuary, church attendance was not an option!

"Well, that's kind of harsh," someone might say. I allowed my sons to make certain decisions for themselves as they grew older, but if they ever began sliding off wisdom's path, I was right there to step in and make the right decision for them until they got their heads straight. If I had to sit with my sons in Sunday School and follow them from the classroom to the sanctuary and then sit with them among all their friends during the main service, then so be it: I was willing to do it. That was my stand, because I was committed. And you are going to have to be just that committed to stand by your own values and ideals.

Number Two: Trust

Commitment is the first godly characteristic of a successful man and the secret to his success. The second secret to success is the characteristic of trust. To be a successful leader in your home, you have to be trustworthy, and your spouse has to be trustworthy. For example, you have to be trustworthy in the way you handle the household's finances, and you have to be able to trust your spouse to handle money, too.

A lack of trust causes division and separation. That's why this issue of trust is so serious. You must be cautious and guard yourself in this area of integrity. You must work to develop trust both ways. Trust doesn't happen just because you make a decision; it is earned over time in a relationship. In our marriage, this trust issue, where money is concerned was a challenge to us at one time. I was always extremely frugal because I was raised without money. But Maureen's father had butlers working for him. She grew up spending money like water, so to speak. In fact, I once asked her, "Don't you ever look at price tags?" She answered, "No, I've never looked at a price tag a day in my life."

Maureen has always had a knack for selecting the highest-priced item as her favorite when she shops. It's almost uncanny! Without looking at the price, she will zero in on the highest-priced item. But as a responsible leader in our home, if I ever had to tell her that we couldn't spend that much money at the moment, she was fine with it. She trusted me to take care of our household financially, and she has become extremely faithful and trustworthy in the way she handles finances.

When it comes to marital fidelity, Maureen and I made a commitment to never cheat. I trusted her commitment, and she trusted mine. And we have never broken that. I'm not saying that temptation isn't out there, but when you have that level of commitment, temptation can never lead you astray because commitment keeps you on-track and off a destructive path.

Trust also has to be developed with your children. They have to be able to trust you and you must raise them to be trustworthy. You begin to earn your child's trust when he or she is an infant. For instance, when a baby cries because he's wet, hungry, tired, or sick, trust is built when you respond to his cries. Of course, there's another kind of cry that says, *I'm spoiled; pick me up!* I'm not saying you should always respond to that, because that goes beyond trust and into manipulation.

A child also learns to trust his or her parents when the child is disciplined in a consistent manner. In other words, if we want our children to trust us, we can't have a rule in place and then enforce it inconsistently. If we enforce a rule one day and then the next day, we fail to follow through on enforcing that same rule, trust is broken down. Then our children can't trust that we will do what we say we are going to do. Whether you are promising some kind of blessing or reward, or you are promising some form of discipline or punishment, it's so important that you keep your word with your children. I'm not saying you should always follow through on some rash promise that you have made in haste, or in anger to punish your child in a way that's cruel. We need to make these promises with level heads, so that we are firm and resolute, not reckless and harsh.

Number Three: Service

A third godly trait and secret to success is service. Too often, people equate successful leadership with authority over others in subservient roles. In other words, they think that if you are successful, others will constantly be serving you.

But a true godly leader will serve God, his family, and others because he's a leader— not because he's trying to become one. He's not trying to impress anyone; he's simply motivated by what's working in him—a heart for service.

Number Four: Loyalty

A fourth godly trait that a successful man possesses is loyalty. Loyalty is directly associated with thoughts, words, and actions. In other words, loyalty can be outwardly recognized by one's words and actions, but God knows whether a person is loyal in his or her thoughts.

Loyalty in Your Thoughts

As I have already shared, even your thoughts can affect and impact those around you, so you need to be especially careful about thinking negative thoughts about others, especially your spouse. On the other hand, thinking the right thoughts can be powerful, as those thoughts will positively affect those around you. The same is true concerning your children. If you are thinking fearful, pessimistic thoughts, those thoughts will create a certain energy in the home and will affect your children.

If you don't believe there's power attached to fear, think about the times you have felt most afraid. In certain cases, every cell in your body can feel the effects of the presence of fear. That's why the Bible teaches us not to give place to fear—or to anything else that comes from the enemy—and that includes giving place to it in our thought life.

Loyalty in Your Words

What about the words we speak? Loyalty can definitely be communicated through speech. Words are powerful! Doesn't it make sense that we should speak only positively to and about our wife? What about our children? From the time our children were very young—in fact, while they were in the womb—Maureen and I began speaking to them about how intelligent and good-looking they were. We also told them this every day

We realize the power that's manifested with every word, so we are careful to put the right beliefs and attitudes into the lives of our loved ones.

when they were kids. We still do it today, and they are grown and married with families of their own! We realize the power that's manifested with every word, so we are careful to put the right beliefs and attitudes into the lives of our loved ones.

What does that have to do with loyalty? Like trust, feelings of loyalty are built over time. My wife and children understood my loyalty to them because I was always thinking and speaking positive things about them. That built within them a deep sense of security and well-being. They knew I always had their best interest at heart. They could trust that I was looking out for them spiritually and in every area. They depended on me to bear fruit from the Word, and I always did my best not to let them down.

The condition of your family is really the result of your faith—your thoughts, beliefs, and the words you speak. What have you been sowing into them? Do you believe they are a success going somewhere to happen? Do you believe God has a plan and purpose for their lives and that they are going to fulfill it?

Loyalty in Your Actions

Loyalty is expressed in your thoughts and words, but it's also expressed by your actions. For example, what do you do for your wife on her birthday, on Mother's Day, and so forth? Your actions portray loyalty and create feelings of loyalty in others as well. I try to celebrate Maureen's birthday for a whole week leading up to her special day. That way, on her actual birthday, Maureen is already "filled up," because I've made her feel so special. There are any number of creative ways you can show your wife and children, by your actions, that you are loyal to them and that they are your number-one priority in life, next to your relationship with the Lord.

Number Five: Unconditional Love

A fifth godly trait that successful men possess is unconditional love. Unconditional love is about loving the inside person, and it's based on a decision of your heart. People tend to want to love others because they have earned or deserved it in some way. They will love someone because of what the person does for them, how that person makes them feel, or even how he or she looks. Very little of their love is based on the real person on the inside and on their own heartfelt commitment to love him or her unconditionally. My wife is beautiful and takes great care of herself, but even if she didn't look the way she looks, I would still love her the same because of my own heart of love and my commitment to her. In other words, loving others unconditionally has more to do with you, than with the people you are loving

Unconditional Love and Your Happy Marriage

Marriage is about making a heart connection that's eternal in its commitment, based on unconditional love. Marriages don't last because your spouse is changing, but because you are changing and growing in the love of God. You are making commitments in your heart to love forever. "Husbands, love your wives, just as Christ also loved the church and gave Himself for her" (Ephesians 5:25 NKJV).

Of course, the wife is supposed to love her husband, too, but it's interesting that wives are never directly commanded in the Word to love their husband. Remember, we said that Christ is the picture of the husband and the Church is the picture of the wife, or the bride. Husbands are supposed to love their wife as Christ loves the Church. When husbands love their wife as Christ loves the Church, wives will automatically respond to that, and they will love their husband fervently and devotedly.

One thing we know about the way Christ loved the Church is He loved us first before we loved Him (see First John 4:19). Therefore, we as husbands must love our wife first. If we are waiting to be loved by her first, we can forget it. We might enjoy her initiating love for a season, but it won't last. We must ultimately act as the initiator in the relationship; we must be the "sowers," if we expect to reap on a consistent, long-term basis. We will never receive the love that truly fulfills us and makes us happy, until we first give that kind of love away. "He who finds a wife finds a good thing, And obtains favor from the Lord" (Proverbs 18:22 NKJV).

Marriage is about making a heart connection that's eternal in its commitment and that's based on unconditional love.

Think about this. A woman gives up her name to become the wife of her husband. What does he give up? He doesn't give up anything, he gains something: favor with the Lord —that, and the responsibility to love and care for his wife. So another aspect of showing unconditional love toward your wife is to take care of her as the gift from God that she is. Do you see your wife as a gift from God? She could have given herself to someone else, but she chose you. And now that she has entrusted her life to you, what are you going to do with it? She gave you her heart, trusting you to love her unconditionally for the rest of your life.

I have loved Maureen since we were in middle school, and she was still in braces. When she later accepted my marriage proposal, my attitude was, *I'd better take care of this gift from the Lord. I'd better honor her, provide for her, and serve her. I'm going to give her the best in life that I possibly can. She is trusting me, and I'm not going to let her down!*

Love and Sex

Unconditional love is also associated with sex or physical intimacy. A man needs to know that foreplay begins from the time he wakes up in the morning until the time he goes to bed at night. In other words, he must invest in his wife outside the bedroom. If he can get past just what he wants out of sex and get to the place of desiring what his wife wants and needs from the relationship, he and his wife will experience a very rewarding sexual relationship. Closeness of heart is very closely connected with the intimacy of sex.

A man can attempt to blame his failures in life on the people in his life or on the circumstances that surround him. But ultimately, the responsibility for his failure lies squarely with him. Similarly, the secret to success in life—to a happy marriage, a happy family, and a happy life—is as close as your own heart. When you develop the characteristics of commitment, trust, service, loyalty, and unconditional love in your life, success in every area will ultimately find you and envelop you and your family in the blessings of God.

PRAYER OF SALVATION

God loves you—no matter who you are, no matter what your past. God loves you so much that He gave His one and only begotten Son for you. The Bible tells us that "...whoever believes in him shall not perish but have eternal life" (John 3:16 NIV). Jesus laid down His life and rose again so that we could spend eternity with Him in heaven and experience His absolute best on earth. If you would like to receive Jesus into your life, say the following prayer out loud and mean it from your heart.

Heavenly Father, I come to You admitting that I am a sinner. Right now, I choose to turn away from sin, and I ask You to cleanse me of all unrighteousness. I believe that Your Son, Jesus, died on the cross to take away my sins. I also believe that He rose again from the dead so that I might be forgiven of my sins and made righteous through faith in Him. I call upon the name of Jesus Christ to be the Savior and Lord of my life. Jesus, I choose to follow You and ask that You fill me with the power of the Holy Spirit. I declare that right now I am a child of God. I am free from sin and full of the right-eousness of God. I am saved in Jesus' name. Amen.

If you prayed this prayer to receive Jesus Christ as your Savior for the first time, please contact us on the Web at **www.harrisonhouse.com** to receive a free book.

Or you may write to us at
Harrison House • P.O. Box 35035 • Tulsa, Oklahoma 74153

About the Authors

Dr. C. Thomas Anderson and Dr. Maureen Anderson have been in active ministry for more than thirty years. Much of this time has been based in Mesa, Arizona, where they founded and now pastor Living Word Bible Church, an independent ministry that has grown to more than 8,500 members and is the 12th fastest growing church in the nation.

Dr. Tom Anderson is known worldwide for an easy-going teaching style and for the practical, positive, life-changing information that he presents. In recent years, Dr. Anderson has extended the reach of his ministry through development of national television broadcasts, including teaching programs and informal interview and discussion shows. The simple style and the depth of his teaching continue to impact the lives of millions. Dr. Anderson has become a favorite with audiences all over the world.

Maureen Anderson is among the most gifted and respected women in the ministry. Her television programs are broadcast around the world. She speaks at conferences and churches, and has shared the stage with Kenneth and Gloria Copeland, Joyce Meyer, Creflo Dollar, T.D. Jakes and many more.

Maureen Anderson started the Women of Destiny Ministries at Living Word. Under her leadership, Moms of Destiny, Daughters of Destiny, and God's Girls of Destiny reach all women, starting at the age of thirteen. The goal of the Women of Destiny Ministries is that "Every woman would fulfill her destiny, and not one woman would be left behind."

From the beginning, Tom and Maureen have focused on biblical training for building strong families and marriages. They travel extensively, presenting seminars on practical subjects such as marriage, relationships, financial health, leadership and nutrition, as well as a variety of other topics.

Between the two of them, the Andersons have authored numerous books including *Becoming a Millionaire God's Way*, *What in Health Do You Want?* *Wisdom Wins I and II*, *Will the Real America Please Stand Up?*, *Who's the Boss*, *Damaged DNA*, *Making Impossibilities Possible*, *Confessing God's Word*, and *Releasing the Miraculous Through Fasting with Prayer*.

Tom and Maureen are the proud parents of two boys and the grandparents of nine. They have been married for over 40 years.